LEARNING RESOURCES CTR/NEW ENGLAND TECI

3 0147 1000 8479 0

S0-EIJ-495

KF 9223.5 .B86 1997 Copy 2

Bunker, Matthew D.

Justice and the media.

NEW ENGLAND INSTITUTE
OF TECHNOLOGY
LEARNING RESOURCES CENTER

JUSTICE AND THE MEDIA
Reconciling Fair Trials and a Free Press

LEA'S COMMUNICATION SERIES
Jennings Bryant/Dolf Zillmann, General Editors

Select titles in Communication include:

Black • Mixed News: The Public/Civic/Communitarian Journalism Debate

Dennis/Wartella • American Communication Research: The Remembered History

Gonzenbach • The Media, the President, and Public Opinion: A Longitudinal Analysis of the Drug Issue, 1984–1991

Moore • Mass Communication Law and Ethics

Weaver/Wilhoit • The American Journalist in the 1990s: U.S. News People at the End of an Era

For a complete list of other titles in LEA's Communication Series, please contact Lawrence Erlbaum Associates, Publishers.

JUSTICE AND THE MEDIA
Reconciling Fair Trials and a Free Press

❦

Matthew D. Bunker
University of Alabama

 LAWRENCE ERLBAUM ASSOCIATES, PUBLISHERS
1997 Mahwah, New Jersey

NEW ENGLAND INSTITUTE
OF TECHNOLOGY
LEARNING RESOURCES CENTER

Copy 2
5-99

#35243586

Copyright © 1997 by Lawrence Erlbaum Associates, Inc.
   All rights reserved. No part of this book may be repro-
   duced in any form, by photostat, microfilm, retrieval
   system, or any other means, without the prior written
   permission of the publisher.

Lawrence Erlbaum Associates, Inc., Publishers
10 Industrial Avenue
Mahwah, New Jersey 07430

Cover design by Mairav Salomon-Dekel

Library of Congress Cataloging-in-Publication Data

   Bunker, Matthew D.
   Justice and the media : reconciling fair trials and a free
press / Matthew D. Bunker.
       p.   cm.
   Includes bibliographical references and indexes.
   ISBN 0-8058-2168-6 (cloth : alk. paper)
   1. Free press and fair trial—United States. 2. Freedom
of speech—United States.   3. Freedom of the
press—United States.   I. Title.
   KF9223.5.B86   1997
   342.73'0853—dc20
   [347.302853]   96-38168
                                                          CIP

Books published by Lawrence Erlbaum Associates are printed
on acid-free paper, and their bindings are chosen for strength
and durability.

Printed in the United States of America
10 9 8 7 6 5 4 3 2 1

-Contents-

Preface   **vii**

1 SCRUTINIZING THE SCRUTINY STRUCTURE   **1**
   Free Speech and First Amendment Doctrine   *2*
   Theoretical Perspectives   *5*
   Scholars and the Scrutiny Structure   *10*
   Summary of the Book   *13*

2 THE SUPREME COURT AND FIRST AMENDMENT   **15**
   SCRUTINY
   The End of the *Lochner* Era   *16*
   Civil Liberties Ascendant   *18*
   First Amendment Scrutiny Today   *28*
   Conclusion   *33*

3 COURTS AND PREJUDICIAL PUBLICITY   **34**
   Limitations on the Contempt Power   *34*
   Fair Trial Rights and the Search for an Impartial Juror   *41*
   Studies and Guidelines Regarding Prejudicial Publicity   *60*
   Conclusion   *63*

4   PRIOR RESTRAINTS   65
    Prior Restraint Doctrine in the Supreme Court   66
    Cases Striking Down Prior Restraints on Media   70
    Prior Restraint Upheld   75
    Prior Restraints on Participants   78
    Conclusion   84

5   POSTPUBLICATION SANCTIONS   85
    Postpublication Sanctions in the Supreme Court   85
    Lower Court Decisions   90
    Conclusion   93

6   ACCESS TO PROCEEDINGS   94
    The Supreme Court and Access   94
    Lower Court Access Decisions   101
    Conclusion   114

7   DEFECTS IN THE SYSTEM   116
    Summary of Findings   116
    Problems with the Existing Structure   118
    Conclusion   130

8   A PROPOSAL FOR A CATEGORICAL SOLUTION   132
    The Scrutiny Structure and the First Amendment   132
    Rules Versus Standards   134
    A Categorical Rule?   140
    Conclusion   145

    Author Index   146

    Subject Index   148

-Preface-

The First Amendment right of free speech is a fragile one. Its fragility is found no less in legal opinions than in other, less specialized forms of public discourse. Both its fragility and its sometimes surprising resiliency are reflected in the following pages.

This book attempts to examine how courts treat First Amendment claims made by the press in the context of the criminal justice system. Rather than explore the vast universe of such cases, the book focuses on federal courts, where reported opinions by trial courts are more common than at the state level. The hope is to produce a reasonably accurate—if partial—picture of how intermediate appellate and trial courts use U.S. Supreme Court doctrine to decide First Amendment cases. This picture is then used to evaluate and critique the doctrinal system.

For better or worse, this book is haunted by the specter of the O.J. Simpson trial. Although the Simpson case did not make new law, the trial and its outcome seem to be, at this writing, an inescapable part of how many people think about these issues. The simple truth, however, is that the Simpson case was an anomaly that has little relation to the everyday concerns of media coverage of the criminal justice system. Although the venerable "parade of horribles" can be an effective strategy for the legal advocate, it is not always the ideal way to address larger concerns, particularly when fundamental rights are at stake.

No doubt there will be objections to the following pages. First, to the extent that my preferred resolution of the issues discussed herein favors uninhibited speech, there will be some who maintain that I have devalued other interests to which the rights of the press should yield. I remain convinced, however, that there are always effective alternatives preferable to sacrificing one constitutional right in favor of another. Even to those who disagree with me on this point, I hope the descriptive portions of this work prove worthwhile. Second, my preference for clear rules over more discretionary standards makes me vulnerable to the charge of formalism. To this charge I suppose I must plead guilty, although I do so with the caveats discussed in the final chapter. Despite the currently fashionable claims of the advocates of indeterminacy, human beings make rule-based decisions regularly, with roughly the same degrees of success and disappointment that attach to any human enterprise.

I am indebted to a number of people for help in bringing this book into being. In particular, I would like to thank Bill Chamberlin for his constant support and encouragement in the course of the work that led to this book. Professor Chamberlin's suggestion of exploring how courts use strict scrutiny to decide First Amendment cases opened up a rich vein of research, and his comments along the way added tremendously to the project. Thanks are also due to Fletcher Baldwin, Kermit Hall, John Wright, and William McKeen for their insightful comments on an earlier draft. I am very grateful to Jennings Bryant for his enthusiastic support of this project. I also owe a profound debt of gratitude to my wife, Lois Graham, whose patience and friendship through this project have been remarkable, and to my parents, Herbert and Eudora Bunker, whose support has been invaluable.

—*Matthew D. Bunker*

-1-

Scrutinizing the Scrutiny Structure

The First Amendment to the U.S. Constitution states, in relevant part, that "Congress shall make no law. . . abridging the freedom of speech, or of the press . . . ."[1] Yet it has become clear that, despite the claims of a few purported absolutists like Justice Hugo Black, "no law" could never truly mean "no law." Freedom of expression is subject to numerous abridgments, not the least of which are laws regulating false advertising, libel, perjury, obscenity, and solicitation of murder. Once courts begin to draw lines that demarcate "protected speech" from "unprotected speech," as they must, complexities and conflicts almost inevitably proliferate. In fact, judges and scholars have struggled for many years to reconcile free expression with other values that government seeks to advance.

The conflict between the First Amendment rights of the media and the interest in maintaining the integrity of the criminal justice system has been a particularly dramatic example of this struggle. The Sixth Amendment guarantee of an impartial jury, similar state constitutional provisions, and the Fourteenth Amendment's due process clause all require that criminal defendants be tried fairly before a jury that is not prejudiced against them. These "fair trial" guarantees are often seen as inevitably colliding with the rights of the media to gather and disseminate news about the criminal justice system, particularly in high-profile cases. The O.J. Simpson murder prosecution in Los Angeles, for example, offered a stark portrait of the tension between press coverage of an international cause celebre and the attempt to provide a sober, unbiased trial. In recent years, a host of other celebrated trials—including those of the Menendez brothers, William Kennedy Smith, the police officers in the Rodney King case, and boxer Mike Tyson—have seemed to some observers to tax the ability of the justice system to provide a fair trial, in the face of pervasive and sometimes prejudicial media coverage.

---

[1] U.S. Const. Amend. I.

FREE SPEECH AND FIRST AMENDMENT DOCTRINE

Regardless of the excess and sensationalism that sometimes characterize media coverage of criminal trials, the fundamental importance of free expression in a democracy is beyond question. For many scholars, however, the theoretical and doctrinal bases of protecting free expression have often appeared inadequate to the task. In particular, the U.S. Supreme Court's development of a judicial approach to the protection of First Amendment freedoms has been a source of frustration to those who feel that free expression is one of the most basic and fragile rights in our constitutional system. Scholars have long lamented the fragmented state of the Supreme Court's First Amendment jurisprudence—the overall scheme of legal doctrine the Court employs to decide free expression questions. The great First Amendment scholar Thomas Emerson expressed this frustration in the 1960s:

> No one concerned with freedom of expression in the United States today can fail to be alarmed by the unsatisfactory state of First Amendment doctrine. Despite the mounting number of decisions and an ever greater volume of comment, no really adequate or comprehensive theory of the First Amendment has been enunciated, much less agreed upon.[2]

One recurring theme, however, at least since the late 1930s, has been the notion that government must demonstrate some significant competing interest to limit certain types of speech. Judges using this approach to judicial review seek to balance the value of free expression against the need to implement other societal interests. Depending on the type of speech in question, the balancing test may require the competing interest achieve a given level of significance, whether "compelling," "substantial," or "important," or a variety of other descriptive terms, before the competing interest can override the strong interest in freedom of expression. Because judges using this type of review process claim to carefully analyze the strength of the need for government regulation of speech, this form of judicial review is often referred to as *heightened scrutiny*. Heightened scrutiny, which embraces a number of different standards of review, is a more searching form of judicial review than the Court uses in, for example, cases involving economic regulation. In such cases, in which no fundamental rights such as free expression are involved, the Court upholds legislation provided it has a "rational basis." In other words, the Court defers to the wisdom of the legislative body unless the legislation is manifestly unreasonable. Such deference is generally not the Court's *modus operandi* when First Amendment interests are at stake.

Constitutional scholars frequently trace the heightened scrutiny approach to First Amendment speech issues to the famous "footnote four" in Justice Harlan Fiske Stone's 1938 opinion in *U.S. v. Carolene Products*.[3] In that case, Stone declared that "[t]here may be a narrower scope for the operation of the presumption of constitutionality when the legislation appears on its face to be within a specific

---

[2]T. Emerson, Toward a General Theory of the First Amendment vii (1963).

[3]304 U.S. 144 (1938).

prohibition of the Constitution."[4]Although the footnote addressed other constitutional issues as well, its implication for the specific guarantees of the Bill of Rights, in particular the First Amendment, became clear in decisions that followed. The Court reasoned that the text of the Constitution authorized judges to engage in a searching form of judicial review when government sought to restrict textual rights such as the First Amendment speech and press clauses. When such rights were infringed, the mere rationality of legislative enactments would not guarantee deferential treatment by the courts.

The seed planted by Justice Stone blossomed in the development of the so-called "strict scrutiny test." Under strict scrutiny, sometimes called the *compelling state interest test*, First Amendment interests are upheld unless the governmental interest in regulation is compelling and that interest is achieved in the least restrictive manner. Strict scrutiny, at least in the years when Earl Warren was chief justice, most frequently upheld freedom of expression against opposing governmental interests. One commentator has said that the Warren Court used strict scrutiny as "an almost automatic tool for overturning legislation."[5]

In 1968, the Court began using a less protective test for determining the constitutionality of government attempts to limit expression. In *United States v. O'Brien*,[6] the Court constructed a lower level of scrutiny for evaluating laws governing conduct that included both "speech" and "nonspeech" elements. The *O'Brien* test stated that a regulation that only "incidentally" regulates speech (i.e., is not primarily aimed at suppressing speech) passes constitutional muster if it furthers an "important or substantial" governmental interest, is within the constitutional power of government, and "if the incidental restriction on alleged First Amendment freedoms is no greater than is essential to the furtherance of that interest."[7] Variations on the *O'Brien* test have since come to be applied in a number of media contexts.

Communication law scholars have paid inadequate attention to the doctrines of heightened scrutiny, particularly as those doctrines are interpreted by lower courts. This book is intended to examine heightened scrutiny as applied to government restrictions on the media. The heightened scrutiny approach appears in numerous areas of media law, but the present study focuses on constitutional analysis of restrictions on press coverage of the criminal justice system. The book is not intended as a complete review or analysis of the "free press–fair trial" problem, something a number of works have done with great skill. Although it explores various aspects of that enduring problem to provide context, this work is first and foremost a study in the evolution of constitutional jurisprudence. The book attempts to explore how First Amendment doctrine created by the U.S. Supreme Court is interpreted and applied by lower federal courts. Federal courts were chosen because

---

[4]*Id.* at n.4.

[5] Gottlieb, Compelling Governmental Interests: An Essential but Unanalyzed Term in Constitutional Adjudication, 68 B.U.L. Rev. 917, 923 (1988).

[6]391 U.S. 367 (1968).

[7]*Id.* at 377.

trial-level decisions are reported with much greater frequency than those in state courts. In the process, the book critiques both the doctrinal structures created by the Supreme Court and the ways in which those structures are transformed as they are applied by lower courts. The book also seeks to suggest an alternative to the Supreme Court's current jurisprudence in this area.

This study examines both U.S. Supreme Court and lower federal court cases from the beginning of modern Supreme Court jurisprudence in the respective substantive areas under consideration. For example, *Nebraska Press Assn v. Stuart,*[8] decided in 1976, was the seminal case on prior restraints on the press in criminal cases. For prior restraint doctrine, the year of that decision will be the beginning point for study of both Supreme Court and lower court use of heightened scrutiny. Similarly, the Supreme Court's 1980 decision in *Richmond Newspapers, Inc. v. Virginia*[9] was the beginning of its articulation of a First Amendment right to attend criminal trials. Therefore, that case is the beginning point in examination of access to proceedings.

The book's emphasis, as noted earlier, is on the scrutiny doctrines developed by the Supreme Court and their subsequent application in lower court opinions. Federal district court decisions, which are not always reported in the Federal Reporter system, are examined as illustrative of the application of heightened scrutiny, rather than as an exhaustive reporting of all cases. The book's treatment is limited to cases in which government regulation has some impact, or at least potential impact, on media coverage of the criminal justice system. Cases related to cameras in the courtroom are excluded because those cases have generally not been treated as raising significant First Amendment questions. In addition, cases dealing with access to documents, rather than physical access to proceedings by the press, are excluded for two reasons. First, the ability of the press to be present in the courtroom and to report proceedings without inhibition could be argued to provide most of the necessary safeguards to allow public scrutiny of the process. Second, the volume of access cases related to documents would have expanded this study beyond a manageable level. As a result, the study focuses on cases dealing with prior restrictions on publication, postpublication punishment of the press, and access to court proceedings.

The purpose of this book is to explore the techniques of judicial review the Court has developed in a significant body of case law in which the free expression rights of the media have been deemed to be in conflict with some other interest government seeks to advance. The actual mechanics of the scrutiny structure the Court uses in such cases is interesting for a number of reasons. First, the structure seems to suggest that there is some solid jurisprudential basis for making decisions once the judge has identified the respective interests in conflict. Second, it suggests that similar cases will be treated similarly. Third, it professes to hold the government to rigorous standards of proof of the necessity of its regulation when free expression rights are threatened. Fourth, the Court regards its scrutiny structure as giving

---

[8] 427 U.S. 539 (1976).

[9] 448 U.S. 555 (1980).

guidance to lower courts that will assist them in deciding cases in which First Amendment issues are raised.

This study also examines the levels of scrutiny the Court has applied to restrictions on media coverage of the criminal justice system. This area of law was chosen for a number of reasons. The criminal justice system is a domain in which government exercises significant power over the lives of its citizens, and thus arguably requires close observation. The conflict between the press and the courts has generated a significant body of case law, as well as scholarly and public concern. This class of cases, at the federal level, was sufficiently narrow for a study of this type.

This study explores the extent to which the scrutiny structure forms a coherent body of law that protects free expression values while permitting reasonable government regulation. It examines the levels of scrutiny the Court has created as they apply to prior restraint and postpublication sanctions on the press, as well as the right of access to criminal proceedings. The study explores the way in which the Court and lower federal courts have used the doctrines to limit or enhance the ability of the media to provide information to the public on functioning of the criminal justice system. The scrutiny structure is examined to determine whether it adequately guides judicial action.

THEORETICAL PERSPECTIVES

The scrutiny structure in First Amendment law is closely realted to the notion of important societal interests served by free expression. Numerous scholars have explored the theoretical justifications of the First Amendment free speech and press clauses. Although different scholars have classified these justifications in somewhat different ways, a number of rationales for free expression are consistently cited. Among the theoretical explanations for the high value that society has placed on free expression are the following: individual autonomy, diversity, self-government, and checking abuses of official power.[10]

The individual autonomy rationale explains free expression as not directed exclusively toward some pragmatic or instrumental end, but as "valuable in and of itself because it figures prominently in our vague notions of what it means to be human."[11] Under this rationale, freedom of thought and expression create conditions conducive to self-realization, and are valuable as ends in themselves, rather than as means to some other social end.[12] This rationale is tied to broader conceptions of liberal political theory, which assert that individuals should be treated as

---

[10]For a discussion of the theories, see V. Blasi, The Checking Value in First Amendment Theory, 1977 Am. Bar. Found. Res. J. 521, 529-66; T. Emerson, The System of Freedom of Expression 6-9 (1970); L. Tribe, American Constitutional Law 785-89 (1988).

[11]Blasi, *supra* note 10, at 544.

[12]*See generally* Baker, Scope of the First Amendment Freedom of Speech, 25 U.C.L.A. L. Rev. 964 (1978).

rational beings with the ability to grow and develop along lines that they—not the state—choose. As Justice Jackson stated in the 1943 flag salute case, *West Virginia Board of Education v. Barnette*: "If there is any fixed star in our constitutional constellation, it is that no official, high or petty, can prescribe what shall be orthodox in politics, nationalism, religion, or other matters of opinion . . . ."[13]

The autonomy rationale, in some versions, qualifies as an instrumental theory in that it seeks to promote growth and human development. Legal scholar Kent Greenawalt suggested that,

> despite the burden of anxiety that often accompanies serious personal choice, many people can work out for themselves a style of life that is more fulfilling than what they could achieve by simply conforming to standards set by others. Both the valuation of autonomy for its own sake and the belief that it contributes to other satisfactions are aspects of traditional liberal theory.[14]

Another theoretical justification for free expression is the perceived need for a diversity of viewpoints to be freely communicated. The diversity rationale is often expressed by Justice Holmes' *marketplace of ideas* metaphor. This metaphor equates free and open discussion of ideas with the free market for goods and services. Presumably, all citizens are free to offer their views and try to convince other members of society of their validity. Thus, the diversity rationale encourages new and innovative ideas, whether in government policy, science, or the arts. It also serves a safety valve function by allowing those disaffected with the society to express their dissatisfaction through speech, rather than more violent means. Free speech thus contributes to social stability by allowing an outlet for dissent.

The diversity rationale received one of its most famous formulations in John Stuart Mill's essay, "On the Liberty of Thought and Discussion" in "On Liberty."[15] Mill suggested three reasons that free discussion should be unrestrained and even unpopular ideas allowed into public discussion. First, suppression of speech could prevent true ideas from coming to light, thus stifling social progress. Mill's argument suggests that human fallibility may make it difficult to determine in advance which ideas are true or false, and he argues that the safest course is to avoid the authoritarian imposition of particular ideas. Second, even if the unpopular idea is not true, Mill argued that the idea may be partially true, and thus provides a needed supplement to the received or popular view in society. Again, the unpopular idea should not be suppressed because its partial correctness will contribute to a broader or more complete truth. Finally, Mill argued that even if an idea is wholly false and the prevailing wisdom is correct, the unpopular idea will galvanize people into a vigorous examination of their beliefs, and thus enliven what would otherwise be, to them, dead dogma. Mill suggested that, "unless [the prevailing view] is suffered

---

[13]West Virginia State Board of Education v. Barnette, 319 U.S. 624, 642 (1943).

[14]Greenawalt, Free Speech Justifications, 89 Colum. L. Rev. 119, 144 (1989).

[15]J. Mill, On Liberty (1947).

to be, and actually is, vigorously and earnestly contested, it will, by most of those who receive it, be held in the manner of a prejudice, with little comprehension or feeling of its rational grounds."[16]

In contrast, Justice Holmes expressed great skepticism about the nature of "truth" as anything but provisional and contingent. Nonetheless, he viewed a largely unrestrained marketplace in speech as the necessary condition of achieving that provisional kind of "truth" in a democracy. As he stated in his dissent in *Abrams v. United States*, "the best test of truth is the power of thought to get itself accepted in the competition of the market. . . ."[17]

A third justification for free expression is its contribution to effective self-government. This position, most commonly associated with Professor Alexander Meiklejohn, values free expression as the means by which popular sovereignty is realized. The speech protected by the First Amendment, according to Meiklejohn, is speech aimed at enhancing citizen participation in political decisions. "We, the people who govern, must try to understand the issues which, incident by incident, face the nation," Meiklejohn wrote. "We must pass judgment upon the decisions which our agents make upon those issues. And, further, we must share in devising methods by which those decisions can be made wise and effective, or if need be, supplanted by others which promise greater wisdom and effectiveness."[18] Meiklejohn also recognized the need for free expression in literature, science, and other activities beyond the purely political.[19]

First Amendment theorist Rodney Smolla argued that free speech as an adjunct to democratic self-governance includes a number of related values.[20] For example, political participation, in the form of debating, voting, and otherwise participating in political deliberation, is a distinct value that advances individual fulfillment and dignity. Other portions of the self-government rationale focus more on collective well-being, including making certain, through debate, that political decisions actually represent the will of the majority, rather than that of particularly wealthy or vocal segments of society.

The theoretical justification for freedom of expression perhaps most closely related to this study is Professor Vincent Blasi's "checking value."[21] Blasi's theory, while recognizing other purposes of free expression, emphasizes the role of free expression in checking the abuse of official power. "The central premise of the checking value," Blasi wrote, "is that the abuse of official power is an especially serious evil—more serious than the abuse of private power, even by institutions such as large corporations which can affect the lives of millions of people."[22] Blasi

---

[16]*Id.* at 52.

[17]Abrams v. United States, 250 U.S. 616, 630 (1919).

[18]Meiklejohn, The First Amendment is an Absolute, 1961 Sup. Ct. Rev. 245, 255 (1961).

[19]Blasi, *supra* note 10, at 559.

[20]R. Smolla, Free Speech in an Open Society 12 (1992).

[21]Blasi, *supra* note 10.

[22]*Id.* at 538.

maintained that the abuse of official power is particularly dangerous because of the government's monopoly on the sanctioned use of violence. The threat of irresponsible or malevolent use of this monopoly makes close observation of official power particularly critical. No private entity, no matter how powerful, could have conducted the kind of operation the U.S. government did in Vietnam, Blasi argued. Moreover, this monopoly on violence also suggests that only the force of public opinion and outrage can act as an effective check on the abuse of official power—through the polls as well as other techniques of citizen activism. In addition, the government's ability to investigate and conduct surveillance against its citizens through official channels is much greater than the citizenry's ability to watch government activities. This point further supports the claim that abuse of official power is more dangerous than misuse of private power.

The checking value posits that government officials will carry out their duties more fairly and effectively if their activities are closely watched and reported upon. Blasi's theory takes a basically pessimistic view of how human beings react when given the reins of governmental power. The corrupting effect of power is assumed to be a constant. The criminal justice system is one exercise of official power that historically has been open to public scrutiny for exactly such reasons. Police departments, public prosecutors, judges, and juries are all actors endowed with varying degrees of official power subject to tremendous abuse without the watchful eye of press and public. The U.S. Supreme Court has frequently recognized the vital role that press and public examination of criminal proceedings can play in ensuring fairness in those proceedings.

The First Amendment theories cited above may offer some or all of the explanation for the high regard for free expression in our society. One of the more significant judicial tools by which free expression is protected from infringement is the Supreme Court's heightened scrutiny methodology. As previously discussed, however, the Court's First Amendment doctrine lacks a consistent, comprehensive approach. This state of doctrinal disarray certainly appears to be present in the Court's approach to strict judicial review of government action aimed at limiting the media's First Amendment rights. Some restrictions on media expression are subjected to the highest level of review—strict scrutiny—while others are subjected to various lesser levels of scrutiny. Some restrictions can be justified only by compelling governmental interests, some only by overriding governmental interests, others only by serious and imminent harm, and still others by a mere probability that harm may occur. The scrutiny structure seems to lack internal consistency, as well as even-handed application.

Professor Thomas I. Emerson's work suggests a number of criticisms of the use of balancing tests in constitutional adjudication. Emerson's critique is aimed at what he referred to as "ad hoc balancing," which is a less stringent form of judicial review than heightened scrutiny. Emerson's critique of ad hoc balancing, however, raises questions about the use of heightened scrutiny as well. As Emerson described ad hoc balancing: "The formula is that the court must in each case balance the individual and social interest in freedom of expression against the social interest sought by the regulation which restricts expression."[23] Such balancing is similar to the comparison that takes place when courts apply heightened scrutiny to a restriction on the media.

First, Emerson criticized the ambiguity and subjectivity of ad hoc balancing. According to Emerson, such a test lacks a "hard core."[24] Emerson asserted that when ad hoc balancing is applied, the court is "cast loose in a vast space, embracing the broadest possible range of issues, to strike the general balance in light of its own best judgment."[25] If one surveys the application of heightened scrutiny in media cases, this lack of a hard core is evident. The verbal formulation of the tests often does little to increase legal certainty.

Emerson also faulted the balancing approach for the way in which it calls on judges to make broad policy judgments based only on evidence presented by the parties before the court. In using balancing tests, a judge is required to make what amounts to a legislative judgment about conflicting social policy goals. Emerson called the factual determinations necessary to make such judgments "enormously difficult and time-consuming, and quite unsuitable for the judicial process."[26] For example, how is a judge to evaluate the need to maintain the editorial integrity of the news media and then balance that interest against the possible harm to a particular criminal defendant's Sixth Amendment right to a fair trial? How is a judge to measure the value of a free and uninhibited press, or the potentially damaging impact of an open trial on the privacy rights of victims or jurors? Some might maintain that the balance has already been struck by virtue of the First Amendment—no further balancing is necessary. As the scrutiny structure currently stands, however, judges are regularly called on to make broad policy decisions based only on the narrow interests of the litigants.

Emerson further criticized ad hoc balancing for being inordinately weighted toward upholding government regulation. At first glance, this criticism might not seem applicable to heightened scrutiny. But commentators have noted just this feature—exaggerated judicial deference toward legislative judgment—in the application of the intermediate *O'Brien* standard. First Amendment scholar Martin Redish criticized intermediate scrutiny as follows:

> The test nowhere asks whether the asserted governmental interest is sufficiently "substantial" to justify the "incidental" impact on free expression. Under these conditions, it is practically inconceivable that an asserted governmental purpose will not qualify. . . . Ultimately, the *O'Brien* test for content-neutral regulations requires nothing more than what Dean Ely characterizes as "no gratuitous inhibition" on speech, a protection which he correctly suggests is all but useless.[27]

---

[23]Emerson, *supra* note 2, at 53-54.

[24]*Id.* at 54.

[25]*Id.*

[26]*Id.* at 55.

[27]M. Redish, Freedom of Expression: A Critical Analysis 101 (1984).

Thus, at least to the extent that some form of intermediate scrutiny is used, Professor Emerson's view that balancing tends to uphold government regulation facing constitutional challenge may be relevant. Although Professor Emerson's analysis is directed at ad hoc balancing tests—and not the heightened scrutiny formulations examined in this book—it does at least raise questions worth asking about heightened scrutiny.

The application of balancing tests may be particularly fraught with danger for free expression when another constitutional right is placed on the scale opposite the First Amendment. In cases examined in this study, the Sixth Amendment right of a criminal defendant to an impartial trial is frequently cited as opposing the First Amendment rights of the media. The right of a "free press" is seen as being balanced against a defendant's right to a "fair trial." This interpretation of conflicting rights is open to dispute, however. Professor Laurence Tribe pointed out that the "key conflict . . . is not between a defendant's sixth amendment rights and a publisher's first amendment rights." Rather, if the state, which has a duty to provide a fair trial, cannot do so, "the defendant is entitled by the sixth amendment to a dismissal of the charges against him."[28] The burden is on the government to provide a fair trial under the Sixth Amendment, but that amendment does not allow the government to invade other constitutional rights, such as free expression, to accomplish its ends. Regardless of whether one accepts Professor Tribe's distinction, however, the perceived conflict between two constitutional rights in cases involving media coverage of criminal proceedings may affect the application of heightened scrutiny. This study will examine the extent to which that perceived conflict alters the balance.

SCHOLARS AND THE SCRUTINY STRUCTURE

Legal scholars have written fairly extensively on the nature of judicial review when First Amendment interests have been implicated. Moreover, a number of commentators have explored the *nature* of the scrutiny structure. However, these studies have concentrated primarily on Supreme Court opinions, and few have focused on how the cases affect the ability of the media to provide information to the public. This section explores the work of scholars in this field, and points out where this study fits within this literature.

Professor Geoffrey Stone explored the distinction the Supreme Court has recognized between content-based and content-neutral restrictions on speech and the accompanying levels of scrutiny that distinction entails. In *Content Regulation and the First Amendment*,[29] Stone examined the nature of the content distinction and the varying modes of judicial review associated with it, touching on the notions of intermediate and strict scrutiny. Government limitations on speech that are

---

[28]L. Tribe, American Constitutional Law 624-26 (1978).

[29]25 Wm. & Mary L. Rev. 189 (1983).

considered content-neutral restrict speech based on some factor other than the message sought to be communicated. An example would be limitations on bill-boards in some areas. Content-neutral restrictions are generally treated with some deference by the Court, requiring only that government demonstrate that it has some reasonably substantial interest in the regulation, and that the speaker has alternative means of communicating his or her views to others. In contrast, content-based restrictions restrict speech based on the message conveyed. The Court has generally viewed content-based restrictions with some suspicion, although it has allowed such restrictions in the case of "low-value" speech, like obscenity or commercial speech. For higher value speech, particularly speech concerned with political matters or public affairs, the Court has generally applied strict scrutiny or the clear and present danger test, both of which are standards under which restrictions on speech rarely survive. In a subtle and nuanced analysis, Stone concluded that the content distinction was a worthwhile feature of First Amendment doctrine.

Professor Stone more closely analyzed levels of scrutiny in a 1987 article, *Content Neutral Restrictions*.[30] In this article, Stone identified three distinct stand-ards of review: deferential, intermediate, and strict. These three standards were further subdivided into seven verbal formulations the Court has used to describe the process of judicial review it was undertaking.

In *The* O'Brie*ning of Free Speech Methodology*, Professor Keith Werhan examined the "curious omnipresence of *O'Brien* balancing across a considerable landscape of free speech issues."[31] He advocated returning *O'Brien* to its relatively limited role in balancing incidental restrictions on expression where the First Amendment stakes are low.

Professor Thomas Emerson also criticized the scrutiny structure in his 1980 article, *First Amendment Doctrine and the Burger Court.*[32] Emerson expressed concern that the Supreme Court under Chief Justice Warren Burger insisted on engaging in extensive "balancing" or weighing of countervailing interests, even in cases in which it was clear that the government restriction violated the First Amendment. Professor Emerson argued that the Court's elaborate attempts to calculate the social value of particular speech to calibrate the balance of interests thrusts the Court into exactly the sort of value determinations that government should not make under the First Amendment. Emerson also found the intermediate *O'Brien* standard inadequate, arguing that, under most circumstances, "there is virtually no likelihood that the balance will be struck in favor of First Amendment values."[33]

Another examination of the scrutiny structure is provided by Professor David S. Day in *The Hybridization of the Content-Neutral Standards for the Free Speech Clause.*[34] Professor Day criticized the tendency of the Supreme Court to blur the

---

[30] 54 U. Chi. L. Rev 46 (1987).

[31] 19 Ariz. St. L.J. 635, 637-38 (1987).

[32] 68 Calif. L. Rev. 422 (1980).

[33] *Id.* at 451.

[34] 19 Ariz. St. L.J. 195 (1987).

line between heightened scrutiny and weaker standards of constitutional review. In particular, Day found that the so-called "time, place, and manner" doctrine, which allows significant regulation of speech not based on content, was being fused with the ostensibly more-protective *O'Brien* test, used to decide cases in which the burden on speech is "incidental." Day declared this hybridization to be a doctrinal mistake that confuses two standards created for different purposes, and that would ultimately limit the Court's flexibility in deciding free speech cases.

A thorough review of *O'Brien*, as well as the broader implications of heightened scrutiny methodologies, is provided by Professor John Hart Ely in *Flag Desecration: A Case Study in the Roles of Categorization and Balancing in First Amendment Analysis.*[35] Professor Ely explored the assumptions implicit in *O'Brien* and the broader significance of the scrutiny structure in free expression cases.

Chrysta Osborn examined the scrutiny structure in *Constitutional Scrutiny and Speech: Eroding the Bedrock Principles of the First Amendment.*[36] Osborn argued that the Supreme Court's approach to heightened scrutiny "differentiates between acts of speech based on content, resulting in unequal treatment for strikingly similar speech."[37] Osborn also criticized the scrutiny structure for its incomprehensibility.

In *Means-End Scrutiny in American Constitutional Law,*[38] Professor Russell Galloway engaged in an extended analysis of means-end scrutiny as applied not only in First Amendment cases, but in a variety of constitutional contexts. Professor Galloway suggested the Court develop a consistent scrutiny methodology and employ more precision in its use of such terms as *compelling* or *substantial interests.* "Concededly, the levels of scrutiny tend to be sliding scales that blend into a single spectrum, as Justice Marshall has argued," Galloway wrote. "Nevertheless, the Court has an obligation to use words in a consistent and principled way that allows as much certainty and predictability as possible."[39]

Although a number of legal scholars have examined aspects of the scrutiny structure, few communication scholars have ventured into the field. One exception is Professor Patrick Parsons, who explored the application of intermediate scrutiny to cable television in *In the Wake of Preferred: Waiting for Godot.*[40] Professor Parsons, while not concentrating on the notion of heightened scrutiny, found *O'Brien* an inadequate standard for evaluating the complex constitutional considerations raised by cable.

This book differs in at least two important ways from the literature described above. First, no scholar has concentrated on how the scrutiny structure affects the media specifically. Although much has been written concerning flaming draft cards and flags, the impact of the Court's scrutiny devices on the media's ability to gather

---

[35] 88 Harv. L. Rev. 1482 (1975).

[36] 44 Southwestern L.J. 1013 (1990).

[37] *Id.* at 1013.

[38] 21 Loy. L.A. L. Rev. 449 (1988).

[39] *Id.* at 466.

[40] 1989 Mass Comm. Rev. 26.

news and report events in a day-to-day context has been neglected. In particular, little attention has been paid to the ability of the media to gain access to and report on activities in the criminal justice system under the Court's peculiar balancing regime. Second, scholars have not addressed the impact of scrutiny doctrines once transplanted from the rarefied air of the Court to the lower courts. A confusing and somewhat inconsistent system of judicial review may be an inconvenience at the Supreme Court level, but to busy lower courts, where most cases are decided, the problems with the scrutiny structure may be greatly magnified. Few constitutional scholars examine lower court cases, apparently on the assumption that doctrinal transference is accomplished with little difficulty.

Thus, the present study addresses previously unexplored questions regarding the scrutiny structure, and seeks to shed light on the practical and theoretical advantages and disadvantages of the current structure as it applies to the press as it seeks to cover criminal justice. The result should be a clearer picture of how the Court's First Amendment jurisprudence both empowers and constrains the press.

SUMMARY OF THE BOOK

Chapter 2 explores the historical context in which the Supreme Court first advanced something like the notion of heightened scrutiny of First Amendment issues. The chapter traces the beginnings of the doctrine and the theoretical underpinnings of the idea that First Amendment freedoms should be given special protection from infringement by government. The chapter also discusses some of the heightened scrutiny formulations that have been created by the Supreme Court.

Chapter 3 describes the legal background of the "free press–fair trial" issue, both in the Supreme Court and in a series of studies that sought to resolve the issue. In particular, it explores the difficulties inherent in finding unbiased jurors in an era of widespread mass media and the constitutional limitations on the use of judicial power against the press.

Chapter 4 examines the application of heightened scrutiny to prior restraints on the press in cases involving the criminal justice system. It describes how both the Supreme Court and lower federal courts have applied the scrutiny structure to prior restraints on the press.

Chapter 5 discusses the scrutiny structure's application to cases involving postpublication sanctions against the media in connection with the criminal justice system. The chapter examines a line of Supreme Court cases on this point, as well as lower federal court cases in which either criminal or civil sanctions have been sought.

Chapter 6 examines the issue of access by the press to criminal proceedings, both trials and other related proceedings. The chapter discusses the Supreme Court's creation in 1980 of a First Amendment right of access to trials and the cases that followed. It explores how some lower courts have been slow to extend the Court's rationale to its logical conclusion.

Chapter 7 summarizes the findings of the book, and analyzes the extent to which heightened scrutiny is consistent with First Amendment concerns. It also critiques and offers suggestions for strengthening the existing scrutiny structure.

Chapter 8 proposes a new model for deciding First Amendment cases dealing with the criminal justice system. It explores the tension between "rules" and "standards" in legal doctrine, and argues that a clear rule protecting speech about the criminal justice system is a superior approach to this difficult area of the law.

-2-

The Supreme Court and First Amendment Scrutiny

An enduring question in the Supreme Court's approach to the First Amendment has been the extent to which the Court should exercise its power of judicial review to invalidate legislation the Court deems to be in contravention of the First Amendment. Should the Court presume that legislators, who after all are bound by oath to uphold the Constitution, are acting constitutionally when they pass laws restricting purported First Amendment freedoms? If not, how closely should the Court examine such legislation to determine if it passes constitutional muster? In attempting to answer such questions, the Court since the late 1930s has created a number of constitutional tests to guide both itself and lower courts as they examine legislation affecting First Amendment rights.

One of the most important tests created by the Court to determine the constitutionality of legislation limiting free expression is the so-called "strict scrutiny" test. The term *strict scrutiny* means that when certain fundamental rights are restricted by government, judges will exercise a very active form of judicial review to test the constitutionality of the restriction. Strict scrutiny, as the name implies, places a heavy burden on the government to justify the regulation of speech and other important rights. Under strict scrutiny, First Amendment interests are upheld unless the governmental interest in regulation is compelling, and that interest is achieved in the least restrictive manner.[1]

The U.S. Supreme Court's adoption of a strict scrutiny methodology applied to government regulation of free expression is frequently said to have originated in *U.S. v. Carolene Products*.[2] In that 1938 case, Justice Harlan Fiske Stone articulated

---

[1] Consolidated Edison Co. v. Public Service Commission, 447 U.S. 530 (1980); First National Bank of Boston v. Belloti, 435 U.S. 765 (1978).

[2] 304 U.S. 144 (1938).

the rationale for what would become strict scrutiny in perhaps the most famous footnote in the history of Supreme Court jurisprudence.[3] Although it is clear that Stone's famous footnote was not the first suggestion that government must have weighty reasons to restrict expression, the footnote marks the end of one era and the beginning of another. Perhaps for this reason, Justice Stone's footnote is often credited with creating a new methodology of judicial review in cases involving, among other fundamental rights, First Amendment rights of free speech and free press.

The *Carolene Products* footnote came at the end of a period of heated conflict over the appropriate role of the Court in passing on the constitutionality of legislation. For nearly 50 years, the Court had invalidated many state and federal attempts to legislate in the economic sphere. The Court's laissez-faire view of the Constitution led to a major political crisis during the Great Depression, which significantly altered the Court's approach to judicial review.

This chapter examines the end of the so-called *Lochner* era, noted for its protection of property rights and concomitant rejection of governmental regulation of economic matters. The death of *Lochner*-style judicial review—called *substantive due process*—carried with it the seeds of a new judicial activism in the realm of civil liberties, particularly First Amendment rights. The chapter examines the beginnings of this new approach to judicial review, both as suggested in the *Carolene Products* footnote and a number of earlier cases foreshadowing the new doctrine. The chapter then compares the heightened judicial scrutiny suggested in the famous footnote with the closely related preferred position doctrine. Finally, the chapter reviews several significant cases immediately following *Carolene Products,* in which the new doctrine of strict scrutiny achieved majority support on the Court, and considers the modern variations of the scrutiny structure.

THE END OF THE *LOCHNER* ERA

The era symbolized by the Supreme Court's decision in *Lochner v. New York*[4] began in the late 19th century and came to an end in 1937, the year before Justice Stone composed his famous footnote in *Carolene Products*. In *Lochner*, the Court struck down a New York maximum-hours law aimed at limiting the working hours of bakery employees. The Court held that the law violated Fourteenth Amendment's due process clause, which the Court interpreted as protecting the liberty of contract between employees and employers. The *Lochner* era was characterized by the Court's vigorous use of its power of judicial review to strike down legislative attempts to regulate economic matters.[5] As one commentator put it:

---

[3]*Id.* at 152 n. 4.

[4]198 U.S. 45 (1905).

[5]Harris, Judicial Review: Vagaries and Varieties, 38 Journal of Politics 173, 1818-82 (Aug. 1976); Mavrinac, From *Lochner* to *Brown v. Topeka*: The Court and Conflicting Concepts of the Political Process, 52 American Political Science Review 641 (1958). Some recent scholarship suggests that earlier legal historians have overstated the extent to which laissez-faire views dominated constitutional adjudications in this era. *E.g.*, K. Hall, The Magic Mirror 238-46 (1989).

The chief concern of this long era was to guard the sanctity of property. Socio-economic experimentation by the legislatures, such as minimum-wage, maximum-hour, and child-labor regulations, was regarded with almost unshakable disapproval by a solid majority of the Court. Again and again the justices struck down, as unconstitutional violations of substantive due process of law, legislation that large majorities . . . deemed wise and necessary. They reasoned that because of the *substance* (the nature of the content) of the legislation involved—i.e., what the law was all about—such statutory experimentation deprived "persons" (i.e., property owners, chiefly businessmen) of their liberty without due process of law.[6]

This laissez-faire view of the due process clauses of the Fifth and Fourteenth Amendments led to increasing conflict between the Court and the executive and legislative branches during the nation's economic crisis of the 1930s. The Depression caused a national rethinking of the basic tenets of laissez-faire economic policy, including the notion that the economy functioned best free of government regulation.[7] The response came in 1933, with President Franklin D. Roosevelt's "New Deal." The New Deal "stood for the proposition that lawmakers should provide a social and economic security net to catch the victims of an impersonal industrial order and that administrative agencies should bring a scientific coherence to the economy."[8] New Deal legislation, however, ran directly contrary to the conservative Court majority's view of substantive due process. The New Deal "provided an ample hunting ground for judicial marksmen."[9] The Court struck down fifteen acts of Congress from 1930 to 1937, with eleven of those acts ruled unconstitutional in 1935 and 1936 alone.[10]

Not all of the justices supported the constitutional limits placed on economic regulation under substantive due process. Justices Holmes, Brandeis, and Stone, in dissent, attacked the majority's conservative ideology. Concern for the "counter-majoritarian" nature of substantive due process drove the dissenters' attempts to put judicial review in what they regarded as its proper place in a democratic society.[11] As Justice Stone's biographer wrote:

In particular, Stone set for himself the special task of correcting the Court's besetting sin— its tendency to damage itself by overreaching its power. . . . Deeply disturbed by the conflict between the people's elected representatives and the Court, he strove to bridge that gap by rigorous delineation of the judicial function.[12]

---

[6]H. Abraham, Freedom and the Court 12 (5th ed. 1988).

[7]K. Hall, The Magic Mirror 266 (1989).

[8]*Id.* at 267.

[9]Harris, *supra* note 5, at 187.

[10]*Id.*

[11]Cover, The Origins of Judicial Activism in the Protection of Minorities, 91 Yale L.J. 1287, 1288 (1982).

[12]A. Mason, Harlan Fiske Stone: Pillar of the Law 333 (1956).

Despite the efforts of the dissenters, the Court's majority remained intransigent. The Court's conservative wing, dubbed the "Four Horsemen," consisted of Justices Van Devanter, McReynolds, Sutherland, and Butler. Between these four justices and the three dissenters on the ideological spectrum were Chief Justice Hughes and Justice Roberts.[13]

In an attempt to break the Court's conservative stance on economic experimentation, Roosevelt conceived a plan that would allow him to appoint new justices with more congenial constitutional philosophies. The so-called "court-packing plan," ostensibly designed to assist the federal judiciary with its workload, would have allowed Roosevelt to appoint new judges, including Supreme Court justices, when judges of retirement age chose to stay on the bench. The plan was introduced in Congress in early 1937, but never became law.[14]

While Congress considered the court-packing plan, the Court made what appeared to be a strategic retreat from its previous position on the constitutionality of New Deal legislation. In the spring of 1937, Hughes and Roberts joined the three dissenters to uphold state minimum-wage and federal labor legislation.[15] The decisions, and those that followed, were the death knell for the notion of substantive due process in the economic sphere. In a 3-month span, Roosevelt had won "a political victory often styled as 'the switch in time that saved nine.' "[16] Shortly after the end of the decade, Roosevelt had appointed seven new justices to the Court, altering its philosophical makeup drastically.[17]

CIVIL LIBERTIES ASCENDANT

The Carolene Products Footnote

After the so-called "constitutional revolution of 1937," a new standard of review prevailed in cases affecting property rights and economic interests. In the economic sphere, as long as legislation was not "without a rational basis," it would be upheld as constitutional by the Court.[18] But it was not long before Justice Stone announced a significantly more stringent approach to legislation affecting civil liberties. The Court had adopted a new spirit of judicial restraint, but Stone had determined that such restraint was not appropriate for all constitutional freedoms the Court was charged with protecting. "If the baby was not to be thrown out with the bath, the

---

[13]Hall, *supra* note 7, at 277.

[14]*Id.* at 281-82.

[15]*Id.* at 282.

[16]Abraham, *supra* note 6, at 13. Ironically, Stone's biographer contends the showdown between the Court and the president might never have occurred if the conservative justices had been able to retire with assurances that Congress would not reduce their compensation. Mason, *supra*, note 12, at 454-55.

[17]Hall, *supra* note 7, at 283.

[18]W. Swindler, Court and the Constitution in the Twentieth Century 103 (1970).

Court should become concerned with other values."[19] These new values were initially proclaimed in a rather unlikely place—in a footnote in a case that was not remotely related to civil liberties.

U.S. v. Carolene Products Co.[20] dealt with the constitutionality of a federal statute that prohibited interstate shipment of "filled milk," milk from which the fat had been removed and replaced with coconut oil. This was the type of commercial legislation the pre-1937 Court might well have struck down. Under the Court's revised constitutional philosophy, however, the law was presumptively constitutional. While upholding the legislation under the rational basis standard, Justice Stone included the following language in footnote four of the opinion:

> There may be narrower scope for the operation of the presumption of constitutionality when the legislation appears on its face to be within a specific prohibition of the Constitution, such as those of the first ten amendments, which are deemed equally specific when held to be embraced within the Fourteenth.
>
> It is unnecessary to consider now whether legislation which restricts those political processes which can ordinarily be expected to bring about repeal of undesirable legislation, is to be subjected to more exacting judicial scrutiny under the general prohibitions of the Fourteenth Amendment than are most other types of legislation.
>
> Nor need we enquire whether similar considerations enter into the review of statutes directed at particular religious, or national, or racial minorities: whether prejudice against discrete and insular minorities may be a special condition, which tends to curtail the operation of those political processes ordinarily to be relied upon to protect minorities, and which may call for a correspondingly more searching judicial inquiry.[21]

The first paragraph of the footnote, which suggested a more stringent standard of judicial review for rights explicitly protected by the Constitution, was not solely Stone's product. The first draft of the footnote, written by Stone's law clerk Louis Lusky, contained the following language in the first paragraph: "Different considerations may apply, and one attacking the constitutionality of a statute may be thought to bear a lighter burden, when the legislation aims at restricting the corrective political processes, which can ordinarily be expected to bring about repeal of undesirable legislation."[22]

Chief Justice Hughes wrote a letter to Stone questioning the original language of the first paragraph. Hughes was concerned that the paragraph did not adequately explain that it was invasion of rights given in the specific provisions of the Bill of

---

[19]Mason, Judicial Activism: Old and New, 55 Va. L. Rev. 385, 394 (1969).

[20]304 U.S. 144 (1938).

[21]*Id.* at 152 n.4 (citations omitted).

[22]Mason, The Core of Free Government, 1938-40: Mr. Justice Stone and "Preferred Freedoms," 65 Yale L.J. 597, 600 (1956).

Rights that gave rise to active judicial review.[23] As a result, Stone revised the paragraph to highlight Hughes' concern with textual rights.[24] As Louis Lusky observed:

> Some rights, Hughes was suggesting, deserve more judicial attention than others because they are mentioned in the text of the Constitution. . . . The implicit assumption is that this recognition of their special significance by the revered Framers will legitimize extraordinarily intrusive judicial review as implementing the intent of the Framers themselves.[25]

Commentators have suggested a number of social and political factors that may have led Stone and later proponents to advocate the doctrinal approach of footnote four. Although the first paragraph of the footnote speaks of textual constitutional rights in general, it soon became clear that Stone was principally concerned with First Amendment guarantees.[26] Such liberties were in short supply in other parts of the world in the late 1930s. Political repression in Germany, Italy, and Russia had encouraged even politically conservative groups in the United States to advocate protection of personal freedoms in this country.[27] For some members of the Court, "[t]he desire to join in the national civil liberties' crusade was not absent."[28] The *Carolene Products* footnote offered a doctrinal solution for such action, even as the Court was relinquishing its role as guardian of capitalism.

In addition, the Court was entering an era in which it would openly balance governmental and constitutional interests. Such balancing, suggested in Stone's "more exacting scrutiny" formulation, was a repudiation of "the old legal method known as 'mechanical jurisprudence.' No longer did the Court seem bent on presenting the image that judges were merely the instruments through which the law spoke neutrally and impartially and where syllogistic reasoning and literal interpretation were viewed as the life of the law."[29] As legal historian Morton Horwitz has pointed out, American courts and legal scholars from the early 20th century onward had been engaged in a critique of this kind of "categorical thinking" that reflected dissatisfaction with bright-line rules.[30] This critique, which found its strongest expression in the Progressive and Legal Realist movements, encouraged the abandonment of categorical thinking in favor of more nuanced balancing of social interests. From the syllogistic logic of mechanical jurisprudence, the post-

---

[23]Lusky, Footnote Redux: A *Carolene Products* Reminiscence, 82 Colum. L. Rev. 1093, 1097 (1982).

[24]Mason, *supra* note 22, at 600.

[25]Lusky, *supra* note 23, at 1097.

[26]Abraham, *supra* note 6, at 23.

[27]P. Murphy, The Meaning of Freedom of Speech 276-77 (1972).

[28]*Id.* at 279.

[29]E. Corwin, The Constitution and What It Means Today 239 (13th ed. 1974).

[30]M. Horwitz, The Transformation of American Law 1870-1960: The Crisis of Legal Orthodoxy 199 (1992)

1937 Court seemed prepared to embark on a constitutional jurisprudence that "*explicitly* recognize[d] the legislative function in judicial review."[31]

The new doctrine of judicial review articulated in Justice Stone's *Carolene Products* footnote did not win universal acclamation. As Professor Archibald Cox pointed out:

> Many thoughtful persons, however, Learned Hand and Felix Frankfurter among them, found it inconsistent to follow the legislative supremacy approach in sustaining social and economic measures and then to turn around and substitute judicial findings and values for the conclusions of elected representatives in dealing with restraints upon speech or association. The supposed dichotomy between "personal rights" and "property rights" left them unpersuaded because, as Learned Hand used to say, "No one will ever tell me why holding property is not a personal liberty."[32]

Roots of Footnote Four

Although the *Carolene Products* footnote espoused a novel doctrine, the idea of heightened judicial review of government restrictions on personal freedoms was not entirely new. For example, several late 19th– and early 20th–century cases suggested, in a general way, that government regulation of private conduct could only pass constitutional muster if a sufficiently important state interest supported the regulation.[33] In *Jacobson v. Massachusetts* in 1905, the Court noted that, "the rights of the individual in respect of his liberty may at times, under the pressure of great dangers, be subject to . . . restraint."[34] Such cases contained the germ of the idea that civil liberties could be restricted only with some showing of necessity beyond the will of the majority.

In the First Amendment area, the Supreme Court's first significant free expression case, *Schenck v. United States,*[35] was the first case in which the Court required more than mere reasonableness in reviewing a statute regulating speech.[36] In *Schenck*, decided in 1919, Justice Holmes wrote for a majority of the Court, affirming the convictions of defendants charged under federal statutes after they mailed leaflets asserting that the draft was unconstitutional. In the course of the opinion, Holmes formulated the seminal version of the clear and present danger test as follows: "The question in every case is whether the words used are used in such circumstances and are of such a nature as to create a clear and present danger that they will bring about the substantive evils that Congress has a right to

---

[31] C. Wolfe, The Rise of Modern Judicial Review 247 (1986).

[32] A. Cox, The Warren Court 94 (1968).

[33] *E.g.*, Munn v. Illinois, 94 U.S. 113, 125 (1877); Jacobson v. Massachusetts, 197 U.S. 11, 29 (1905) *cited in* Note, Of Interests, Fundamental and Compelling: The Emerging Constitutional Balance, 57 B.U.L. Rev. 462, 465 (1977).

[34] 197 U.S. at 29.

[35] 249 U.S. 47 (1919).

[36] Note, *supra* note 33, at 465-66.

prevent."[37] Although a number of scholars assert that the clear and present danger test, as enunciated in *Schenck,* was not the same test Holmes and Brandeis advocated in later speech cases,[38] the *Schenck* formulation at least suggests a level of judicial review in speech cases that goes well beyond a simple determination of legislative reasonableness.

Later articulations of the clear and present danger test by Justices Holmes and Brandeis more clearly point to a greatly heightened level of judicial scrutiny in free expression cases. In a dissenting opinion in *Abrams v. United States,*[39] Holmes, joined by Brandeis, criticized the majority's approach in upholding the conviction of defendants who had distributed leaflets claiming the United States' war effort in Europe was intended to crush the Russian Revolution. The leaflets urged readers to stop supporting the war effort. Holmes' dissent urged a much stricter standard of review than the majority's "bad tendency" analysis: "I think that we should be eternally vigilant against attempts to check the expression of opinions that we loathe and believe to be fraught with death, unless they so imminently threaten immediate interference with the lawful and pressing purposes of the law that an immediate check is required to save the country."[40]

Similarly, in 1926, Brandeis, joined by Holmes, wrote a concurrence in *Whitney v. California*[41] in which he emphasized the immediacy of the danger necessary to support governmental regulation of speech. Stone had joined in the majority opinion in *Whitney*—an opinion that required only a rational basis for government to restrict speech. But, by the time he wrote the famous footnote in *Carolene Products,* Stone had apparently become convinced that a more active approach to judicial review was required in speech cases.[42]

The Holmes–Brandeis clear and present danger formulation clearly provided some of the underpinnings of Stone's *Carolene Products* footnote.[43] *Whitney* was one of the cases cited by Justice Stone in the footnote. Although the clear and present danger test was applied to a narrower class of cases than First Amendment strict scrutiny, both express a similar notion of judicial review. When speech interests are implicated, courts carefully examine the necessity of governmental regulation and only uphold such regulation when compelling circumstances require it. One commentator has expressed the relationship between strict scrutiny and the clear and present danger test as follows: "[The clear and present danger test] may be reconciled with the compelling state interest standard [strict scrutiny] by viewing the test as a subclass of the standard. Thus, it could be said that in cases of direct

---

[37]249 U.S. at 52.

[38]*E.g.,* Gunther, Learned Hand and the Origins of Modern First Amendment Doctrine: Some Fragments of History, 27 Stan. L. Rev. 719 (1975).

[39]250 U.S. 616 (1919).

[40]*Id.* at 630.

[41]274 U.S. 357 (1926).

[42]H. Kalven Jr., A Worthy Tradition 177 (1988).

[43]Wolfe, *supra* note 31, at 247.

infringement of speech, the state only has a compelling interest when there is a clear and present danger."[44]

A number of other pre-*Carolene Products* cases seem to have been important precursors to the ideas expressed by Justice Stone in footnote four. Chief Justice Hughes' majority opinion in the 1931 prior restraint case of *Near v. Minnesota*[45] was one such case. In *Near*, the Court struck down a Minnesota statute that allowed a permanent injunction against "malicious, scandalous and defamatory" publications.[46] At least one scholar has cited *Near* as the first case in which the Holmes–Brandeis approach to free expression gained majority support on the Court.[47] "Beginning with *Near v. Minnesota*, legislation affecting speech and press was, in fact, no longer presumed constitutional," A. T. Mason wrote.[48] Although the *Near* opinion did not employ clear and present danger language, it suggested that prior restraints were presumptively unconstitutional except in a few narrow areas, such as national security and obscenity. *Near* did not set forth a doctrinal formula, but the underlying assumption was that prior restraints were invalid. However, Chief Justice Hughes never articulated this doctrine in any formal way—a task that was left for Justice Stone in *Carolene Products*.

The year before Justice Stone wrote *Carolene Products*, Justice Cardozo wrote a majority opinion in *Palko v. Connecticut*[49] that seems to have had some influence on Justice Stone's thought. Although *Palko* dealt with an issue of the application of the Bill of Rights to the states through the Fourteenth Amendment, Justice Cardozo, in dicta, extolled freedom of speech and thought as "the matrix, the indispensable condition, of nearly every other form of freedom."[50] Justice Cardozo made it clear that only certain rights were "of the very essence of a scheme of ordered liberty,"[51] and among these were free expression rights. Those rights that were "of the very essence" justified judicial overriding of legislative preferences. Justice Stone advanced his notion of active judicial review in cases affecting civil liberties "with Cardozo's distinction in mind."[52]

As these and a number of other cases demonstrate, the *Carolene Products* footnote was not conceived in a jurisprudential vacuum. The idea of active judicial review of legislation regulating civil liberties, and in particular freedom of speech and press, had been in existence for a number of years prior to 1938. For whatever reason, Justice Stone's formulation seems to have been the catalyst for increased judicial activism in civil liberties cases.

---

[44] Anton, When Speech is not Speech: A Perspective on Categorization in First Amendment Adjudication, 19 Wake Forest L. Rev. 33, 47 (1983).

[45] 283 U.S. 697 (1931).

[46] *Id.* at 701-02.

[47] A. Mason, The Supreme Court from Taft to Warren 135-36 (1958).

[48] *Id.*

[49] 302 U.S. 319 (1937).

[50] *Id.* at 327.

[51] 302 U.S. at 325.

[52] Abraham, *supra* note 6, at 22.

The Preferred Position Doctrine

The *Carolene Products* footnote has not only been cited as the doctrinal beginning of heightened judicial review, or strict scrutiny, in First Amendment cases, but has also been credited as the origin of the "preferred position" or "preferred freedoms" doctrine. Under the preferred position doctrine, First Amendment freedoms enjoyed a unique status in the constitutional system, and any attempted governmental regulation of those rights was presumptively unconstitutional.[53] The preferred position doctrine flourished in the 10 years between *Carolene Products* and *Kovacs v. Cooper*,[54] in which Justice Frankfurter's concurrence delivered a stinging attack on the doctrine, calling it, among other things, "a mischievous doctrine."[55] The first use of the phrase "preferred position" by a member of the Court is credited to Justice Stone in dissent in *Jones v. Opelika*.[56] In *Jones*, the Court's majority upheld a city ordinance requiring that door-to-door booksellers obtain a license. The ordinance had been challenged by a Jehovah's Witness. In dissent, Chief Justice Stone wrote that the ordinance was unconstitutional, although it was applied in a nondiscriminatory manner: "The First Amendment is not confined to safeguarding freedom of speech and freedom of religion against discriminatory attempts to wipe them out. On the contrary, the Constitution, by virtue of the First and Fourteenth Amendments, has put those freedoms in a preferred position."[57] In 1943, Justice Douglas, writing for the Court, struck down a Pennsylvania municipal ordinance requiring a license tax to sell literature in *Murdock v. Pennsylvania*.[58] The ordinance, as in *Jones*, had been challenged by Jehovah's Witnesses who sought to carry out their literature distribution free of the local ordinance. Justice Douglas wrote, without citation to previous authority, that "[f]reedom of the press, freedom of speech, freedom of religion are in a preferred position."[59]

The preferred position doctrine is closely related to the notion of strict scrutiny in free expression cases. It seems clear that both share the principle that legislation abridging First Amendment guarantees is "infected with presumptive invalidity," as Justice Frankfurter put it in *Kovacs*.[60] This is so, however, only if the word presumption is used as a legal term of art, imposing "on the party against whom it is directed the burden of going forward with evidence to rebut or meet the presumption. . . ."[61] Neither strict scrutiny nor the preferred position doctrine, as

---

[53]Encyclopedia of the American Constitution 1439 (1986).

[54]*See, e.g.,* H. Stonecipher, Safeguarding Speech and Press Guarantees: Preferred Position Postulate Reexamined 96 n.49, in B. Chamberlin and C. Brown, The First Amendment Reconsidered (1982).

[55]336 U.S. 77, 90 (Frankfurter, J., concurring) (1949).

[56]316 U.S. 584, 608 (Stone, C.J., dissenting) (1941), *rev'd on rehearing*, 318 U.S. 796 (1943).

[57]*Id.* at 608 (Stone, C.J., dissenting).

[58]319 U.S. 105 (1943).

[59]*Id.* at 115.

[60]336 U.S. at 90.

[61]Black's Law Dictionary 1067 (5th ed. 1979).

used by the Court, ever gave rise to a presumption of unconstitutionality in the everyday sense, in which a presumption is "the act of presuming or accepting as true."[62] Under strict scrutiny, as later articulated by the Court, First Amendment interests are upheld unless the governmental interest in regulation is compelling, and that interest is achieved in the least restrictive manner.[63] Under the preferred position doctrine, as one commentator described it, the requirement was that "legislative infringement of [First Amendment] values must be shown to be not only 'reasonably' adapted to attaining valid social goals but justified by overwhelmingly conclusive considerations."[64] Thus, whether the formulation requires a "compelling interest" or "overwhelmingly conclusive considerations," both doctrines balance First Amendment interests against other social interests with a strong weighting of the scale toward the former. Meeting such tests involves evidentiary showings that are not inconsequential, but does not involve anything of the magnitude of overcoming a presumption in its everyday sense (e.g., the presumption that the sun sets in the west). Thus, the presumption of unconstitutionality is not an impenetrable barrier to legislation, but merely requires that government come forward with a sufficient showing to meet the test. Once that burden is met, the presumption effectively vanishes.

Explicit mention of the preferred position doctrine seemed to fade after Justice Frankfurter's attack in *Kovacs*. A few commentators contend that the doctrine lost currency with the Court,[65] whereas others imply that, although nominally absent from Court opinions, preferred position doctrine became a basic, if unspoken, element of the Court's First Amendment jurisprudence.[66] Most seem to agree that preferred position doctrine and strict scrutiny are closely related parts of the same constitutional movement begun by the *Carolene* footnote.[67] First Amendment scholar Leonard Levy explained the connection between preferred position doctrine and strict scrutiny as follows: "Although the Court rarely speaks of a preferred freedoms doctrine today, the substance of the doctrine has been absorbed in the concepts of strict scrutiny, fundamental rights, and selective incorporation."[68]

---

[62]The American Heritage Dictionary of the English Language 1037 (1975).

[63]Consolidated Edison Co. v. Public Service Commission, 447 U.S. 530 (1980); First National Bank of Boston v. Bellotti, 435 U.S. 765 (1978).

[64]H. Stonecipher, Safeguarding Speech and Press Guarantees: Preferred Position Postulate Reexamined 96 in B. Chamberlin and C. Brown, The First Amendment Reconsidered (1982).

[65]Lusky, *supra* note 23, at 1102.

[66]Mason, *supra* note 22, at 627-28; Abraham, *supra* note 6, at 24.

[67]*E.g.,* Powell, Carolene Products Revisited, 82 Colum. L. Rev. 1087, 1089 (footnote four "is recognized as the primary source of 'strict scrutiny'"); Rawlings, Employment Division, Department of Human Resources v. Smith: The Supreme Court Deserts the Free Exercise Clause, 25 Ga. L. Rev. 567, 579 (1991); Gottlieb, Compelling Governmental Interests: An Essential But Unanalyzed Term in Constitutional Adjudication, 68 B.U.L. Rev. 917, 923 (1988); W. Murphy et al., American Constitutional Interpretation 490, 493 (1986).

[68]L. Levy, Preferred Freedoms 1440, in L. Levy (Ed.) Encyclopedia of the American Constitution (1986).

The Immediate Aftermath of Footnote Four

The year after *Carolene Products* was decided, the Court issued an opinion that put
the idea of heightened scrutiny into effect. In *Schneider v. State*,[69] the Court held
unconstitutional four separate municipal ordinances restricting either the distribution of handbills on a public street or house-to-house canvassing. Justice Roberts,
writing for the majority, stated that freedom of speech and press were "fundamental
personal rights and liberties."[70] Justice Roberts expressed the standard for determining the constitutionality of restrictions on such rights as follows:

> In every case, therefore, where legislative abridgment of the rights is asserted, the
> courts should be astute to examine the effect of the challenged legislation. Mere
> legislative preferences or beliefs respecting matters of public convenience may well
> support regulation directed at other personal activities, but be insufficient to justify
> such as diminishes the exercise of rights so vital to the maintenance of democratic
> institutions. And so, as cases arise, the delicate and difficult task falls upon the courts
> to weigh the circumstances and to appraise the substantiality of the reasons advanced
> in support of the regulation. . . .[71]

In *Schneider*, the free expression rights of those who wished to distribute
literature were being restricted, and the Court was requiring government to produce
some substantial justification for the ordinances. The mere desire of the munici-
palities to prevent littering, for example, was insufficient under the Court's new
heightened standard of review.[72]

Other decisions using more exacting scrutiny soon followed. In 1942, the phrase
"strict scrutiny" first entered into the Court's vocabulary in *Skinner v. Oklahoma*.[73]
Skinner dealt not with First Amendment free expression rights, but with an
Oklahoma statute that allowed sterilization of persons deemed "habitual criminals"
under Oklahoma law. Justice Douglas, writing for the majority, struck down the
statute as a violation of the equal protection clause of the Fourteenth Amendment.
Justice Douglas, after finding that marriage and procreation were fundamental
rights, wrote that "strict scrutiny of the classification which a State makes in a
sterilization law is essential, lest unwittingly, or otherwise, invidious discrimina-
tions are made against groups or types of individuals in violation of the constitutional guaranty of just and equal laws."[74]

Although *Skinner* dealt with equal protection, another 1943 decision has been
cited as the case in which the First Amendment strict scrutiny suggested in footnote

---

[69]308 U. S. 147 (1939).

[70]*Id*. at 161.

[71]*Id*.

[72]308 U.S. at 162.

[73]316 U.S. 535 (1942).

[74]*Id*. at 541.

four first triumphed.[75] In *Board of Education v. Barnette*,[76] the Court invalidated a West Virginia requirement that public school students regularly participate in the flag salute. Those who declined were subject to expulsion. The *Barnette* case, brought by Jehovah's Witnesses, overruled a decision only 3 years earlier by the Court upholding a similar flag salute requirement by a vote of 8–1 in *Minersville District v. Gobitis*.[77] Scholars have suggested that the wave of national insecurity caused by Germany's invasion of much of Europe, and the resulting "patriotic fervor," may have contributed to the lopsided ruling by the *Gobitis* Court.[78] Justice Frankfurter's majority opinion in *Gobitis* advocated judicial restraint and majoritarian solutions to questionable laws, suggesting that "education in the abandonment of foolish legislation is itself a training in liberty."[79] The sole dissenter in *Gobitis* was Justice Stone, urging the "searching judicial inquiry" he had advocated in footnote four.[80]

Justice Jackson, writing for the *Barnette* majority, repudiated the *Gobitis* ruling. Jackson acknowledged that, under the due process clause of the Fourteenth Amendment, state legislation had only to meet the rational basis test. However, where legislation contravened the guarantees of the First Amendment as applied to the states through the Fourteenth, a different standard prevailed. "[F]reedoms of speech and of press, of assembly, and of worship may not be infringed on such slender grounds," Jackson wrote. "They are susceptible of restriction only to prevent grave and immediate danger to interests which the State may lawfully protect."[81]

Some 5 years after the *Carolene Products* footnote, a majority of the Court had, in *Barnette*, unambiguously supported Justice Stone's notion of heightened judicial review in a First Amendment case. As Professor Cox wrote: "Justice Jackson's opinion marks the Court's first clear-cut commitment to strict review of legislation challenged under the First Amendment, either directly or as incorporated into the Fourteenth Amendment."[82]

Although the details of strict scrutiny analysis remained to be worked out, particularly during the Warren years, the doctrine had established a place in the constitutional arsenal of the Court. One commentator described the transformation of the famous footnote into the modern strict scrutiny formulation as follows:

> The Court's solution was to subject the means and purposes of legislative or administrative action to careful scrutiny; a legislative or administrative enactment impinging

---

[75]Cox, *supra* note 32, at 195.

[76]319 U.S. 624 (1943).

[77]310 U.S. 586 (1939).

[78]C. Pritchett, The Roosevelt Court 95 (1948).

[79]310 U.S. at 600.

[80]*Id.* at 606.

[81]319 U.S. at 624.

[82]Cox, *supra* note 32, at 195.

on the critical rights defined in *Carolene Products* could be sustained only where a compelling governmental purpose was furthered by the least restrictive means.[83]

FIRST AMENDMENT SCRUTINY TODAY

In the years since the beginning of modern First Amendment jurisprudence, the Supreme Court has adopted a variety of tests for balancing constitutional rights — in particular, free expression rights — with other social interests that are deemed important. These tests, sometimes called *standards of review* or *levels of scrutiny*, purport to provide a framework with which the Court, and lower courts, can make a principled determination of the strength of the opposing interest, and whether it should "trump" the constitutional right. Although the tests have been mentioned in prior sections, this section sets forth the particulars of each test.

Clear and Present Danger Test

The clear and present danger test runs through much of the Supreme Court's 20th-century First Amendment jurisprudence. The test, which at first seemed designed primarily to decide cases involving seditious speech, has in later incarnations served to guide courts in free press–fair trial decisions. The clear and present danger test's relationship to other forms of heightened scrutiny can at times seem murky, although for the most part the test seems to operate in a manner similar to strict scrutiny.

The clear and present danger test was first stated, as noted earlier, in 1919 in *Schenck v. United States*.[84] Prior to *Schenck*, the Court had mostly relied on the so-called "bad-tendency" test in speech cases. The bad-tendency standard allowed punishment for speech if it had even a relatively slight propensity to cause harm to some social interest. As stated by Justice Holmes in *Schenck*, the clear and present danger test posed the following question: "The question in every case is whether the words used are used in such circumstances and are of such a nature as to create a clear and present danger that they will bring about the substantive evil the Congress has a right to prevent."[85]

Despite the implication that the new test required a substantial showing to restrain speech, *Schenck* broke little ground. The Court affirmed the conviction of the defendant, a socialist who had circulated leaflets opposing the draft. The clear and present danger test, as applied in *Schenck*, did not add any perceptible rigor to the Court's protection of speech. "Holmes' clear and present danger test was the

---

[83]Gottlieb, Compelling Governmental Interests: An Essential but Unanalyzed Term in Constitutional Adjudication, 68 B.U.L. Rev. 917, 923 (1988) (citing Shelton v. Tucker, 364 U.S. 479, 488 [1960]).

[84]249 U.S. 47 (1919).

[85]*Id.* at 52.

old bad-tendency test wrapped up in new judicial wording," wrote one legal historian. "The Court drew on it to sustain the convictions of radicals in two other cases" decided shortly after *Schenck*.[86]

However, during the Court's next term, Holmes transformed the clear and present danger test. The test became significantly more protective of speech, at least as described by Holmes in dissent in *Abrams v. U.S.* While defending the result in *Schenck*, Holmes asserted that the government, consistent with the Constitution, could only "punish speech that produces or is intended to produce a clear and imminent danger that it will bring about forthwith certain substantive evils . . . ."[87] This new emphasis on imminent harm brought a rigor to the test that had been lacking in *Schenck*.[88] The growing demands of the clear and present danger test, although not yet accepted by a majority of the Court, were underscored in Justice Brandeis' concurrence, joined by Holmes, in the 1927 decision in *Whitney v. California*.[89] Brandeis stated that "no danger flowing from speech can be deemed clear and present, unless the incidence of the evil apprehended is so imminent that it may befall before there is opportunity for full discussion."[90]

The clear and present danger test underwent another transformation when its vitality was reduced in *Dennis v. U.S.* in 1951.[91] The *Dennis* Court, faced with the prosecution of Communist Party members during one of the high points of the cold war, accepted a reformulation of the clear and present danger test proposed by renowned federal appellate judge Learned Hand. This reformulation stated the test as "whether the gravity of the 'evil,' discounted by its improbability, justifies such invasion of free speech as is necessary to avoid the danger."[92] The new version of the test seemed to provide less protection to speech in cases where the "gravity of the evil," or the potential harm to society, was great (in particular, in cases in which groups advocated overthrow of government). In such cases, the gravity or harm was so great that suppression might be justified even if its "probability" was quite low. Thus, for example, the chances that a cell of Communist Party members would actually topple the government of the United States during the 1950s Red Scare were probably infinitesimal, but the potential harm was so great that suppression of speech could be justified nonetheless. However, the 1969 case of *Brandenburg v. Ohio*[93] created a revitalized version of the test by emphasizing the immediacy of the harm that must be threatened in order for government to limit expression. The *Brandenberg* version of the clear and present danger test stated that only that speech directed at producing imminent lawless action could be constitutionally punished.

---

[86]K. Hall, The Magic Mirror 263 (1989).

[87]Abrams v. U.S., 250 U.S. 616, 627 (1919) (Holmes, J., dissenting).

[88]See generally, Gunther, Learned Hand and the Origins of Modern First Amendment Doctrine: Some Fragments of History, 27 Stan. L. Rev. 719 (1975).

[89]274 U.S. 357 (1927).

[90]*Id.* at 377 (Brandeis and Holmes, J.J., concurring).

[91]341 U.S. 494 (1951).

[92]*Id.* at 510.

[93]395 U.S. 444 (1969).

Strict Scrutiny

The highest tier on the scrutiny structure is strict scrutiny. Under this standard, also called the *compelling state interest test*, courts presume government regulation to be unconstitutional. Government must demonstrate a compelling interest in its regulation, and show that it has achieved that interest in the least restrictive manner. Although the Supreme Court has made no definitive statement as to what constitutes a compelling interest, the cases suggest that only governmental objectives of great importance are sufficient to meet the standard. As a result, First Amendment interests often prevail in cases in which courts invoke strict scrutiny. In the 1970s one commentator went so far as to write that strict scrutiny was " 'strict' in theory and fatal in fact. . . ."[94]

An example of the modern strict scrutiny formulation is the Supreme Court's 1995 decision in *McIntyre v. Ohio Elections Commission.*[95] In *McIntyre*, the Court struck down an Ohio law that banned the distribution of anonymous literature aimed at influencing voters in an election. The plaintiff in the case was an Ohio woman who had distributed leaflets regarding a proposed school tax levy signed only "Concerned Parents and Tax Payers." She was eventually fined $100 under Ohio election law.

The Court pointed out that the speech in question was political speech, and thus resided at the core of First Amendment protection. Because the speech was "high-value" speech, the Court applied a version of strict scrutiny — called *exacting scrutiny* in this case—which meant, the Court said, that the Ohio restriction would be upheld only if it were narrowly tailored to serve an overriding interest. In *MacIntyre*, as in many cases, the exact wording of the test varied somewhat from the classic formulation (requiring a "compelling" interest), but the terms seem clearly synonymous, particularly because the Court also used the term *compelling* in other portions of its opinion.

To apply the test, the Court considered the magnitude of Ohio's interest in its election law. The state argued that requiring identification in campaign messages was important because knowing the source helped voters evaluate the veracity of the message. Further, the state claimed, the disclosure requirement helped prevent fraud and libel. The Court found that neither interest was sufficiently compelling to warrant the restriction on speech. The Court reasoned that the first interest — assisting voters in evaluating campaign messages — was not particularly compelling because if the information were distributed by a private citizen, most recipients would not know the source personally anyway. Moreover, the fact that a political message is anonymous is just one more factor that citizens can use to determine its worth. The Court also found the state's interest in preventing fraud and libel insufficiently compelling, in part because Ohio had other laws that adequately addressed that interest. In summary, Ohio had not shown a compelling interest in its regulation, and therefore the Court declared it unconstitutional.

---

[94]Gunther, Foreword: In Search of Evolving Doctrine on a Changing Court: A Model for Newer Equal Protection, 86 Harv. L. Rev. 1, 8 (1972).

[95]115 S.Ct. 1511 (1995).

Even if the Court finds the government interest in its restriction to be sufficiently compelling, the restriction may still fail if it is not narrowly tailored enough. For example, in *Simon & Schuster v. New York State Crime Victims Board*,[96] decided in 1991, the Supreme Court struck down a New York law that required confessed, accused, or convicted criminals to deposit all profits from books or other works describing their crimes in an escrow account. The Court conceded that the state had a compelling interest in compensating victims of crime, as it did in ensuring that criminals did not profit from crime. However, the statute was not narrowly tailored enough because it applied not only to convicted criminals, but to any author who admitted in a work of literature to committing a crime. This aspect of the law was much too broad, the Court found:

> Had [the law] been in effect at the time and place of publication, it would have escrowed payment for such works as the Autobiography of Malcolm X, which describes crimes committed by the civil rights leader before he became a public figure; Civil Disobedience, in which Thoreau acknowledges his refusal to pay taxes . . . and even the Confessions of Saint Augustine, in which the author laments "my past foulness and the carnal corruptions of my soul," one instance of which involved the theft of pears from a neighboring vineyard."[97]

Thus, the law applied to a vast range of communicative materials that did not serve the state's compelling interests.

Intermediate Scrutiny

Intermediate scrutiny, as the name implies, allows courts to make some independent assessment of the regulation at issue. However, this midlevel scrutiny, sometimes called the *O'Brien* test, still seems to operate with considerable deference to the government regulation of speech. As a number of commentators have noted, the choice of test between strict scrutiny and *O'Brien* is often of more importance to the outcome of the case than any particular weighing of interests. The choice-of-test procedure may in fact be the deciding factor in the litigation. For example, in a number of lower court cases that considered the constitutionality of requiring cable operators to provide local "access channels," those courts that applied strict scrutiny struck down the access requirements, whereas those that applied *O'Brien* upheld them.[98]

A 1994 U.S. Supreme Court decision, *Turner Broadcasting System v. FCC*,[99] illustrates the frequent ambiguity of the choice-of-test issue. In *Turner*, the Court was called on to decide whether congressionally mandated "must-carry" rules were consistent with the First Amendment. The must-carry rules require cable operators to carry the signals of local broadcasters. The cable operators argued that the case

---

[96]112 S.Ct. 501 (1991).

[97]*Id.* at 121.

[98]Bunker, Levels of First Amendment Scrutiny and Cable Access Channel Requirements, 15 Commun. & Law 3 (1993).

[99]114 S.Ct. 2445 (1994).

should be decided using strict scrutiny, contending that the requirement was clearly based on content, particularly in light of congressional findings praising the offerings of local broadcasters. Under settled First Amendment jurisprudence, if a government restriction on speech is content-based, strict scrutiny generally applies. A slim majority of the Court disagreed, ruling instead that the must-carry requirement was content-neutral, thus triggering *O'Brien* review. The majority reasoned that the rules applied to all cable operators, regardless of the particular content of their offerings. The majority also contended that the rules were not intended to favor broadcasters' messages, but were designed merely to preserve free broadcast television for those viewers who could not afford cable. Justices who dissented from the majority's opinion were equally convinced that the regulation was based on content, and thus triggered strict scrutiny. Although the Court did not decide the case on the merits, its specification of the appropriate level of scrutiny as the *O'Brien* test was an important strategic defeat for the cable forces.

Various formulations of the intermediate scrutiny test have been devised. The most frequently used version requires that government demonstrate that the interest it seeks to advance is "important" or "substantial," and that the regulation is no greater than is essential to further that interest.

In the case from which the test takes its name, *United States v. O'Brien*,[100] the Supreme Court used the test to uphold a statute prohibiting the destruction of draft cards. Chief Justice Warren, writing for the Court, said that the government's interest in an efficient system of conscription was of sufficient magnitude to constitute a "substantial" interest. Moreover, the Court held that the government's regulation was tailored so that it infringed free expression as little as possible to accomplish that end.

Intermediate scrutiny has also been used extensively in the Court's commercial speech cases. For example, the Court used a version of intermediate scrutiny in 1986 to uphold Puerto Rico's ban on casino advertising directed toward Puerto Rican residents. In *Posadas de Puerto Rico Associates v. Tourism Co.*,[101] the Court ruled that the ban, which did not apply to casino advertising aimed at tourists, involved a "substantial" government interest because it was intended to protect Puerto Rican residents from the infiltration of organized crime, prostitution, and other evils associated with gambling. Moreover, the ban was not too extensive because it affected only ads aimed at residents, not those targeted to the island's tourists.

The Rational Basis Test

The rational basis test, also referred to as the *rational relation* or *reasonableness test*, is a low-level form of scrutiny that presumes the constitutionality of the regulation before the Court. This is the standard of review the Supreme Court has routinely applied to economic matters since the constitutional revolution of 1937.

---

[100]391 U.S. 367 (1968).

[101]478 U.S. 328 (1986).

The Court has also frequently applied the rational basis test to certain low-level categories of expression, including obscenity. A court applying the rational basis test typically defers to the legislative judgment made in the statute or regulation before it. As one commentator has stated: "The Court does not seriously inquire into the substantiality of the government interest, and it does not seriously examine the alternate means by which the government could achieve its objective."[102]

Justice Stone applied the rational basis test in *U.S. v. Carolene Products*,[103] the same case in which the famous footnote announced the beginning of heightened scrutiny for civil liberties. In *Carolene Products*, the defendant challenged a federal statute making it a crime to ship "filled milk" (i.e., milk mixed with other fats or oils) in interstate commerce. The defendant had been charged with shipping "Milnut," a blend of condensed skim milk and coconut oil, in violation of the statute. Justice Stone upheld the lower court's application of the statute against the defendant's argument that Congress lacked the power under the Constitution to regulate such a product. Stone, in the sentence to which his famous "footnote four" was appended, stated that "regulatory legislation affecting ordinary commercial transactions is not to be pronounced unconstitutional unless in light of the facts made known or generally assumed it is of such a character as to preclude the assumption that it rests upon some rational basis within the knowledge and experience of the legislators."[104] Governmental action reviewed under this deferential test is likely to pass constitutional muster unless the policy choice is without any logical foundation in the eyes of the reviewing court.

CONCLUSION

First Amendment strict scrutiny represents a decision by the Supreme Court that certain fundamental freedoms guaranteed by the Constitution need special protection by the judiciary. That special protection takes the form of active judicial review of government regulation that limits First Amendment rights. Government bears the burden of establishing compelling reasons for the restriction, and, as the modern doctrine has come to be formulated, demonstrating that the regulation achieves its purpose in the least restrictive possible manner.

Although it is clear that the idea of heightened judicial review of free expression regulation did not originate with the *Carolene Products* footnote, the footnote provided a doctrinal bridge from the *Lochner* era to a new period in which the Court focused on individual rights. In doing so, it ushered in an era in which free expression guarantees would be significantly expanded. The actual application of the scrutiny structure that has emerged from *Carolene Products* remains problematic.

---

[102]Stone, Content-Neutral Restrictions, 54 Univ. of Chicago L. Rev. 46, 50 (1987).

[103]304 U.S. 144 (1937).

[104]*Id.* at 152 (citations omitted).

-3-

Courts and Prejudicial Publicity

Although the scrutiny structure has only developed in the last 50 years or so, concern about the effects of publicity on the rights of criminal defendants is not new. As long ago as the 1807 trial of Aaron Burr, the legal system has worried that widespread publicity could have detrimental effects on trials, especially by predisposing jurors to accept media versions of events. In the Burr case, "defense counsel urged that jurors had been prejudiced against Colonel Burr by inflammatory articles carried in the Alexandria *Expositor* and other newspapers."[1]

The issue of prejudicial publicity's effect on criminal trials received substantial attention in the 1960s, in part because of a series of sensational cases that eventually found their way to the U.S. Supreme Court. This chapter first discusses a series of contempt cases that established a judicial reluctance to use the contempt power to control out-of-court speech. Next, the chapter traces some of the history of the Court's "fair trial" jurisprudence, in which the question arises of how one determines who is an impartial juror. Finally, the chapter touches briefly on a number of government and private studies that took place in the wake of the 1960s prejudicial publicity cases. The era of extensive study of the "free press–fair trial" controversy set the stage for later attempts to restrain press coverage of criminal trials.

LIMITATIONS ON THE CONTEMPT POWER

A series of U.S. Supreme Court cases beginning in 1941 severely limited the ability of courts to use their contempt power to punish out-of-court statements and press reports about judicial proceedings. This line of cases would be particularly significant in later consideration of sanctions against the media for creating prejudice in high-profile cases. Although the four cases discussed here did not absolutely rule

---

[1] Report of the Committee on the Operation of the Jury System on the "Free Press–Fair Trial" Issue, 45 F.R.D. 391, 394, n.2 (1968).

out punishment by contempt for out-of-court statements, they made such punishment a rather remote possibility under the Constitution.

In *Bridges v. California*,[2] decided in 1941, the Court considered two cases in which defendants were found in contempt for statements concerning pending cases. In one, editorials in the *Los Angeles Times* seemed aimed at influencing sentencing decisions in criminal cases. One *Times* editorial came as a local judge was contemplating the sentencing of two members of a labor union who had been convicted of assaulting nonunion truck drivers. The editorial was titled "Probation for Gorillas?," and stated that "Judge A. A. Scott will make a serious mistake if he grants probation to Matthew Shannon and Kennan Holmes. This community needs the example of their assignment to the jute mill."[3]

In the other case consolidated in *Bridges*, a union leader allowed publication of a telegram in which he called a judge's decision in a labor dispute "outrageous."[4] The union leader also stated that any attempted enforcement of the decision would tie up the Port of Los Angeles, and that "the C.I.O. union, representing some twelve thousand members, did 'not intend to allow state courts to override the majority vote of members in choosing its officers and representatives and to override the National Labor Relations Board.'"[5] In both cases, the contempt citations were based upon a perceived attempt to intimidate a sitting judge toward a certain result. State courts had upheld the contempt charges on the grounds that the state was empowered to take appropriate measures to provide fair trials and prevent attempts at coercion, even if they took place outside of the courtroom.

The Supreme Court reversed the findings of contempt. Justice Black, writing for the majority, made the memorable observation that "free speech and fair trials are two of the most cherished policies of our civilization, and it would be a trying task to choose between them."[6] Justice Black reasoned that the clear and present danger test was the appropriate standard for considering First Amendment challenges to the contempt citations. Justice Black characterized the clear and present danger test as "a working principle that the substantive evil must be extremely serious and the degree of imminence extremely high before utterances can be punished."[7] He acknowledged that the test was not subject to tremendous precision, but nonetheless maintained that it could provide practical guidance when freedom of expression was threatened by government power. He further described the First Amendment interest in allowing open discussion as "a command of the broadest scope that explicit language, read in the context of a liberty-loving society, will allow."[8]

---

[2]314 U.S. 252 (1941).

[3]*Id.* at 272.

[4]*Id.* at 277.

[5]*Id.* at 276.

[6]*Id.* at 260.

[7]*Id.* at 263.

[8]*Id.*

The majority noted that the kind of contempt citations issued in *Bridges* would, as a practical matter, have severe consequences for free speech. For it was precisely during the pendency of controversial cases that public interest was aroused and public comment most likely. However, the First Amendment gave no indication, Justice Black reasoned, that its provisions bore

> an inverse ratio to the timeliness and importance of the ideas seeking expression. Yet, it would follow as a practical result of the decisions below that anyone who might wish to give public expression to his views on a pending case involving no matter what problem of public interest, just at the time his audience would be most receptive, would be as effectively discouraged as if a deliberate statutory scheme of censorship had been adopted.[9]

The lower courts had allowed the contempt citations to stand based on the "reasonable tendency" of the statements to interfere with the administration of justice. The *Bridges* majority reversed the findings of contempt by reasoning that, even under the reasonable tendency standard, which was less robust than the clear and present danger test, the published statements were not sufficiently intimidating to judges to warrant the finding of contempt. For example, as to the newspaper editorial quoted earlier, the majority noted that to find a threat to the administration of justice "would be to impute to judges a lack of firmness, wisdom or honor,—which we cannot accept as a major premise."[10] The editorial, which stated that the judge would make a "serious mistake" if he granted probation to the union members, threatened nothing more than "future adverse criticism which was reasonably to be expected anyway in the event of a lenient disposition of the pending case."[11] This kind of threat was not, Justice Black argued, true intimidation that justified judicial restraint of speech. The majority also rejected the proposition that respect for the judiciary could be created by holding those who criticize judges in contempt. Rather than enhancing judicial dignity and authority, contempt citations could only create resentment and suspicion.

The Court regarded the telegram, with its implied threat of a strike in the event of an unfavorable ruling, as likewise presenting insufficient danger to warrant the trial judge's use of the contempt power. California law did not forbid a strike, Justice Black noted. In any event, the trial judge was well aware, even without the contents of the telegram, that a strike might well follow his decision in the case before him if it displeased the union. "If he was not intimidated by the facts themselves, we do not believe that the most explicit statement of them could have sidetracked the course of justice," Justice Black wrote. "Again, we find exaggeration in the conclusion that the utterance even 'tended' to interfere with justice."[12] Assuming that the judge had even "reasonable fortitude," nothing in the telegram should have affected the disposition of the case in any degree.

---

[9]*Id.* at 269.
[10]*Id.* at 273.
[11]*Id.* at 273.
[12]*Id.* at 278.

Justice Frankfurter, joined by three other justices in dissent, argued that the majority's opinion was an unprecedented elevation of First Amendment rights over the need to maintain an uncoerced justice system. "Free speech is not so absolute or irrational a conception as to imply paralysis of the means for effective protection of all the freedoms secured by the Bill of Rights," Justice Frankfurter wrote.[13] The dissent contended that the time-tested methods of ensuring the fair administration of justice—including the contempt power—could not conceivably violate the First Amendment's protection of speech and press, as applied to the states. The contempt power, properly exercised, simply had no connection to suppressing unorthodox viewpoints on important social issues. Rather, it was the necessary means to ensure citizens that their courts would adjudicate controversies fairly.

The Court struck down another contempt citation in 1946, in *Pennekamp v. Florida.*[14] In *Pennekamp*, employees of the *Miami Herald* were cited for contempt for two editorials and a cartoon critical of state trial courts' actions in criminal cases. One editorial accused Dade County judges of using delay and technicalities to avoid just results in cases before the courts. "Every accused person has a right to his day in court," the editorial stated. "But when judicial instance and interpretative procedure recognize and accept, even go out to find, every possible technicality of the law to protect the defendant, to block, thwart, hinder, embarrass and nullify prosecution, then the people's rights are jeopardized and the basic reason of courts stultified."[15] The cartoon depicted a robed judge throwing out charges against a criminal defendant as a figure identified as "public interest" stands by protesting.

As in *Bridges*, the U.S. Supreme Court reversed the contempt citations applying the clear and present danger test. Justice Reed, writing for the Court, noted that the only issue in *Pennekamp* concerned criticism of judicial actions taken prior to the publication of the items in question, although there was a possibility of later proceedings and decisions on other aspects of the cases. As a result, the publications could not be interpreted as attempting to influence pending decisions. Justice Reed held that the danger to the administration of justice was not sufficiently clear or immediate to warrant punishment for public comment and criticism. In *dicta*, Justice Reed suggested that a clear and present danger might be present in the case of a "judge of less than ordinary fortitude without friends or support or a powerful and vindictive newspaper bent upon a rule or ruin policy, and a public unconcerned with or uninterested in the truth or the protection of their judicial institutions."[16]

Justice Frankfurter concurred, but criticized the Court's use of the clear and present danger test as a standard of decision. He noted that "[f]ormulas embodying vague and uncritical generalizations offer tempting opportunities to evade the need for continuous thought."[17] The clear and present danger standard, Frankfurter

---

[13]*Id.* at 282.

[14]328 U.S. 331 (1946).

[15]*Id.* at 339.

[16]*Id.* at 349.

[17]*Id.* at 351 (Frankfurter, J., concurring).

argued, was "a literary phrase" used by Justice Holmes in a series of celebrated cases, and was not intended "to express a technical legal doctrine or to convey a formula for adjudicating cases."[18]

Justice Frankfurter also argued that English judges had wide contempt powers to ensure that their proceedings were impartial in the face of media criticism or sensationalism, and that the English example was compelling. "'Trial by newspaper,' like all catch phrases, may be loosely used but it summarizes an evil influence upon the administration of criminal justice in this country," Frankfurter wrote. "Its absence in England, at least its narrow confinement there, furnishes an illuminating commentary."[19] Nonetheless, Frankfurter agreed that no contempt should have been issued in *Pennekamp* because the cases had been decided, and thus the newspaper could not be viewed as trying to influence their outcome.

Craig v. Harney,[20] decided in 1947, extended the *Pennekamp* rationale by striking down a contempt citation directed at newspaper employees for articles and editorials calling a judge's action in a civil case, among other things, a "travesty on justice."[21] The case involved a disputed lease in Corpus Christi; both parties sought to be the rightful tenant of the "Playboy Cafe." The judge had repeatedly ordered a jury to return a directed verdict for one party in the suit. The jury finally did so, after disobeying the instruction three times and finding instead for the other party, who was a war veteran and the subject of considerable patriotic sentiment. When the jury finally obeyed and ruled for the veteran's opponent, it stated "that it acted under coercion of the court and against its conscience."[22] Although the case was complete at the time the articles and editorials were published, a motion for a new trial was pending.

The newspaper articles reported on the proceedings and the public outrage they engendered, while the editorial that followed deplored the fact that the judge in the case was a layperson rather than a trained lawyer. The editorial contended that the judge's action was a

> "gross miscarriage of justice." It was also said that the judge's behavior had properly brought down "the wrath of public opinion upon his head," that the people were aroused because a service man "seems to be getting a raw deal," and that there was "no way of knowing whether justice was done, because the first rule of justice, giving both sides an opportunity to be heard, was repudiated."[23]

The judge cited the newspaper employees for contempt for attempting to influence the court in its ruling on a new trial in the case.

The U.S. Supreme Court, in an opinion written by Justice Douglas, struck down the contempt citations. The articles about the case, and about subsequent public

---

[18]*Id.* at 353 (Frankfurter, J., concurring).

[19]*Id.* at 359.

[20]331 U.S. 367 (1947).

[21]*Id.* at 369.

[22]*Id.* at 369.

[23]*Id.* at 370.

reaction, were protected speech, although the description of the facts and issues before the court were one-sided and not entirely accurate, Justice Douglas wrote. It might be possible for willfully biased reporting to endanger the fair administration of justice, but these articles simply did not constitute such a risk to a resolute judge, the Court reasoned.

The editorial raised a more serious issue, according to Justice Douglas. Its criticism of the judge was harsh, but still not sufficiently dangerous to warrant application of the contempt power. "The vehemence of the language used is not alone the measure of the power to punish for contempt," the majority wrote. "The fires which it kindles must constitute an imminent, not merely a likely, threat to the administration of justice. The danger must not be remote or even probable; it must immediately imperil."[24] Applying the clear and present danger test, the Court reasoned that some of the newspaper's accusations were unfair, but did not rise to the level of a clear and present danger to the administration of justice. Any threat created by the criticism was simply not serious and imminent enough.

Justice Douglas rejected the argument that *Craig* should be treated differently than *Bridges* because the former involved only a private civil action, whereas the latter concerned public labor controversies, some of which were criminal cases. The nature of the "danger" as the Court applied the clear and present danger test might vary as between cases that dealt with matters of public concern to a greater or lesser degree, Justice Douglas reasoned, but the type of case should have no impact on the extension of fully protected rights of public comment and criticism.

Justice Frankfurter, joined by one other justice, dissented. He argued that the publications before the Court were not merely a critique of lay judges, nor of the particular actions of the judge in this case. Rather, they were aimed directly at influencing the judge in his decision on the motion for a new trial that was before him. "We cannot say that the Texas Court could not properly find that these newspapers asked of the judge, and instigated powerful sections of the community to ask of the judge, that which no one has any business to ask of a judge, namely, that he should decide one way rather than another," Justice Frankfurter wrote. In deference to the state courts that had reviewed the matter, he argued that the Supreme Court should uphold the finding of a "clear and present danger" based on conditions in Corpus Christi at the time of the trial.

In the final major contempt case following *Bridges*, *Wood v. Georgia*,[25] the Court held that a public official's criticism of a judge's action was protected by the First Amendment. In *Wood*, an elected Georgia sheriff criticized a local judge's instruction to a grand jury to investigate suspected "Negro bloc voting."[26] This bloc voting was alleged to have been the result of bribes paid to voters by elected county officials. The judge told the grand jury that "certain Negro leaders, after having met and endorsed a candidate, have switched their support to an opposing candidate

---

[24]*Id.* at 376.

[25]370 U.S. 375 (1962).

[26]*Id.* at 376.

who put up a large sum of money. . . ."[27] The investigation was launched with some fanfare, including a media presence in the courtroom, in the midst of a local election.

The following day, Sheriff James Wood issued a press release in which he condemned the judge's action and stated that, at a time "when all thinking people want to preserve the good will and cooperation between the races in Bibb County, this action appears either as a crude attempt at judicial intimidation of negro voters and leaders, or, at best, as agitation for a 'negro vote' issue in local politics."[28] The press release also compared the intimidation inherent in the investigation to that practiced by the Ku Klux Klan. The following day, Wood distributed "An Open Letter to the Bibb County Grand Jury" to the grand jury. The letter suggested that the judge's statements about bloc voting were erroneous, and contended that the Bibb County Democratic Executive Committee was responsible for any electoral corruption that might exist in the county. The court found Wood to be in contempt because the critical statements were contemptuous of the court and interfered with the grand jury investigation.

The Supreme Court, citing *Bridges, Pennekamp,* and *Craig,* held that the sheriff's statements did not present a sufficient danger to the administration of justice to allow the contempt to stand. A grand jury, the Court wrote, has historically served the function of providing a voice of reason between the accuser and the accused in a criminal case. The grand jury is charged with determining whether criminal prosecutions are brought on reasonable grounds or are based on malice or ill will. "Particularly in matters of local political corruption and investigations it is important that freedom of communication be kept open and that the real issues not become obscured to the grand jury," the Court wrote. "It cannot effectively operate in a vacuum."[29] In the case at hand, in which a panel of judges, themselves elected officers, sought to silence another elected officer through the contempt power, the need for enlightened public knowledge of the dispute was great.

As to the clear and present danger of Wood's statements, the Court noted that the record failed to disclose any actual interference with the work of the grand jury. Moreover, Wood's attack would have had little effect on the grand jury unless the claims of bloc voting were clearly incorrect. Finally, the Court rejected the claim that Wood's position as sheriff made his statements particularly dangerous. Wood had communicated his views as a private citizen. It was not as if, the Court reasoned, Wood's statements had somehow interfered with his duties in any way—he had simply expressed his opinion on a matter of public import. "The petitioner was an elected official and had the right to enter the field of political controversy, particularly where his political life was at stake," the Court wrote.[30]

Taken together, *Bridges* and its progeny placed tight limits on the ability of courts to use the contempt power to silence public criticism of their proceedings. Robust,

---

[27]*Id.* at 376.

[28]*Id.* at 379.

[29]*Id.* at 390.

[30]*Id.* at 394-95.

sometimes harsh, political discourse—and judges of sturdy mettle—were presumed to be the rule by the Court. The cases, although vague on exactly what might constitute a clear and present danger to the administration of justice, clearly created a jurisprudential climate of tolerance for criticism of judicial proceedings.

FAIR TRIAL RIGHTS AND THE SEARCH
FOR AN IMPARTIAL JUROR

Trial by an impartial jury is one of the rights guaranteed to criminal defendants by the Sixth Amendment. Moreover, in state and federal courts, allowing a case to be tried by biased jurors is a fundamental denial of due process of law. The U.S. Supreme Court has stated that, "[i]n the ultimate analysis, only the jury can strip a man of his liberty or his life. . . . This is true, regardless of the heinousness of the crime charged, the apparent guilt of the offender or the station in life which he occupies."[31] A jury of one's peers has long been recognized in Anglo-American law as an important safeguard against arbitrary government action. As one historian noted, "The presence of jurors precluded secret trials, secured the citizenry from venal judges, purchased testimony, or threatening officials, and protected them from other abuses by governments unconcerned with the liberties of its people."[32] But the problem of defining exactly what constitutes an impartial jury has vexed courts for many years. The problem has been exacerbated by the pervasive nature of the mass media.

When trial by jury first evolved in English law, jurors were not expected to be ignorant of the facts of the case or strangers to the defendant or witnesses. On the contrary, jurors were gathered from the vicinity of the incident, often knew the parties, and sometimes had even witnessed the crime in question. As Ronald Goldfarb pointed out, early jurors "were chosen for their knowledge of the events that caused the accused to be suspect, not for their freedom from bias."[33] However, gradually, as criminal procedure and the rules of evidence became more formalized, it became important to find jurors sufficiently unbiased and removed from the facts to decide the case based solely on the evidence presented in court, and not by extra-judicial knowledge.

A series of U.S. Supreme Court cases through the 19th and 20th centuries explored the question of when jurors were sufficiently impartial to produce a fair trial.[34] One of the earliest, and perhaps one of the most famous, American cases on the subject was not a Supreme Court case, however, but an 1807 lower court

---

[31]Irvin v. Dowd, 366 U.S. 717, 722 (1961).

[32]D. Bodenhamer, Fair Trial: Rights of the Accused in American History 32 (1992).

[33]Goldfarb, Public Information, Criminal Trials, and the Cause Celebre, 36 N.Y.U. L. Rev. 810 (1961).

[34]An excellent introduction to these cases, with helpful commentary, can be found in D. Campbell, Free Press v. Fair Trial: Supreme Court Decisions Since 1807 (1994).

decision in the treason trial of Aaron Burr. The great Chief Justice John Marshall presided over the trial, which resulted in Burr's acquittal, sitting as judge of a circuit court in Virginia. The case, *United States v. Burr*,[35] provides one of the most important early statements in American law on the problem of fair jury trials.

Marshall began his opinion by noting that the "great value of the trial by jury certainly consists in its fairness and impartiality. Those who most prize the institution, prize it because it furnishes a tribunal which may be expected to be uninfluenced by an undue bias of the mind."[36] Marshall pointed out that a juror possessing a fixed opinion about the guilt of the accused was in the same position as a juror who had some personal connection with the defendant: Both might claim to be able to render an impartial verdict, and in fact might be able to, but the law nonetheless could not depend on such claims. "Such a person may believe that he will be regulated by testimony," Marshall wrote, "but the law suspects him, and certainly not without reason. He will listen with more favor to that testimony which confirms, than to that which would change his opinion; it is not to be expected that he will weigh evidence or argument as fairly as a man whose judgment is not made up in the case."[37]

Marshall pointed out that not all preconceptions about a case necessarily render a juror so partial as to be subject to challenge. According to Marshall, the crucial distinction is whether the impressions the juror has formed about the guilt or innocence of the accused are "light" or deeply ingrained. Marshall wrote,

> The opinion which has been avowed by the court is, that light impressions, which may fairly be supposed to yield to the testimony that may be offered, which may leave the mind open to a fair consideration of that testimony, constitute no sufficient objection to a juror; but that those strong and deep impressions which will close the mind against the testimony that may be offered in opposition to them, which will combat that testimony, and resist its force, do constitute a sufficient objection to him. Those who try the impartiality of any juror ought to test him by this rule.[38]

In the case before the court, Marshall ruled that a juror who formulated and expressed an opinion that Burr had committed at least some portions of the acts with which he was charged was subject to removal from the jury.

In 1878, in *Reynolds v. United States*,[39] the U.S. Supreme Court considered a claim by a convicted bigamist, George Reynolds, that he had not received a fair trial because the jurors in his case were not impartial. For example, one juror, Charles Read, had the following exchange with the district attorney after Read was asked if he had formed an opinion about Reynolds' guilt or innocence:

---

[35] 25 F. Cas. 49 (No. 14,692g) (CC Va. 1807).

[36] *Id.* at 50.

[37] *Id.* at 50.

[38] *Id.* at 51.

[39] 98 U.S. 145 (1878).

A. I believe I have formed an opinion.
By the court: Have you formed and expressed an opinion?
A. No, sir; I believe not.
Q. You say you have formed an opinion?
A. I have.
Q. Is that based upon evidence?
A. Nothing produced in court.
Q. Would that opinion influence your verdict?
A. I don't think it would.
By defendant: I understood you to say that you had formed an opinion, but not expressed it.
A. I don't know that I have expressed an opinion: I have formed one.
Q. Do you now entertain that opinion?
A. I do.[40]

Both Read and Eli Ransohoff, another juror, were allowed to remain on the jury despite challenges by Reynolds. Ransohoff admitted that he had read newspaper reports of a previous trial in the case, but maintained that he could nonetheless remain impartial. On appeal, the Supreme Court held that it was not error for the trial court to permit the jurors to serve.

Chief Justice Waite, writing for the Court, quoted Coke's definition of an *impartial juror* as one who must "be indifferent as he stands unsworn."[41] Waite stressed that *impartiality* did not mean the juror was ignorant of the case or had not formed any impression of the defendant's guilt or innocence. Rather, impartiality meant that the proposed juror's mind was not completely closed to evidence and testimony that would tend to alter the initial impression. Chief Justice Waite expressed an oddly modern-sounding sentiment when he noted that,

in these days of newspaper enterprise and universal education, every case of public interest is almost, as a matter of necessity, brought to the attention of all the intelligent people in the vicinity, and scarcely any one can be found among those best fitted for jurors who has not read or heard of it, and who has not some impression or some opinion in respect to its merits.[42]

The trial court, being in a better position than an appellate court to determine whether a juror was impartial, should be given considerable latitude in its findings on the issue. Thus, Chief Justice Waite wrote, a trial court's finding that a juror was sufficiently impartial would be reversed on appeal only if the appellate court found "manifest" error. "It must be made clearly to appear that upon the evidence the court ought to have found the juror had formed such an opinion that he could not in law be deemed impartial," Chief Justice Waite wrote. "The case must be one in which

[40]*Id.*

[41]*Id.* at 154.

[42]*Id.* at 155-56.

it is manifest the law left nothing to the 'conscience or discretion' of the court."[43]
This standard in effect meant that few trial courts would be reversed because the
challenging party's burden was so daunting.

Turning to the specific challenge against juror Charles Read, the Court noted
that, although Read stated during voir dire that he had formed an opinion about the
case, he also stated that he did not think the opinion he had formed would influence
his decision after he heard the evidence at trial. The Court held that this kind of
statement by a juror did not indicate that Read could not be impartial. "The reading
of the evidence leaves the impression that the juror had some hypothetical opinion
about the case, but it falls short of raising a manifest presumption of partiality," the
Court wrote.[44] Moreover, the demeanor of the juror—which the trial court could
observe, but which the Supreme Court, with only a dry record before it, could not
see—frequently meant more than the exact words spoken by the juror. For this
reason, the Court wrote, only clear cases of partiality should be disturbed on appeal,
and the burden rested on the defendant when a juror had been retained over the
defendant's objection. "The affirmative of the issue is upon the challenger," Chief
Justice Waite wrote. "Unless he shows the actual existence of such an opinion in
the mind of the juror as will raise the presumption of partiality, the juror need not
necessarily be set aside, and it will not be error in the court to refuse to do so."[45]

The Supreme Court ruled that the defendant had not demonstrated clearly that
Read was not impartial. Moreover, the statements of the other juror who had been
challenged, Ransohoff, were even less compelling than those of Read. Thus, the
Court found no error in the selection of jurors in *Reynolds*.

An 1887 Supreme Court case further clarified the nature of the prejudice
necessary for a juror to render a trial unfair. The case also made it clear that trial
court rulings on jurors who were eventually removed from the panel could not be
the basis for reversal. In *Hopt v. Utah*,[46] the Court applied a law that forbade
excluding jurors based on opinions they had formed from reading newspaper
accounts unless the trial court was convinced that the juror could not be impartial
despite that opinion. In *Hopt*, the Court considered the fourth conviction of
Frederick Hopt for murder; three previous convictions had been reversed. Among
other things, Hopt claimed that the trial court's rulings that accepted four jurors,
three of whom had subsequently been removed from the panel by peremptory
challenges, were reversible error.

The only juror of the four who remained on the panel, Gabott, had stated that he
had read about the case in the newspaper,

> that he had talked about it since that time; that he did not think he had ever expressed
> an opinion on the case, but that he had formed a qualified opinion; that is, if the
> evidence were true, or the reports were true; that he had an opinion touching the guilt

---

[43]*Id.* at 156.

[44]*Id.*

[45]*Id.* at 157.

[46]120 U.S. 430 (1887).

or innocence of the accused which it would take evidence to remove; but that he thought he could go into the jury-box and sit as if he had never heard of the case. . . .[47]

A statute in the Utah territory, in which the trial was held, specifically stated that a juror could not be disqualified merely because he or she had formed or expressed an opinion about a case "founded upon public rumor, statements in public journals, or common notoriety,"[48] as long as the trial court believed that the juror could act impartially despite that exposure.

The Supreme Court upheld the trial court's action and the statutory language as follows: "We think that evidence, or what purports to be evidence, printed in a newspaper is a 'statement in a public journal' within the meaning of the statute; and that judgment of the court upon the competency of the juror in such cases is conclusive."[49] The Court also noted that, because Hopt had several peremptory challenges remaining at the end of voir dire, he could not then complain on appeal because the trial court had refused to remove the other three jurors, who had subsequently been removed by peremptory challenge. "Those jurors were not on the jury, and impartial and competent jurors were obtained in their place, to whom no objection was made," the Court wrote.[50]

Another 1887 Supreme Court case, *Spies v. Illinois*,[51] helped further clarify the extent to which the Court was willing to leave decisions about juror impartiality to the discretion of trial courts. The case also raised, without resolving, the applicability of the Sixth Amendment to state trials. The *Spies* case arose out of a spectacular trial in Illinois of a number of individuals identified as union organizers, socialists, and anarchists who were charged with a bombing and subsequent riot that killed both Chicago police officers and bystanders at a mass meeting in Haymarket Square.[52] Spies, one of the defendants, contended that the trial was unfair, in part, because of the trial judge's rulings on certain jurors. Part of Spies' argument to the Court claimed that the protections of the Fourteenth Amendment due process clause extended the Sixth Amendment fair trial guarantees to the states. The Bill of Rights, including the Sixth Amendment, had been interpreted as imposing restrictions on the federal government, but not on state governments. Spies also argued that an Illinois statute, similar to the Utah law the Court examined in *Hopt*, was unconstitutional. The Illinois statute stated that a potential juror could not be disqualified from serving because the juror had read a newspaper account of the case, or formed an opinion about the case "based upon rumor or newspaper statements," as long as the juror could state under oath that he or she could reach an impartial verdict and the court was satisfied the juror was telling the truth.

---

[47]*Id.* at 434.

[48]*Id.* at 434.

[49]*Id.* at 435.

[50]*Id.* at 436.

[51]123 U.S. 131 (1887).

[52]For more information on the facts of this celebrated case, see the excellent historical information in D. Campbell, *Free Press v. Fair Trial: Supreme Court Decisions Since 1807* (1994).

The Court upheld the constitutionality of the statute without reaching the question of whether the Sixth Amendment applied to the states. With little analysis, the Court agreed with the Supreme Court of Illinois that the statute was constitutional under a provision of the Illinois constitution, which was nearly identical to the Sixth Amendment. Because of the similarity of the state and federal provisions, the Court said it was unnecessary to decide whether the Sixth Amendment was incorporated through the Fourteenth Amendment.

In *Hopt*, the Supreme Court affirmed its stance that a trial judge's failure to exclude jurors for cause was not error if the defendant nonetheless peremptorily challenged the jurors and still had remaining peremptory challenges unused when voir dire was complete. Therefore, the Court confined its analysis to two jurors, Denker and Sanford, who actually sat in the case. The Court included lengthy excerpts from the voir dire of these two jurors. For example, Denker's examination included the following exchanges:

Q. You heard of this Haymarket meeting, I suppose?
A. Yes.
Q. Have you formed an opinion upon the question of the defendants' guilt or innocence upon the charge of murder, or any of them?
A. I have.
Q. Have you expressed this opinion?
A. Yes.
Q. You still entertain it?
A. Yes.
Q. You believe what you have read and what you heard?
A. I believe it; yes.
Q. Is that opinion such as to prevent you from rendering an impartial verdict in the case sitting as a juror under the testimony and the law?
A. I think it is.[53]

Under further questioning, however, Denker reversed his stand.

Q. If you were taken and sworn as a juror in the case, can't you determine the innocence or guilt of the defendants upon the proof that is presented to you here in court, regardless of your having any prejudice or opinion?
A. I think I could.
Q. You could determine their guilt or innocence upon the proof presented to you here in court, regardless of your prejudice and regardless of your opinion, and regardless of what you have read?
A. Yes.[54]

---

[53]123 U.S. at 170.
[54]*Id.* at 171.

Later questioning revealed that Denker had some bias against some of the defendants' political beliefs.

Q. Do you know anything about socialism, anarchism, or communism?
A. No, sir; I do not.
Q. Have you any prejudice against this class of persons?
A. I think I am a little prejudiced against socialism. I don't know that I am against anarchism. In fact, I don't really understand what they are. I do not know what their principles are at all.[55]

Sanford, the other juror challenged by Spies, also said he held an opinion on the case based on newspaper reporting.

Q. Have you any opinion as to the guilt or innocence or the defendants, or any of them, of the murder of Matthias J. Degan?
A. I have.
Q. All right, have you an opinion as to whether or not there was an offense committed at the Haymarket meeting by the throwing of a bomb?
A. Yes.
Q. Now, from all that you have read and all that you have heard, have you an opinion as to the guilt or innocence of any of the eight defendants of the throwing of that bomb?
A. Yes.[56]

Later in the voir dire, Sanford was asked about his feelings toward the political philosophies of the defendants.

Q. Have you any knowledge of the principles contended for by socialists, communists, and anarchists?
A. Nothing, except what I read in the papers.
Q. Just general reading?
A. Yes.
Q. You are not a socialist, I presume, or a communist?
A. No, sir.
Q. Have you a prejudice against them from what you have read in the papers?
A. Decided.
Q. A decided prejudice against them? Do you believe that that would influence your verdict in this case, or would you try the real issue, which is here, as to whether these defendants were guilty of the murder of Mr. Degan or not, or would you try the question of socialism or anarchism, which really has nothing to do with the case?

---

[55]*Id.* at 172.
[56]*Id.* at 175.

A. Well, as I know so little about it in reality at present, it is a pretty hard question to answer.

Q. You would undertake—you would attempt, of course, to try the case upon the evidence introduced here—upon the issue which is presented here?

A. Yes, sir.[57]

With little explicit analysis, the Supreme Court held that the trial court had not erred in refusing to exclude the two jurors. The Court stated that, consistent with *Reynolds v. United States*, an appellate challenge to the fairness of a trial based on juror partiality could be upheld only if manifest error were established. "It must be made clearly to appear that upon the evidence the court ought to have found the juror had formed such an opinion that he could not in law be deemed impartial," the Court wrote. "We are unhesitatingly of opinion that no such case is disclosed by this record."[58]

The Supreme Court again upheld the discretion of a trial judge in *Simmons v. United States*, decided in 1891.[59] In *Simmons*, however, that discretion was not used to keep a juror on the panel, but to dismiss an entire jury. Simmons was charged with aiding and abetting an embezzler. One of the jurors, Goodnow, claimed during voir dire that he did not know Simmons. But during the trial, a third party, Ward, notified the district attorney that Simmons and Goodnow had in the past shared nearby office space and had frequently talked to each other in the hall. Simmons' lawyer then sent a letter to the district attorney denying the allegations, claiming that Ward had made the charge because of a long-standing quarrel with Simmons. The letter was also sent to the daily newspapers, where it was subsequently published.

The prosecution sought to remove the juror, but the trial judge instead chose to discharge the entire jury. The judge noted that, "the knowledge respecting the statement made by Ward, conveyed to the jury by the publication of the defendant's counsel, makes it impossible that in the future consideration of this case by the jury there can be that true independence and freedom of action on the part of each juror which is necessary to a fair trial of the accused."[60] Simmons opposed this action; when his case was tried before another jury, he was found guilty.

The Supreme Court upheld the propriety of the trial court in discharging the jury after the defense counsel's letter was published in several newspapers. The Court ruled that the trial judge was "fully justified in concluding that such a publication, under the peculiar circumstances attending it, made it impossible for that jury, in considering the case, to act with the independence and freedom on the part of each juror requisite to a fair trial of the issue between the parties."[61] Thus, the trial court

---

[57] *Id.* at 176.

[58] *Id.* at 179-180.

[59] 142 U.S. 148 (1891).

[60] *Id.* at 148.

[61] *Id.* at 155.

properly dismissed the jury, and the retrial before a new jury did not constitute double jeopardy under the Constitution.

One year after the *Simmons* case, in 1892, the Court was again called on to decide a case involving the influence of a newspaper report on a jury. In *Mattox v. United States*,[62] Mattox had been convicted of murder at a trial in Wichita, Kansas. Mattox appealed on the grounds that, among other things, as the jury was deliberating his fate, someone brought a copy of *The Wichita Daily Eagle* into the jury room and read an article in the paper to the jury. The newspaper article gave a rather dim view of Mattox's chances: "The destiny of Clyde Mattox is now in the hands of the twelve citizens of Kansas composing the jury in this case. If he is not found guilty of murder he will be a lucky man for the evidence against him was very strong, or at least appeared to be to an outsider."[63] The newspaper reported that observers did not expect the jury to deliberate more than 1 hour before returning a verdict. The article also referred to the closing argument of the prosecutor as "so strong that the friends of Mattox gave up all hope of any result but conviction," and stated that, as the jury filed out, Mattox's mother was "very pale and her face indicated that she had but very little hope."[64] After reporting that Mattox had been on trial for his life once before, the article closed by noting that the evidence against Mattox was "purely circumstantial, but very strong, it is claimed, by those who heard all the testimony."[65]

The Supreme Court noted the general rule that matters within the private knowledge of one juror were generally not sufficient to reverse a jury's verdict. However, where an overt act had taken place that brought prejudicial information to the attention of all of the jurors, as in this case, a new trial might be necessary. The Court ruled that the refusal of the trial court to consider the affidavits regarding the newspaper article—as well as prejudicial statements by a bailiff—required that the Court reverse the judgment. "It is not open to reasonable doubt that the tendency of that article was injurious to the defendant," the Court wrote.[66]

In *Holt v. United States*,[67] decided in 1910, the Court again reaffirmed the principle that, despite possible juror prejudice, trial courts could be reversed in only the most extreme circumstances. In the *Holt* case, James Holt was convicted of a murder on a military reservation and sentenced to life imprisonment. Holt challenged the conviction based, in part, on several indications of jury prejudice created by newspaper articles.

During voir dire, one potential juror said he had read a newspaper account of the murder, presumably implicating the defendant. The juror stated that although he believed the newspaper report to be factual, evidence to the contrary could

---

[62]146 U.S. 140 (1892).

[63]*Id.* at 140.

[64]*Id.*

[65]*Id.*

[66]*Id.* at 150.

[67]218 U.S. 245 (1910).

change his opinion of the case, "although it would take some evidence to remove it."[68] The juror also said that he thought he could decide the case solely on the evidence presented in court. Justice Holmes, writing for the Supreme Court, stated that there was no "manifest" error in keeping this juror on the panel, citing *Reynolds, Hopt,* and *Spies.*

Holt also demanded a new trial based on the fact that "members of the jury had stated to him that they had read the Seattle daily papers with articles on the case while the trial was going on."[69] When presented with Holt's affidavit to this effect, the trial judge decided against Holt's motion for a new trial under the assumption that the jurors had indeed read the newspaper articles. The Supreme Court affirmed the lower court's refusal to grant a new trial. Justice Holmes noted that many states allowed jurors to "separate," even in capital cases. The mere fact that jurors had read the newspaper accounts, however, was not sufficient to create a presumption of partiality. Moreover, such determinations were the unique province of the trial judge, who would only be reversed if clear error were demonstrated. "If the mere opportunity for prejudice or corruption is to raise a presumption that they exist, it will be hard to maintain jury trial under the conditions of the present day," Holmes wrote. "Without intimating that the judge did not go further than we should think desirable on general principles, we do not see in the facts before us any conclusive ground for saying that his expressed belief that the trial was fair and that the prisoner has nothing to complain of is wrong."[70]

In 1919, the Supreme Court ruled on one of the methods of finding an impartial jury when the local jury pool has been exposed to significant prejudicial publicity about a case. In *Stroud v. United States,*[71] the Court considered Robert Stroud's appeal of his murder conviction. Stroud, the so-called "Birdman of Alcatraz," contended that the trial judge should have granted his motion for a change of venue. Stroud made the motion after residents of Leavenworth, Kansas, where the trial was held, were exposed to local press reports of prosecution evidence from former trials of Stroud for the same offense. Local newspapers had reported only prosecution evidence, and, according to Stroud, "its wide circulation by the medium of the press created prejudice in the minds of the inhabitants of Leavenworth County against him. . . ."[72]

In response, the trial judge excluded from the jury pool all residents of Leavenworth County—for all practical purposes a "change of venire"—but Stroud contended that this jury, although not containing county residents, was still influenced by the prejudice that had been created by the newspaper reports. Once again affirming trial court discretion on issues of juror impartiality, the Supreme Court ruled that the record in the case disclosed no "abuse of discretion" by the trial court,

---

[68] *Id.* at 248.

[69] *Id.* at 250-51.

[70] *Id.* at 251.

[71] 251 U.S. 15 (1919).

[72] *Id.* at 18-19.

"such as would authorize an appellate court to interfere with the judgment."[73] Thus, *Stroud*, like the cases before it, created a wide zone of discretion for trial judges to make on-the-spot determinations of prejudice without appellate second-guessing.

In the 1950s, the Supreme Court again took up a series of cases exploring what constituted a fair trial by an impartial jury. In *Shepherd v. Florida*,[74] the Court considered the rape convictions of four African-American men who had been accused by a 17-year-old White girl in Lake County, Florida, in 1949. The defendants adduced ample evidence that theirs had been an unusual trial—so unusual, in fact, that the *per curiam* opinion of the Court simply reversed the judgment without further explanation.

In a concurrence by Justice Jackson, joined by Justice Frankfurter, it became clear why the Court had taken this unusual step. Justice Jackson characterized the atmosphere in Lake County as so prejudiced against the defendants that "the trial was but a legal gesture to register a verdict already dictated by the press and the public opinion which it generated."[75]

Prior to the trial, local newspapers had published reports that the sheriff had confessions from the defendants. Although these reports were not officially repudiated, no confessions had been offered at the trial. Justice Jackson noted that, had such a statement about confessions been made by a prosecutor in the courtroom, a mistrial would have resulted. "But neither counsel nor court can control the admission of evidence if unproven, and probably unprovable, 'confessions' are put before the jury by newspapers and radio," Justice Jackson wrote. "Rights of the defendant to be confronted by witnesses against him and to cross-examine them are thereby circumvented."[76]

The local press also enthusiastically reported on—*exploited*, in Justice Jackson's words—a number of other events preceding the trial. These included the appearance of a lynch mob at the jail where the defendants were held, a mob burning of the home of one of the defendant's parents, attempts to lynch other local African Americans, and an eventual call for the National Guard to restore order. Moreover, "every detail of these passion-arousing events was reported by the press under such headlines as, 'Night Riders Burn Lake Negro Homes' and 'Flames From Negro Homes Light Night Sky in Lake County,'" Justice Jackson wrote. "These and many other articles were highly prejudicial, including a cartoon published at the time of the grand jury, picturing four electric chairs and headed, 'No Compromise—Supreme Penalty.'"[77]

Justice Jackson reasoned that, under the circumstances surrounding the trial, a fair proceeding was simply impossible. Although the *per curiam* reversal was based on racial discrimination in jury selection, Justice Jackson wrote that the discrimi-

[73]*Id.* at 20.

[74]341 U.S. 50 (1951).

[75]*Id.* at 51.

[76]*Id.* at 52.

[77]*Id.* at 53.

nation was of only "theoretical importance." In reality, it was the poisoned atmosphere created by the media that posed the greatest threat to the defendants. Few jurors of either race, Justice Jackson argued, would have had the courage to vote for an acquittal given the local conditions. Justice Jackson's concurrence, although acknowledging that the Court's First Amendment jurisprudence made it quite difficult for trial judges to remedy prejudicial publicity, nonetheless called attention to the danger to defendants' Sixth Amendment rights when prejudicial coverage is unchecked. However, as noted earlier, a majority of the justices reversed the lower court on grounds not involving the relation between the press and juror impartiality.

In 1952, the Court refused to reverse a conviction despite arguments that newspaper accounts had made a fair trial impossible. In *Stroble v. California*,[78] Stroble had been convicted in Los Angeles of the gruesome murder of a 6-year-old girl. On appeal, Stroble contended that he could not obtain a fair trial in the Los Angeles area because of newspaper articles published weeks before his trial began that had referred to him "as a 'werewolf,' a 'fiend,' a 'sex-mad killer,' and the like."[79] Moreover, after Stroble confessed to the killing, the Los Angeles district attorney had released excerpts from the confession to the newspapers during the time Stroble was being interrogated. These excerpts had been printed, as had the full text of Stroble's confession when it was read into the court record at Stroble's preliminary hearing.

The Supreme Court declined to reverse the conviction. The Court noted that, although the district attorney perhaps should not have released the confession excerpts, by the time the confession was read into the record at the preliminary hearing, it was then a matter of public record. Further, the Court found inadequate support for the argument that the newspaper accounts created a sufficiently prejudicial atmosphere to prevent a fair trial. The Court noted that,

> in an effort to determine whether there was public hysteria or widespread community prejudice against petitioner at the time of his trial, we think it significant that two deputy public defenders who were vigorous in petitioner's defense throughout the trial, saw no occasion to seek a transfer . . . to another county on the ground that prejudicial newspaper accounts had made it impossible for petitioner to obtain a fair trial in . . . Los Angeles County.[80]

In addition, the Court stated that the jurors had been thoroughly examined, and had given no indication that they had read the prejudicial articles or that they could not reach an impartial verdict. "It is also significant," the Court wrote, "that in this case the confession which was one of the most prominent features of the newspaper accounts was made voluntarily and was introduced in evidence at the trial itself."[81]

---

[78]343 U.S. 181 (1952).

[79]*Id.* at 192.

[80]*Id.* at 194.

[81]*Id.* at 195.

Justice Frankfurter dissented, expressing concern with the extent to which media coverage might have affected the fundamental fairness of the trial. Frankfurter seemed particularly troubled by the prosecutor's participation in "trial by newspaper." Frankfurter wrote that,

> [s]cience with all its advances has not given us instruments for determining when the impact of such newspaper exploitation has spent itself or whether the powerful impression bound to be made by such inflaming articles as here preceded the trial can be dissipated in the mind of the average juror by the tame and often pedestrian proceedings in court.[82]

Justice Frankfurter argued that the conviction should have been obtained "wholly through the processes of law unaided by the infusion of extraneous passion."[83]

The Court rejected another appeal involving prejudicial publicity in 1956, this one involving publicity from one trial that was claimed to have affected a later trial. In *United States ex rel. Darcy v. Handy*,[84] a convicted murderer, David Darcy, brought a habeas corpus action contending that prejudicial publicity from a separate trial of Darcy's associates in the armed robbery during which the murder occurred resulted in an unfair trial for Darcy. Darcy's confederates in the robbery, Foster and Zeitz, were found guilty in a trial that ended 3 days before Darcy's trial began. Darcy's claim to the Court, among other claims, was that the publicity surrounding the robbery and the Foster–Zeitz trial "created such an atmosphere of hysteria and prejudice that it prevented him from having a fair trial."[85]

The Supreme Court denied the claim, noting that those seeking to show unfairness must do so "not as a matter of speculation but as a demonstrable reality."[86] The Court found that an opportunity for prejudice had existed, but that Darcy had failed to demonstrate actual prejudice. The Court noted in particular that Darcy's lawyer did not use all of the available peremptory challenges to potential jurors, nor did he seek a continuance or change of venue. The Court found that the failure to exercise these potential remedies for juror bias, although not proving that widespread prejudice did not exist, militated against such a finding. The Court also expressed skepticism toward the claim of prejudice because it had not been raised until nearly 3 years after the trial. Moreover, the Court accepted a lower court's description of the news coverage of the events and subsequent proceedings as "factual, with an occasional descriptive word or phrase, and, on occasion, words of compassion or commendation."[87] All of these factors tended to diminish, rather than support, Darcy's claim of widespread community prejudice and hysteria resulting in a biased jury.

---

[82]*Id.* at 201.

[83]*Id.* at 202.

[84]351 U.S. 454 (1956).

[85]*Id.* at 461.

[86]*Id.* at 462.

[87]*Id.* at 463.

A 1959 decision by the Court did reverse a conviction based on prejudicial publicity, although the Court stated it was not deciding the case on constitutional grounds. In *Marshall v. United States*,[88] the Court reversed the conviction of Howard R. Marshall for dispensing amphetamine tablets unlawfully. Marshall sold the pills to a government agent who claimed to be a salesman who had trouble staying awake during long automobile trips. At the trial, the prosecution sought to introduce evidence that Marshall had once practiced medicine without a license, but the trial judge declared the evidence to be insufficiently relevant to the case at hand and prejudicial to Marshall. As the trial progressed, the evidence was published in two newspapers in the area. One article even identified Marshall as an unlicensed physician who had prescribed drugs for country music legend Hank Williams. Another article stated that Marshall, in testimony before an Oklahoma legislative committee, "told the committee that although he had only a high school education, he practiced medicine with a $25 diploma he received through the mail. He told in detail of the ease in which he wrote and passed prescriptions for dangerous drugs."[89]

When the trial judge learned of the news articles, he questioned the jurors about whether they had read the articles containing the inadmissible evidence. Seven of the jurors had either read or scanned one or both of the articles. All of the seven, however, maintained that they could still decide the case impartially based on the evidence in court.

The Supreme Court, in a *per curiam* opinion, reversed the conviction. The Court reiterated the wide discretion it had granted to trial judges in determining jury prejudice. However, in this case, that discretion had been exceeded. "We have here the exposure of jurors to information of a character which the trial judge ruled so prejudicial it could not be directly offered as evidence," the Court wrote. "The prejudice to the defendant is almost certain to be as great when that evidence reaches the jury through news accounts as when it is a part of the prosecution's evidence. It may indeed be greater for it is then not tempered by protective procedures."[90] The Court stated that it was reversing the conviction based on its supervisory power over standards of criminal law enforcement in the federal courts, suggesting that the reversal was not on due process or other constitutional grounds.

In 1960, the U.S. Supreme Court reversed a lower court's denial of habeas corpus relief because of prejudicial publicity in the significant case of *Irvin v. Dowd*.[91] In *Dowd*, the defendant, Leslie Irvin, was convicted of murder in the Evansville, Indiana, vicinity. The murder of which he was convicted was but one of six apparently related murders that were intensely publicized and created tremendous concern in both Indiana and Kentucky.

Irvin, who was eventually sentenced to death by an Indiana state court, had been the subject of intense pretrial publicity before his trial for one of the murders. The

[88]360 U.S. 310 (1959).

[89]*Id.* at 311.

[90]*Id.* at 312-13.

[91]366 U.S. 717 (1960).

police and prosecutor in Vanderburg County, where Evansville was located, issued a variety of press releases, including one stating that Irvin had confessed to all six murders. "The headlines announced his police line-up identification, that he faced a lie detector test, had been placed at the scene of the crime and that the six murders were solved but petitioner refused to confess," the Court wrote. "Finally, they announced his confession to the six murders and the fact of his indictment for four of them in Indiana."[92]

Although the accused was granted a change of venue, it was only to an adjoining county, Gibson County, where massive publicity regarding his background and involvement in the murders was also underway. After the case was moved to Gibson County, his counsel sought another change of venue, but Indiana law allowed only a single change of venue in a given case. Evansville newspapers and broadcast stations reached most homes in Gibson County, so that most news stories originating in Evansville also reached potential jurors in the more rural Gibson County. After the change of venue, Irvin's case became a cause celebre in Gibson County, the residents of which soon learned of Irvin's juvenile crimes and his prior convictions for burglary and arson, as well as a military court-martial. The media reported not only Irvin's "offer to plead guilty if promised a 99-year sentence, but also the determination, on the other hand, of the prosecutor to secure the death penalty, and that [Irvin] had confessed to 24 burglaries (the modus operandi of these robberies was compared to that of the murders and the similarity noted)," the Court wrote.[93] News stories related Irvin's remorselessness, as well as the determination of a Kentucky sheriff to "devote his life" to make certain that Irvin was executed. The day before the trial was to begin, news stories reported Irvin's purported confessions to additional murders.

The effect of this onslaught of publicity on potential Gibson County jurors was dramatic. The voir dire produced a great deal of bitterness and anger. "Spectator comments, as printed by the newspapers, were 'my mind is made up'; 'I think he is guilty'; and 'he should be hanged,' " the Court wrote.[94] From a panel of 430 potential jurors, 370 (nearly 90 %) expressed some opinion as to the guilt of Irvin. This percentage is even more remarkable considering that 10 jurors were never even asked if they had an opinion on the matter. The feelings of those jurors who expressed an opinion on Irvin's guilt ranged "in intensity from mere suspicion to absolute certainty. A number admitted that, if they were in the accused's place in the dock and he in theirs on the jury with their opinions, they would not want him on a jury."[95] The trial court eventually settled on 12 jurors, of whom 8 expressed the opinion that Irvin was guilty.

The *Irvin* Court seemed less sanguine than in past cases about jurors who, while admitting to opinions about guilt, nonetheless maintained they could weigh the

---

[92] *Id.* at 725.

[93] *Id.* at 725-26.

[94] *Id.* at 727.

[95] *Id.* at 727.

evidence impartially. The overwhelming nature of the publicity, as well as the jurors' familiarity with Irvin's alleged involvement in other murders, led the Court to doubt the possibility of the jury, in these circumstances, to consider the case impartially. "No doubt each juror was sincere when he said that he would be fair and impartial to petitioner, but the psychological impact requiring such a declaration before one's fellows is often its father," the Court wrote. "Where so many, so many times, admitted prejudice, such a statement of impartiality can be given little weight."[96]

In reversing Irvin's conviction, the Court's majority opinion expressed no opinion on the means of halting such intense prejudicial coverage in the future. However, Justice Frankfurter's concurrence noted that the Court had not addressed the conflict between the fair trial rights of criminal defendants and freedom of the press. Every term, Frankfurter wrote, the Court was asked to reverse convictions because of "inflammatory" media coverage—in many cases, created in collaboration with prosecutors, as in the *Irvin* case. Justice Frankfurter noted that the Supreme Court had not yet considered whether freedom of the press necessarily trumped the right to fair judicial proceedings. "The Court has not yet decided that, while convictions must be reversed and miscarriages of justice result because the minds of jurors or potential jurors were poisoned, the poisoner is constitutionally protected in plying his trade," he wrote.[97] Although somewhat ambiguous, Frankfurter's concurrence suggested that at least one member of the Court was dissatisfied with reversing criminal convictions while the press had a virtually unfettered right to publish prejudicial information.

Two years after *Irvin*, the Court reversed a conviction in another highly publicized murder trial. In *Rideau v. Louisiana*,[98] Wilbert Rideau was charged with kidnapping and murder after a bank robbery in Louisiana. While Rideau was in custody, officials filmed him during an interview with the sheriff of Calcasieu Parish. During the interview, Rideau confessed to the crimes. That filmed confession was subsequently broadcast on television three times by a Lake Charles television station and viewed by a large percentage of the population of Calcasieu Parish, where the trial was held. Rideau's lawyers sought a change of venue based on the televised confession. The motion was denied, and Rideau was convicted and sentenced to death.

Characterizing the trial as "Kangaroo court proceedings," the Supreme Court reversed the conviction.[99] The majority reasoned that the conviction was inherently invalid under the due process clause, even without any specific showing of prejudice. This approach was in contrast to *Irvin* and earlier cases, in which the Court had required extensive factual proof that prejudice actually existed. The Court noted that the jury contained three members who admitted seeing the filmed confession at least once, as well as two who were deputy sheriffs in Calcasieu Parish. The Court pointed out that to the jurors who had witnessed the film, the

---

[96]*Id.* at 728.

[97]*Id.* at 730 (Frankfurter, J., concurring).

[98]373 U.S. 723 (1962).

televised confession in effect *was* the trial, while the actual judicial proceeding was but a "hollow formality." Rideau's counsel asked that these jurors be removed for cause, having exhausted all peremptory challenges, but the trial judge denied the challenges for cause.

The Court noted that it was unclear from the record

> whose idea it was to make the sound film, and broadcast it over the local television station, but we know from the conceded circumstances that the plan was carried out with active cooperation and participation of the local law enforcement officers. And certainly no one has suggested that it was Rideau's idea, or even that he was aware of what was going on when the sound film was being made.[100]

The Court held that due process entitled Rideau to a jury composed of persons who had not seen the televised confession, and ruled that the change of venue should have been granted.

Justice Clark, joined by Justice Harlan, dissented on the ground that the majority had failed to establish a clear nexus between the interview and an unfair trial. Clark argued that, "[u]nless that adverse publicity is shown by the record to have fatally infected the trial, there is simply no basis for the Court's inference that the publicity, epitomized by the televised interview, called up some informal and illicit analogy to res judicata, making petitioner's trial a meaningless formality."[101] Justice Clark wrote that, unless circumstances were "unusually compelling," as in the *Irvin* case, courts should give substantial deference to juror statements that they can ignore outside factors and decide the case impartially. Although not defining exactly what would constitute such compelling circumstances, Clark argued that Rideau had not met the burden of establishing a violation of due process.

In a 1965 case, *Estes v. Texas*,[102] four justices concluded that televising a criminal trial was a *per se* violation of the accused's due process rights.[103] In *Estes*, the Court reversed the swindling conviction of notorious financier Billie Sol Estes in a Texas state court. Estes' trial generated huge pretrial publicity, and venue was changed to a court nearly 500 miles away from the original site of the trial. The proceedings were covered by television and radio, although after some disastrous pretrial coverage, the trial was covered with significant restrictions. These included little live broadcasting, with the exception of the prosecutions's opening and closing arguments and the return of the jury's verdict. Moreover, only sporadic camera operation—without sound—was allowed for taping proceedings for later use during regularly scheduled newscasts.

---

[99] *Id.* at 726.

[100] *Id.* at 725.

[101] *Id.* at 729.

[102] 381 U.S. 532 (1965).

[103] *But see* Chandler v. Florida, 449 U.S. 560 (1981) (reading *Estes* as not creating an absolute ban on state experimentation with televising trials).

At least four justices in the *Estes* majority followed the *per se* approach taken in *Rideau*, finding inherent prejudice in any televised proceedings without any factual showing of actual prejudice. "Television in its present state and by its very nature reaches into a variety of areas in which it may cause prejudice to the accused," Justice Clark wrote. "Still one cannot put his finger on its specific mischief and prove with particularity wherein he was prejudiced."[104] The majority's fifth vote, Justice Harlan, agreed that Estes' due process rights were violated in this particular case, but declined to adopt an absolute constitutional rule as to all televised proceedings.

Four dissenters in *Estes* agreed that televised trials could create constitutional risks, but argued against reversing the conviction. Justice Stewart wrote that an *amicus curiae* brief filed by the American Bar Association had catalogued the risks, including jurors watching selectively edited news reports in the evening, jurors being subjected to pressure from friends and family who watch the televised coverage, and jurors becoming "recognizable celebrities, likely to be stopped by passing strangers, or perhaps harried by intruding telephone calls."[105] While acknowledging these risks, Justice Stewart noted that, in Estes' trial, none of these things had taken place because the jury was sequestered, and thus completely insulated from both the televised coverage and members of the public who watched it. Moreover, during the trial, the courtroom was notable for showing almost no evidence of the media presence. "In appearance the courtroom was practically unaltered," Justice Stewart wrote. "There was no obtrusiveness and no distraction, no noise and no special lighting."[106] The dissent thus concluded that the television cameras had no effect on Estes' constitutional rights.

In 1966, the Court suggested methods for controlling prejudicial publicity in *Sheppard v. Maxwell*.[107] This celebrated case, which later became the basis for parts of the storyline of the fictional television series and motion picture "The Fugitive," had it beginnings on the night that Marilyn Sheppard was found bludgeoned to death in 1954. Ms. Sheppard was the wife of Dr. Sam Sheppard, a Cleveland surgeon, who was present in the couple's house on the night of the murder. Dr. Sheppard claimed that he had fallen asleep on the couch, but was awakened by his wife's cries. Rushing to her bed, Sheppard claimed he saw a "form" standing over his wife. Sheppard said he struggled with the form and was knocked unconscious. Sometime later, Sheppard claimed, he awoke, found his wife dead, pursued the "form" to the lakeshore near the couple's home, and was again knocked unconscious.

Dr. Sheppard's account of the murder was apparently unconvincing to authorities, who immediately began to focus their investigation on him. Police and prosecutors also began supplying fodder for newspapers stories about Sheppard's

---

[104]381 U.S. at 544.

[105]*Id.* at 612-13.

[106]*Id.* at 613.

[107]384 U.S. 333 (1966).

alleged lack of cooperation with authorities, including his unwillingness to take a lie detector test. Newspapers began making front-page editorial assertions to the effect that someone was "getting away with murder."[108] Media accounts also emphasized Sheppard's relationship with a woman named Susan Hayes as a possible motive for the murder. As the investigation progressed, newspaper editorials became ever more strident, with front-page editorials asking, "Why Isn't Sam Sheppard in Jail?," and demanding that authorities "Quit Stalling—Bring Him In."[109] The publicity grew even further in intensity in the period preceding Sheppard's indictment for the crime.

When Sheppard's trial was about to begin, Cleveland newspapers published the names and addresses of prospective jurors, who received letters and telephone calls regarding the case. The papers also published photographs of the prospective jurors, as well as photographs of the jury proper as the trial progressed. With one exception, the jurors admitted exposure to pretrial publicity about the case. Moreover, the jurors were not sequestered during the trial, and the trial judge gave only rather anemic "suggestions" that they avoid media coverage of the case while the trial was in progress. Although jurors were sequestered to deliberate the verdict, they were allowed to make unmonitored telephone calls during deliberations. While the case was being tried, the courtroom was filled with reporters who created what Justice Clark, writing for the majority, characterized as a "carnival atmosphere." "The fact is that bedlam reigned at the courthouse during the trial and newsmen took over practically the entire courtroom, hounding most of the participants in the trial, especially Sheppard," Justice Clark wrote.[110] The media also carried extensive accounts of statements of witnesses and officials that were never presented at the trial.

In *Sheppard*, the Court ruled that the trial was unfair based on "the massive, pervasive and prejudicial publicity that attended his prosecution."[111] Thus, the Court granted Sheppard federal habeas corpus relief based on the unfair trial in an Ohio court. The Court "assumed" that significant amounts of prejudicial material had reached the jury, in part because the trial judge had refused most defense requests to interview jurors about their exposure to prejudicial reports.

The Supreme Court suggested a number of measures the trial court might have taken to ensure a fair trial. For example, the Court wrote, "the trial court might well have proscribed extrajudicial statements by any lawyer, party, witness, or court official which divulged prejudicial matters. . . ."[112] Such matters would have included Sheppard's willingness to be questioned or take a lie detector test, Sheppard's statements to police, and statements about Sheppard's guilt or the merits of the case against him. Thus, the Supreme Court in *Sheppard* expressly encouraged

---

[108]*Id.* at 339.

[109]*Id.* at 341.

[110]*Id.* at 355.

[111]*Id.* at 335.

[112]*Id.* at 361.

gag orders against participants as a valid, and presumably constitutional, means of ensuring a fair trial. The Court made it clear, however, that there was nothing to prevent the press from reporting what went on in the courtroom. The Court also suggested alternative measures in high-profile cases, such as sequestering the jury, postponing the trial until publicity died down, transferring the case to another locale, or, if all else failed, ordering a new trial. The Court placed the requirement of providing a fair trial squarely on the trial court, not on the press. Throughout the *Sheppard* opinion, the Court seemed reluctant even to suggest any direct restraint against the press. While acknowledging the vital importance of a fair trial, the Court emphasized the value of the media's role as the "handmaiden" of a fair judicial system. This role, in which the press "guards against the miscarriage of justice by subjecting the police, prosecutors, and judicial processes to extensive public scrutiny and criticism," made the Court particularly unwilling to consider direct limitations on press freedom.[113]

STUDIES AND GUIDELINES REGARDING PREJUDICIAL PUBLICITY

In the years that followed *Sheppard*, a number of organizations issued studies and reports analyzing the so-called "free press–fair trial" controversy. A number of events converged in the mid-1960s to bring about the extraordinary attention paid to prejudicial publicity and its effect on criminal justice. As one scholar described this era: "The general determination to act was generated by cases like *Irvin v. Dowd,* and by the season of introspection which came upon the courts as a result of the assassinations of President Kennedy and Lee Harvey Oswald."[114] Many concerned observers wondered how Oswald could have ever received a fair trial in light of the publicity surrounding Kennedy's death. This concern helped lead to a major reassessment of the media's impact on the criminal justice system.

A 1968 American Bar Association report, known as the Reardon Report, contained recommendations for ensuring fair trials despite intense news coverage.[115] The Reardon Report generally advocated restrictions on lawyers and court officers, rather than restrictions on the media. In extreme cases, however, such as instances in which a person disseminated information for the purpose of affecting the outcome of a trial, the report advocated a balancing methodology in invoking the judge's contempt power against the media or others: "The clear and present danger of an immediately discernible substantive evil plainly exists; the period of judicial concern is limited and carefully defined; and the conduct in question must be plainly egregious—for example, a campaign to convict—in order to warrant

---

[113]*Id.* at 350.

[114]J. Gerald, News of Crime 66 (1983).

[115]Advisory Committee on Fair Trial and Free Press, Standards Relating to Fair Trial and Free Press (1968).

punishment."[116] Using this test, the press and others could constitutionally be punished using the contempt power. The appeal to the clear and present danger standard reflected the common legal perception of the time that clear and present danger review was the answer to preserving free expression rights while protecting criminal defendants from an unrestrained press.

Another influential study, issued in 1967, was the Medina Report, drafted by a committee of the Association of the Bar of the City of New York.[117] The Medina Report, unlike the Reardon Report, urged that courts eschew direct controls on the media, including the contempt power. The committee stated that it was

> of the opinion that the guarantees of the First Amendment will prevent the use of the contempt power to control the news media even where the impartiality of a petit jury is endangered. Moreover, the Committee feels that the "clear and present danger" test would be applied as well to criminal prosecutions and nonsummary contempt proceedings, thereby making it unlikely that they would pass constitutional muster.[118]

The Medina Report instead advocated tighter controls on statements by lawyers. For example, the committee recommended revising the canons of lawyer conduct promulgated by the American Bar Association to prohibit lawyers from making or sanctioning out-of-court statements on a variety of subjects in pending cases. The proposed canon was to prohibit statements as to the guilt of an accused, the existence or contents of confessions, proposed testimony or evidence, the credibility of witnesses, prior convictions of an accused, and other matters that might prejudice a trial.

The Medina Report also proposed stricter regulation on statements by police and other law enforcement agencies. The committee proposed that police should be limited to release of information that concerned matters such as an arrested defendant's name, age, and occupation, but not his or her criminal record, psychiatric history, or the contents or results of any statements or tests. News media should not be allowed to interview or photograph a defendant in custody. Under the proposed code, police were prohibited from releasing gruesome photographs or descriptions of crime scenes, or making comments about the motive or character of the accused. Moreover, the committee called on trial judges to take strong action to avoid the kind of "Roman holiday" trial described in the *Sheppard* case.

Another 1967 report, this one prepared by a committee of the American Newspaper Publishers Association, also rejected controls on the press.[119] The ANPA report argued that there was no genuine conflict between the right of a free press and the right to trial by an impartial jury. On the contrary, citizens in a democracy

---

[116]*Id.* at 150.

[117]Special Committee on Radio, Television, and the Administration of Justice of the Association of the Bar of the City of New York, Freedom of the Press and Fair Trial (1967).

[118]*Id.* at 6.

[119]American Newspaper Publishers Association Special Committee on Free Press and Fair Trial, Free Press and Fair Trial (1967).

must have access to information to make informed judgments about the criminal justice system. The report argued both for an absence of governmental restraints on press coverage of trials and for full access to government information concerning arrests and criminal prosecutions. "When the people are denied information about criminal charges, the denial provides a breeding ground for rumor," the report stated. "If there is no reliable source of information, such as an authentic news story, rumor and exaggeration can unduly excite and arouse the public."[120]

In 1968, the Committee on the Operation of the Jury System of the United States Judicial Conference, composed of federal judges, issued a report advocating measures substantially similar to those in the Medina Report.[121] The committee suggested controls on comments by lawyers and court officials, as well as prohibition of photography and radio and television broadcasting in the courtroom. The report, like the Medina Report, expressed opposition to restraints on the press. The Judicial Conference committee opined that direct control on publication by the press would be mistaken as a policy matter and probably unconstitutional as well. The committee said it had "firmly kept in mind the substantial contributions which the news media has made, and will continue to make, to virtually every phase of the administration of criminal justice, from the exposure of corruption and miscarriages of justice to the uncovering of evidence germane to establishing guilt or innocence."[122] The committee rejected suggestions aimed at limiting release of information by federal law enforcement agencies, citing concurrent actions by the Justice Department and other agencies to limit release of information by their employees.

The Judicial Conference committee report also urged individual federal district courts to adopt local rules that regulated discussion of pending cases by attorneys practicing in those courts. The committee cited the frequency with which prejudicial reports originate from either the prosecution or defense counsel, and suggested that those sources, at least, were within the control of the court. The report listed a number of topics that lawyers should be prohibited from discussing. The topics included the following: prior criminal records of defendants; statements, including confessions by defendants; the identity, testimony, and credibility of potential witnesses; statements concerning possible plea bargains; and opinions about a defendant's guilt or innocence, or the merits of the case. The proposed rule also forbade lawyers during a trial from giving statements or interviews to the press, except to quote from public court records without comment.

The committee further recommended that federal district courts make more extensive use of traditional methods of ensuring an impartial jury. Techniques suggested by the *Sheppard* Court—such as continuance, change of venue, sequestration of jurors, sequestration of witnesses, extensive voir dire, and judicial

---

[120]*Id.* at 5.

[121]Report of the Judicial Conference Committee on the Operation of the Jury System on the "Free Press–Fair Trial" Issue, 45 F.R.D. 391 (1968) *revised* at 87 F.R.D. 519 (1980).

[122]*Id.* at 393-94.

admonition—should be used to preserve a fair trial despite extensive pretrial publicity. The committee noted, however, that

> in many cases, particularly those of a highly sensational nature, the use of one or more of these traditional measures has not proven sufficient to assure the defendant a fair trial. Moreover, some of them will involve additional complications such as, in the case of a protracted continuance, prejudice to the right of a defendant to a speedy trial and the interest of the public in the prompt administration of justice.[123]

The concerns about perceived conflicts between First Amendment and Sixth Amendment rights also led to a number of voluntary agreements between the press and the judicial establishment. These agreements, commonly called *bench-bar-press guidelines*, suggest what sort of material should be released concerning criminal cases and how reporters can report on pending cases without prejudicing the trial. Often based on guidelines promulgated by the American Bar Association, such agreements suggest limits on dissemination of information on matters such as confessions and statements by participants about the defendant's guilt or innocence, or the credibility of witnesses. One count found that 28 states have bench-bar-press guidelines in existence.[124]

Scholars who have studied the guidelines have questioned their effectiveness. One study conducted in 1976 concluded, surprisingly, that violations of the ABA's guidelines occur with slightly more frequency in states that have press-bar agreements than in those that do not.[125] Although guidelines may sometimes foster a spirit of cooperation among judges, lawyers, and journalists, the agreements do not guarantee consensus, and may well lead to conflict in individual cases.[126]

CONCLUSION

The concern with prejudicial publicity in criminal trials is long-standing, as the cases discussed in this chapter reveal. However, the issue drew particular attention during the middle decades of this century. During the 1960s, the Supreme Court and numerous private and public groups sought to resolve the perceived tension between a free press and fair trials. Although both the justices and others seemed reluctant to inhibit media coverage of the criminal justice system, the consensus view seemed to be that, at some point, free expression concerns had to give way to the need to preserve a criminal defendant's right to a fair trial.

---

[123] *Id.* at 413.

[124] D. Pember, Mass Media Law 400 (1987).

[125] Tankard, Middleton, & Rimmer, Compliance with American Bar Association Fair Trial–Free Press Guidelines, 56 Journalism Q. 464 (1979).

[126] *See, e.g.,* Drechsel, An Alternative View of Media–Judiciary Relations: What the Non-Legal Evidence Suggests About the Fair Trial–Free Press Issue, 18 Hofstra L. Rev. 1, 10-11 (1989).

The next chapter examines the evolution of the Supreme Court's prior restraint jurisprudence, particularly as applied in cases involving criminal proceedings. Prior restraints have traditionally been anathema in First Amendment law. Nevertheless, as the next chapter demonstrates, even prior restraints have not been absolutely barred, but have only been subject to balancing formulas such as the clear and present danger test.

-4-

Prior Restraints

Prior restraints have historically been perhaps the least tolerated infringements on free speech in Anglo-American law. In its most common form, a *prior restraint* is a judicial order preventing the media from publishing material already in its hands. In the 18th century, Sir William Blackstone stated the legal aversion to prior restraints in its classic formulation: "The *liberty of the press* is indeed essential to the nature of a free state; but this consists in laying no *previous* restraints upon publications, and not in freedom from censure for criminal matter when published."[1] Prior restraints were regarded as pernicious because they stopped speech from ever being heard. A scheme of subsequent punishment might discourage potential speakers, but prior restraints allowed ideas to be silenced before they even saw the light of day. As Chief Justice Burger put it: "If it can be said that a threat of criminal or civil sanctions after publication 'chills' speech, prior restraint 'freezes' it at least for the time."[2]

The traditional common law doctrine of prior restraint grew out of the licensing system in England. Under licensing, the Crown exercised control over printers and punished those who published without a license. The licensing system ended in 1694.[3] It was not until the 20th century that the U.S. Supreme Court decided a major case involving a prior restraint, and constitutionalized the Blackstonian common law doctrine that prior restraints were rarely, if ever, allowable.

---

[1]W. Blackstone, Commentaries on the Laws of England (1765-69), book 4, chap. II, 151-152, reprinted in L. Levy, ed., Freedom of the Press from Zenger to Jefferson 104-05 (1966).

[2]Nebraska Press Assn v. Stuart, 427 U.S. 539, 559 (1975).

[3]L. Levy, Emergence of a Free Press 6-7, 12 (1985).

That decision, *Near v. Minnesota*,[4] and another landmark case decided in 1976, *Nebraska Press Assn v. Stuart*,[5] seemed to establish a constitutional regime under which prior restraints would have great difficulty passing constitutional muster. For the most part, lower federal courts have rejected direct prior restraints on the press in criminal cases. Nonetheless, in at least one case, a federal district court and appellate court have upheld a temporary restraint on material in the hands of the media concerning the criminal justice system. Moreover, even in those cases striking down prior restraints on the press, federal courts have often seemed to lack any firm jurisprudential ground for decision, relying instead on vague generalizations that offer little guidance for future cases.

As an alternate means to control prejudicial publicity, many courts have chosen to restrict the comments of trial participants through gag orders, rather than impose restrictions directly on the press. Those federal court decisions focusing on media challenges to gag orders on trial participants are sharply divided. Some courts have held that such gag orders cannot be classified as prior restraints at all, whereas others have treated such orders as functionally equivalent to prior restraints, and applied appropriately higher levels of scrutiny.

PRIOR RESTRAINT DOCTRINE
IN THE SUPREME COURT

In *Near v. Minnesota*,[6] the landmark 20th-century prior restraint case, the Court struck down a Minnesota statute allowing courts to enjoin, as a public nuisance, a "malicious, scandalous and defamatory newspaper, magazine or other periodical."[7] The publication in question in *Near* was *The Saturday Press*, an anti-Semitic Minneapolis newspaper owned by Near. Near's newspaper routinely charged city officials with dereliction of duty and corruption. The trial court in *Near* issued a permanent injunction against Near's publication of *The Saturday Press* or any other publication "whatsoever which is a malicious, scandalous or defamatory newspaper. . . ."[8]

Chief Justice Hughes, writing for the Court, declared the statute unconstitutional under the First and Fourteenth Amendments. According to Hughes, the statute was an impermissible prior restraint because it allowed a publication to be completely suppressed. The *Near* majority did not assert that prior restraints were never constitutionally permissible; rather, Chief Justice Hughes, in *dicta*, noted some circumstances under which prior restraints might pass constitutional muster. These included publication of military information in wartime, obscenity, and incitement

---

[4]283 U.S. 697 (1931).

[5]427 U.S. 539 (1975).

[6]283 U.S. 697 (1931).

[7]*Id.* at 701-702.

[8]*Id.* at 706.

to overthrow government.[9] The *Near* opinion did not set forth any test to measure when prior restraints might be constitutional. Hughes wrote that limitations on the "no prior restraint" rule would only apply in "exceptional cases."[10] The language of the opinion, however, seemed to suggest that prior restraints would be difficult to reconcile with free expression.

In 1971, the Court issued another landmark opinion concerning prior restraints in *New York Times Co. v. U.S.*[11] This case, known as the "Pentagon Papers case," reemphasized the difficulty inherent in establishing prior restraints that could stand under the First Amendment. The Pentagon Papers case involved a governmental attempt to enjoin publication of a classified government study of U.S. policy in Vietnam by *The New York Times* and the *Washington Post.*

In a brief *per curiam* opinion, the Court pointed out that "[a]ny system of prior restraints of expression comes to this Court bearing a heavy presumption against its constitutional validity."[12] The Court's *per curiam* opinion did not set forth any formal test for determining when government might overcome that heavy presumption. It merely held that the government had not done so in the case at hand. Among the nine concurrences and dissents spawned by the case, a few justices sought to state a standard by which prior restraints might be balanced against other needs. Justice Brennan wrote that only "proof that publication must inevitably, directly, and immediately cause the occurrence of an event kindred to imperiling the safety of a transport already at sea"[13] would be sufficient to overcome the presumption against restraints on publication. In opinions that rejected balancing, Justices Black and Douglas would have held that the First Amendment left no room for prior restraints. Both called for a categorical rule against such restraints, with no governmental interest balancing to dilute the "no law" language of the framers.

Justice Blackmun, in dissent, advocated "a weighing, on properly developed standards, of the broad right of the press to print and of the very narrow right of the Government to prevent,"[14] noting that such standards had not been formulated. However, Justice Blackmun alluded to Justice Holmes' clear and present danger test from *Schenck v. United States*[15] as one possible source of such standards. Justice Stewart, joined by Justice White, suggested the Court could act, in the absence of a specific statute or regulation, only if disclosure of the documents would "surely result in direct, immediate, and irreparable damage to our Nation or its people."[16] Because this standard was not met in the case before the Court, Justice Stewart wrote that the Court was required to overturn the restraint.

---

[9]*Id.* at 716.

[10]*Id.* at 716.

[11]403 U.S. 713 (1971).

[12]*Id.* at 714, quoting *Bantam Books, Inc. v. Sullivan*, 372 U.S. 58, 70 (1963).

[13]*Id.* at 726-27.

[14]*Id.* at 761.

[15]249 U.S. 47 (1919).

[16]403 U.S. at 730.

It was not until 1976, in *Nebraska Press Assn v. Stuart*,[17] that the Court applied prior restraint doctrine to a court order aimed at silencing the press in a criminal case. In *Nebraska Press*, the Court struck down an injunction restraining the press from reporting facts that might prejudice the trial of a murder suspect, including the existence of a confession by the suspect. The accused, Erwin Charles Simants, was charged with killing six family members in a small Nebraska town. The trial court, citing the difficulty of seating an impartial jury amidst massive coverage of the proceedings leading up to the trial, prohibited those attending from publishing "any testimony given or evidence adduced."[18] A higher state court later limited the order to a narrower group of subjects, including Simants' confession and other incriminating evidence.

The U.S. Supreme Court, in an opinion written by Chief Justice Burger, struck down the restraint as failing to meet the heavy burden required by the First Amendment. Chief Justice Burger's opinion acknowledged the command of the Sixth Amendment that an accused must be provided with a trial by an impartial jury, but held that, under the facts of *Nebraska Press*, the First Amendment rights of the press outweighed those Sixth Amendment rights. The Court formulated the issue as essentially one of conflict between the two constitutional rights—a conflict that could be resolved differently in different cases depending on their facts. Chief Justice Burger stated that, "[t]he authors of the Bill of Rights did not undertake to assign priorities as between First Amendment and Sixth Amendment rights," and that the *Nebraska Press* Court would not do so either.[19]

The Court set forth a three-part balancing test designed to accommodate the opposing First and Sixth Amendment interests. According to Chief Justice Burger, the test was based on Judge Learned Hand's formulation of the clear and present danger test: whether "the gravity of the 'evil,' discounted by its improbability, justifies such invasion of free speech as is necessary to avoid the danger."[20] Based on that test, the *Nebraska Press* Court wrote, a judge evaluating a prior restraint in a criminal trial context was required to determine: (a) "the nature and extent of pretrial coverage,"[21]; (b) whether some alternative judicial action could reduce the effect of the coverage, and (c) whether a prior restraint would effectively protect the defendant's right to a fair trial under the Sixth Amendment. Examining these factors, the Court concluded on the facts before it that a prior restraint was not constitutionally permissible.

In a concurrence in the judgment that read as if it had been prepared as a majority opinion, Justice Brennan, joined by Justices Stewart and Marshall, rejected Burger's balancing approach. Justice Brennan advocated the categorical position "that to resort to prior restraints on the freedom of the press is a constitutionally

---

[17]427 U.S. 539 (1976).

[18]*Id.* at 542.

[19]*Id.* at 561.

[20]*Id.* at 562, quoting United States v. Dennis, 183 F.2d 201, 212 (CA 1950).

[21]427 U.S. at 562.

impermissible method for enforcing [the right to a fair trial]." Justice Brennan argued that the use of alternative devices, such a sequestering jurors and limiting release of information, could adequately protect defendants' Sixth Amendment rights. Brennan pointed out that the suggested exceptions to prior restraint doctrine in *Near* and the Pentagon Papers case had centered on matters of national security, not criminal trials.

Justice Brennan's concurrence seemed to come close to garnering a majority of the Court's members. Aside from the two justices joining Brennan, two other justices stated a willingness to adopt a tougher standard than that contained in Chief Justice Burger's majority opinion. Justice Stevens' concurrence in the judgment expressed hesitance to lay down an absolute rule that prior restraints in criminal cases were unconstitutional. Nonetheless, Justice Stevens stated that he did "subscribe to most of what Mr. Justice Brennan says and, if ever required to face the issue squarely, may well accept his ultimate conclusion."[22] Similarly, Justice White, concurring, expressed "grave doubt in my mind whether orders with respect to the press such as were entered in this case would ever be justifiable."[23] However, Justice White, like Justice Stevens, chose not to adopt a general rule based only on the facts before the Court. Thus, it appears that five justices evinced some degree of support for a bright-line rule that prior restraints could not constitutionally issue in criminal trials. However, the need to preserve future flexibility apparently resulted in the majority's acceptance of Chief Justice Burger's balancing formulation.

The Court reinforced its aversion to prior restraints in criminal cases by striking down a restraint in the 1977 case of *Oklahoma Publishing Co. v. District Court.*[24] In *Oklahoma Publishing*, the Court confronted a state court order, based on an Oklahoma statute, forbidding the press to publish the name or photograph of an 11-year-old juvenile murder defendant. Despite the order, the media used both the name and photograph of the boy after attending hearings in the case. The issue, the Court stated, was whether a court could "prohibit the publication of widely disseminated information obtained at court proceedings which were in fact open to the public."[25]

In a *per curiam* opinion, the Court held the order unconstitutional under *Nebraska Press* and *Cox Broadcasting Corp. v. Cohn,*[26] in which the Court had ruled that the First Amendment forbade criminal punishment of the press for publishing truthful information obtained in criminal proceedings. The Court in *Oklahoma Publishing* noted that the presiding judge knew that members of the media were present at the juvenile hearing, but made no attempt to exclude them.

---

[22] *Id.* at 617 (Stevens, J., concurring in the judgment).

[23] *Id.* at 570 (White, J., concurring).

[24] 430 U.S. 308 (1977).

[25] *Id.* at 310.

[26] 420 U.S. 469 (1975).

CASES STRIKING DOWN PRIOR RESTRAINTS
ON MEDIA

The strong presumption against prior restraints found in Supreme Court cases such as *Near* and *Nebraska Press* has resulted in an almost universal rejection of prior restraints on the press in lower federal court cases involving the criminal justice system.[27] For example, in *WXYZ, Inc. v. Hurd,*[28] the U.S. Court of Appeals for the Sixth Circuit in 1981 held unconstitutional an order suppressing the details of an alleged sexual assault and the names of the victim and suspect. The order was entered pursuant to a Michigan statute allowing such suppression until "the actor is arraigned on the information, the charge is dismissed, or the case is otherwise concluded, whichever occurs first."[29] The judge who entered the order warned media representatives that the order applied to them, and that violators would be subject to being held in contempt.

Before the Sixth Circuit, the judge argued that the order, and the statute under which it was issued, served "a different and *far less speculative* social objective than the one considered in *Nebraska Press*."[30] That interest consisted of the privacy rights of both the victim and the accused in the sexual assault case, not the Sixth Amendment interest in a fair trial cited in *Nebraska Press*. Protection of this privacy interest was essential to shielding victims from psychological harm and rehabilitating sex offenders, the judge argued.

The Sixth Circuit decided that the order and the underlying statute violated the First Amendment. The Sixth Circuit held that the alleged harms the statute prevented were simply too speculative to support a prior restraint. In reaching this conclusion, the court adopted Justice Brennan's Pentagon Papers balancing test, requiring that "publication must inevitably, directly and immediately cause the occurrence of an event kindred to imperiling the safety of a transport already at sea."[31] This formulation, which appears to be a particularly strong version of the clear and present danger test, led the Sixth Circuit to conclude that the state trial judge in *WXYZ* had not met the burden necessary to justify a prior restraint.

The Sixth Circuit also affirmed the lower court's holding that the statute underlying the order was unconstitutional on its face. The court stated that, even if the statute did not contemplate a prior restraint, but allowed only subsequent punishment for revealing information about sexual offenses, it could not pass muster under the *Cox Broadcasting Corp. v. Cohn*[32] and *Smith v. Daily Mail*

[27]In addition to the cases discussed in the text, *see, e.g.*, Corbitt v. NBC, 20 Media L. Rep. 2037 (N.D. Ill. 1992); Menendez v. Fox Broadcasting Co., 22 Media L. Rep. 1702 (C.D. Cal. 1994); Lambert v. Polk County, 723 F.Supp. 128 (S.D. Iowa 1989); Huron Publishing Co. v. Martin, 5 Media L. Rep. 1871 (D.S.D. 1979).

[28]658 F.2d 420 (6th Cir. 1981).

[29]*Id.* at 421 (quoting MCLA sec. 750-520K).

[30]*Id.* at 425.

[31]New York Times v. U.S., 403 U.S. 713, 726-27 (1971).

[32]420 U.S. 469 (1975).

Publishing Co.[33] line of cases. These cases held unconstitutional attempts to punish the press for revealing unlawfully obtained information about judicial proceedings. Even assuming, for purposes of argument, that the privacy interests underlying the Michigan statute were sufficiently compelling, the Sixth Circuit held that the statute allowed the legislature to decide, without a separate judicial determination, that privacy interests were sufficient in every case involving sexual offenses to warrant sanctions for publication of the names of those involved and the details of the offense. "Deference to such legislative judgments is impossible when First Amendment interests are at stake," the court wrote.[34] The court also noted that the statute was overbroad because the details of the offense could never be suppressed, regardless of the asserted state interest in privacy.

Frequently, lower federal courts do not use any balancing language at all in their prior restraint opinions. Instead, they often rely on generalized statements that prior restraints are presumptively unconstitutional. For example, a 1990 decision by the U.S. Court of Appeals for the Fourth Circuit readily disposed of a prior restraint issued by a South Carolina federal district court. In *In re Charlotte Observer*, the Fourth Circuit struck down two oral injunctions forbidding newspaper reporters from naming an attorney identified in open court as the subject of an ongoing grand jury investigation.[35] The attorney was mentioned because he had not been allowed to represent a defendant pleading guilty in a related case. After the attorney had been identified as a target of the investigation, the judge realized that two reporters from area newspapers were in the courtroom. The judge then directed the reporters not to publish information about the attorney, stating that "I do not want to jeopardize any person's right to a fair trial."[36]

The Fourth Circuit cited a number of cases, including *Nebraska Press*, for the proposition that prior restraints were generally impermissible. The appeals court seemed to regard *Nebraska Press* as determinative because that case also involved a judge's attempt to enjoin publication of statements made in open court. However, the Fourth Circuit did not engage in any attempt to balance the interests in *Charlotte Observer* independently under the *Nebraska Press* test. Apparently viewing itself as bound by the facts of *Nebraska Press*, the Fourth Circuit simply held the restraint unconstitutional with little discussion. The court also rejected arguments that a federal statute protecting grand jury secrecy somehow dictated a different result.[37]

Another example of a prior restraint case with little explicit analysis is a 1983 decision by the U.S. Court of Appeals for the Fifth Circuit. In *U.S. v. McKenzie*, the Fifth Circuit struck down a restraint on a "60 Minutes" segment that related to a criminal trial.[38] The Fifth Circuit stayed a lower court order enjoining the broadcast.

---

[33]443 U.S. 97 (1979).

[34]658 F.2d at 427.

[35]921 F.2d 47 (4th Cir. 1990).

[36]*Id.* at 49.

[37]Fed. R. Crim. P. 6 (e)(3)(C).

[38]697 F.2d 1225 (5th Cir. 1983).

In reaching its decision, the *McKenzie* court stated the *Nebraska Press* three-prong test, but predicated its holding on the one-sentence lower court order, devoid of "any findings whatsoever."[39] When the case was again appealed, after the lower court held proceedings and issued an order limited both geographically and temporally, the Fifth Circuit panel, with one dissent, again struck down the injunction. With almost no analysis, the Fifth Circuit simply declared that "the evidence is too speculative to support the relief granted."[40] The Fifth Circuit's opinion, consisting of a single paragraph, did little to explicitly test the injunction against the *Nebraska Press* criteria.

Although *Charlotte Observer* and *McKenzie* exemplify a judicial minimalism that strikes down prior restraints with little analysis, other cases involve extensive weighing of the facts under the *Nebraska Press* three-prong test. In *CBS v. U.S. Dist. Ct. for C.D. of California*, the U.S. Court of Appeals for the Ninth Circuit struck down a temporary restraining order enjoining CBS from broadcasting government surveillance tapes from the celebrated drug trial of John DeLorean.[41] Applying *Nebraska Press*, the Ninth Circuit found that, despite "enormously incessant and continually increasing publicity,"[42] there was an insufficient showing that an impartial jury could not be selected to try DeLorean. Citing highly publicized cases, such as the prosecutions that arose from the Watergate cover-up, the Ninth Circuit stated that extensive news coverage did not necessarily taint potential jurors. The appellate court presented no empirical or social scientific evidence for this conclusion, but cited "precedent and experience,"[43] including the Watergate prosecutions.

The Ninth Circuit addressed the first prong of the *Nebraska Press* test, which requires the judge to determine the nature and extent of the prejudicial publicity. The Ninth Circuit cited language from the majority opinion in *Nebraska Press*, stating that a prior restraint could be constitutionally valid only if it is "clear that further publicity, unchecked, would so distort the views of potential jurors that 12 could not be found who would . . . fulfill their sworn duty."[44] By invoking what is arguably some of the strongest language from Chief Justice Burger's majority opinion in *Nebraska Press*, the Ninth Circuit set forth a standard that may be impossibly high—practically, if not theoretically, upholding Justice Brennan's proposed categorical ban on prior restraints in fair trial settings. The test for a constitutional prior restraint, the Ninth Circuit said, must not be based on the effect of the coverage on individual viewers, but on "its capacity to inflame and prejudice the entire community."[45] The Ninth Circuit also pointed out that the DeLorean case

[39]*Id.* at 1227.

[40]U.S. v. McKenzie, 697 F.2d 1228, 1228 (5th Cir. 1983).

[41]729 F.2d 1174 (9th Cir. 1983).

[42]*Id.* at 1179.

[43]*Id.* at 1180.

[44]427 U.S. at 569.

[45]729 F.2d at 1180.

did not involve a "lurid" subject matter, nor would the venire be chosen from a small rural community—both factors that had, in prior Supreme Court cases, tended to support findings of unfair trials.

Next, the Ninth Circuit held that the second prong of *Nebraska Press* had not been met (i.e., the determination that other measures short of a prior restraint could not ensure a fair trial). The lower court, the Ninth Circuit concluded, had not adequately examined such alternatives as careful voir dire and special instructions to jurors. The lower court had rejected these alternative techniques in a conclusory manner, according the appellate court. In light of the Supreme Court's express support for such techniques, "there may be no reason for courts ever to conclude that traditional methods are inadequate and that the extraordinary remedy of prohibiting expression is required," the court wrote.[46] Because the prior restraint in *CBS* failed the first two prongs of *Nebraska Press*, the Ninth Circuit chose not to examine the third prong.

At the close of its opinion, the Ninth Circuit quoted Justice Brennan's test from his Pentagon Papers concurrence, requiring that the publication "must inevitably, directly and immediately cause the occurrence of an event kindred to imperiling the safety of a transport already at sea. . . ."[47] Noting the rigor of this test, which never attained a majority following on the Court, the Ninth Circuit questioned whether any publicity surrounding a trial would ever be sufficient to justify a prior restraint. By selecting the most severe language from both *Nebraska Press* and the Pentagon Papers case, the court rendered the outcome in *CBS* unavoidable.

In a concurring opinion, Judge Alfred Goodwin pointed out the view of some jurists and scholars that the Sixth Amendment, as a restraint on government, could never support a prior restraint on the press. The Sixth Amendment is a command directed at government, Judge Goodwin reasoned, and does not empower government to invade the liberties of its citizens, including those of free speech and press. Under this view, there is not, and could not be, any conflict between the First and Sixth Amendments. "The Sixth Amendment tells the government that it cannot deprive individuals of their liberty without a fair trial, and by judicial decision that guarantee has come to mean that the government may not perform governmental acts that deprive a person of a fair trial," Judge Goodwin wrote.[48] This position, also taken by constitutional scholar Laurence Tribe, holds that the government must act to provide a fair trial—the Sixth Amendment cannot be used as justification to limit private actors, including the press. If government cannot provide a fair trial, it must dismiss the charges against the accused. Judge Goodwin's reasoning received a second vote on the three-judge panel, when Judge Reinhart indicated his "complete agreement" with Judge Goodwin's opinion.[49]

---

[46]*Id.* at 1183.

[47]U.S. at 726-27 (Brennan, J., concurring).

[48]729 F.2d at 1184 (Goodwin, J., concurring) citing Linde, Fair Trials and Press Freedom—Two Rights Against the State, 13 Willamette Law Journal 211 (1977).

[49]*Id.* at 1184 (Reinhardt, J., concurring).

The Ninth Circuit affirmed the unconstitutionality of another prior restraint in *Hunt v. National Broadcasting Co., Inc.*[50] *Hunt* involved an NBC docudrama, "Billionaire Boys Club," which depicted Hunt planning and committing a murder, for which he was to be tried. The docudrama also portrayed Hunt committing another murder of which he had already been convicted. Hunt was seeking a new trial for this murder conviction at the time of the broadcast. Hunt sought to restrain the telecast as an infringement of his Sixth Amendment right to a fair trial.

The Ninth Circuit in *Hunt* agreed with the trial judge that Hunt had met none of the three prongs of the *Nebraska Press* test. Addressing the first prong, the court noted that the population of San Mateo County, where the trial would take place, was more than 530,000. Based on the determination that 21.3% of adults watched NBC's broadcast, the court declared that impartial jurors could be found: "Even taking into account any possible 'ripple effect' of the broadcast, there remains an extremely large pool of untainted jurors from which to draw twelve."[51]

As to the existence of alternatives to a prior restraint—*Nebraska Press'* second prong—with little discussion the court found that Hunt had not established that voir dire, jury instructions, and other alternative methods were inadequate to protect his right to a fair trial. Similarly, the Ninth Circuit summarily declared that Hunt had not met the third prong of *Nebraska Press*. That prong required a showing that the prior restraint would effectively protect his Sixth Amendment rights. "NBC's docudrama aside, substantial and unrestrained publicity concerning Hunt and the Billionaire Boys Club has already been exposed to the public," the court wrote.[52]

The *Hunt* court declined to adopt Judge Goodwin's position in his *CBS* concurrence that the Sixth Amendment was only a limit on government, and could not authorize restraint of a private actor. Acknowledging that Judge Reinhardt's agreement with Judge Goodwin "may constitute a majority vote on that issue"[53] in *CBS*, the court nevertheless chose not to address the issue because it had already determined that the district court's decision to deny the restraint was not an abuse of discretion. Although somewhat cryptic, the Ninth Circuit panel seemed to take the position that, because the district court reached the correct result under *Nebraska Press*, the more controversial rationale contained in Judge Goodwin's *CBS* concurrence need not be considered. Presumably, this follows the traditional judicial reluctance to decide any more than necessary to resolve the case at hand.

In 1978, the Ninth Circuit used a somewhat enigmatic approach to hold that an order to provide a court with a copy of a film for review was *itself* a prior restraint. In *Goldblum v. National Broadcasting Corp.*, Stanley Goldblum, imprisoned on fraud charges, sought to enjoin broadcast of an NBC docudrama entitled "Billion Dollar Bubble."[54] The film depicted securities and insurance fraud at a company of which Goldblum was a former officer. Goldblum claimed that the film depicted

---

[50]872 F.2d 289 (9th Cir. 1989).

[51]*Id.* at 295.

[52]*Id.* at 296.

[53]*Id.* at 296.

[54]584 F.2d 904 (9th Cir. 1978).

both the company and Goldblum inaccurately, and would "jeopardize his release on parole, his right to trial by an impartial jury in any future state or federal criminal action . . . and also his right to a fair trial in a pending civil matter. . . ."[55]

The Ninth Circuit struck down a lower court order to provide a copy of the film in an opinion written by Judge Anthony Kennedy, who was later elevated to the U.S. Supreme Court. The appellate court held that such a procedure, calling for prepublication review, was "an inherent threat to expression, one that chills speech." The Ninth Circuit did not set forth any standard under which the decision had been made, although the court cited *Nebraska Press* for the general proposition that prior restraints were presumptively unconstitutional. The *Goldblum* court noted that no court had ever suggested that a prior restraint might be upheld based on the possibility the material would prejudice parole officials or a jury in some as-yet nonexistent future criminal trial.

PRIOR RESTRAINT UPHELD

Cases in which prior restraints against the media in criminal proceedings have been allowed to stand are rare. Apparently, the only reported case since *Nebraska Press* in which federal courts have upheld a restraint on criminal justice-related material already in the hands of the press is *U.S. v. Noriega.*[56] In *Noriega*, the U.S. Court of Appeals for the Eleventh Circuit approved a temporary restraint on the Cable News Network, forbidding it to cablecast audiotapes of telephone conversations between deposed Panamanian strongman Manuel Noriega and his defense team. Noriega had been deposed and brought to the United States by force to stand trial for various drug-related charges. Officials at the prison where Noriega was held regularly tape recorded inmate telephone conversations, but were required to allow inmates to have unmonitored conversations with attorneys on request. CNN managed to obtain a number of tapes of Noriega's conversations with his attorneys.

After CNN verified the authenticity of the tapes with Noriega's attorney, Noriega filed a motion in federal court to enjoin the network from broadcasting the tapes. Noriega argued that the tapes were privileged by virtue of the attorney–client privilege, and that their dissemination would aid the prosecution by disclosing Noriega's trial strategy.

The district judge granted the injunction, noting that the attorney–client privilege does not ordinarily rise to constitutional dimensions. In *Noriega*, however, the privilege had a constitutional aspect because "it serves to protect a criminal defendant's Sixth Amendment right to effective assistance of counsel by ensuring unimpeded communication and disclosure by the defendant to his attorney."[57] Because one purpose of the privilege is to prevent disclosure that might damage a criminal defendant's case, the judge said the real issue before the court was not the privilege per se, but the right to a fair trial under the Sixth Amendment.

---

[55]*Id.* at 905.

[56]917 F.2d 1543 (11th Cir. 1990).

[57]U.S. v. Noriega, 752 F.Supp. 1032, 1033 (S.D. Fla. 1990).

The district judge concluded that, despite the "heavy burden" required to justify a prior restraint, cases involving a criminal defendant's fair trial rights were "[a]mong the very narrow range of cases which might justify a restraint."[58] The judge cited the three-prong test used by the U.S. Supreme Court in the *Nebraska Press* case as the applicable standard. Although the *Nebraska Press* test was fashioned to guide courts in cases involving prejudicial pretrial publicity, the judge concluded that the standard also applied to Noriega's attempt to keep his trial strategy private. The real danger posed by the tapes was that the tactics of Noriega's defense team would become known to the prosecution. The problem was that, before the judge could apply the *Nebraska Press* test, he would have to review the tapes. Because CNN had resisted providing the tapes to the court for review, the judge decided that a temporary injunction against airing the tapes would remain in effect until CNN made the tapes available. The district judge wrote that it seemed "fundamentally unfair" to allow CNN to avoid turning over the tapes and to use that refusal to justify a finding that no harm to Noriega's rights was imminent "when the only reason that no clear and immediate harm yet appears is because CNN has so far prevented this court from reviewing the contents of the tapes. . . ."[59]

The district court's Supplemental Order to its decision took on an almost apologetic tone as the judge emphasized that the restraint did not constitute a decision on the merits of CNN's right to broadcast. Noting the *Nebraska Press* holding that even a temporary restraint required a showing of immediate harm, the judge nonetheless concluded that "the unique nature of the problem" required that broadcast of the tapes be halted until the court could review them and decide whether a permanent injunction should be issued.[60]

On appeal, the U.S. Court of Appeals for the Eleventh Circuit denied CNN's request to overturn the temporary restraining order.[61] The Eleventh Circuit began its discussion by noting that trial judges have broad discretion to take steps to ensure that Sixth Amendment rights of criminal defendants are protected. That discretion, the court wrote, includes steps that might negatively affect First Amendment interests. The court left little doubt that First Amendment rights could be trumped by fair trial rights if the two directly conflicted. The court wrote: "When the exercise of free press rights actually tramples upon Sixth Amendment rights, the former must nevertheless yield to the latter."[62]

Nevertheless, the Eleventh Circuit said, some showing of immediate danger to a defendant's fair trial rights is necessary before First Amendment protections can be overcome. With only one indirect reference to *Nebraska Press*, the Eleventh Circuit's opinion embarked on a somewhat confusing discussion of cases involving access to court proceedings. The court did not cite the three-prong test from

---

[58]*Id.* at 1033.

[59]*Id.* at 1035.

[60]*Id.* at 1036.

[61]U.S. v. Noriega, 917 F.2d 1543 (11th Cir. 1990).

[62]*Id.* at 1548, quoting In re Application of Dow Jones and Co., 842 F.2d 603, 609 (2nd Cir.), *cert. denied*, 488 U.S. 946 (1988).

Nebraska Press, but apparently erroneously quoted the test from *Press-Enterprise v. Superior Court ("Press-Enterprise II")*[63] —a Supreme Court case dealing with public and press access to a preliminary hearing. The less rigorous test of *Press-Enterprise II* was not created for cases involving restraint of material already in the hands of the media. The *Press-Enterprise* test requires, first, a substantial probability that publicity will prejudice the Sixth Amendment rights of the accused. This "substantial probability" prong is weaker from a First Amendment perspective than the stronger readings of *Nebraska Press,* requiring a virtual certainty that 12 impartial jurors could not be located after the publicity. Second, *Press-Enterprise II* requires a substantial probability that closure of the hearing would prevent the prejudice. Again, the degree of permitted judicial speculation is higher than the *Nebraska Press* requirement that the restraining order "serve its intended purpose," without reference to degrees of probability, statistical or otherwise.[64] The *Press-Enterprise II* prong requiring examination of alternatives seems analogous to that of the *Nebraska Press* test.

Perhaps more important than the semantic differences between the standards of *Press-Enterprise II* and *Nebraska Press* is the fundamental difference between the strength of the First Amendment interest in preventing prior restraints and the more attenuated interest in allowing press access to proceedings. The weaker interest in access was suggested by the *Noriega* court when it chose, inexplicably, to apply the *Press-Enterprise II* test, rather than that of *Nebraska Press*. The Eleventh Circuit's *Noriega* decision also seemed to misstate the holding in the 1981 Fifth Circuit decision of *Belo Broadcasting Corp. v. Clark.*[65] *Belo* denied a broadcaster access to FBI audiotapes in the possession of a court, whereas the Eleventh Circuit seemed to cite *Belo* for the proposition that broadcasters could be forbidden to air tapes already in their possession in the interest of a fair trial. The Eleventh Circuit also ignored the district court's emphasis on the dangers of disclosing trial strategy to the prosecution, focusing rather on the perils of seating an unbiased jury after the tapes were broadcast.

With no explanation of how the balance was struck, the Eleventh Circuit concluded that the court had properly restrained CNN. The opinion seemed less concerned with the burden necessary to impose a prior restraint than with CNN's refusal to provide the tapes for review. "While appealing to our nation's judicial system for relief, CNN is at the same time defiant of that system's reasonable directions," the court wrote at the close of its opinion.

After its loss before the Eleventh Circuit, CNN filed an application to stay the restraining orders and a petition for a writ of certiorari with the U.S. Supreme Court. The Court, without opinion, denied both requests.[66] Two justices dissented from the denials.

---

[63]478 U.S. 1 (1986).

[64]427 U.S. at 569.

[65]654 F.2d 423 (5th Cir. 1981).

[66]Cable News Network v. Noriega, 111 S.Ct. 451 (1990).

Justice Marshall, in an opinion joined by Justice O'Connor, wrote that "this case is of extraordinary consequence for freedom of the press."[67] Marshall was concerned that the Court had left intact lower court decisions that allowed a prior restraint to stand with no showing that the restrained material would harm Noriega's right to a fair trial, or that no less restrictive means were available to prevent any harm. Citing *Nebraska Press*, Marshall reminded the majority of the strong presumption against prior restraints and the significant burden on a party seeking to justify such restraints. "I do not see how the prior restraint imposed in this case can be reconciled with these teachings," Marshall wrote.[68]

PRIOR RESTRAINTS ON PARTICIPANTS

Although restraints directed at the press in criminal cases have been routinely held to violate the First Amendment, gag orders directed at trial participants, when challenged by the media, have received varying treatment in the federal courts. Some courts have contended that the participant gag orders challenged by media entities are not prior restraints at all, thus allowing a low level of scrutiny approaching mere reasonableness. Other courts have treated media-challenged gag orders as the equivalent of prior restraints, and have applied corresponding higher levels of scrutiny, including the *Nebraska Press* version of the clear and present danger test.

In 1988, the U.S. Court of Appeals for the Second Circuit held that a gag order aimed at trial participants was not a prior restraint when challenged by the media. In *Application of Dow Jones & Co., Inc.*, the Second Circuit upheld a trial court order that prohibited "virtually all extrajudicial speech" not part of the public proceedings in the courtroom by prosecutors, defendants, and defense counsel.[69] The proceedings, which had generated intense publicity, concerned allegations of fraud, bribery, and racketeering against defendants associated with Wedtech, a New York military contractor. One defendant was a member of Congress.

The *Dow Jones* court first considered whether news media had the standing to challenge a gag order directed not at the media, but at trial participants. The doctrine of standing requires that the party must be subject to some injury or threat of injury that is " 'distinct and palpable' and 'concrete.' "[70] Some real harm must threaten the party whose standing is challenged. In *Dow Jones*, the Second Circuit held that the media had standing to challenge the order by virtue of a line of U.S. Supreme Court cases upholding First Amendment standing for "recipients" of speech. For example, the Court held in *Virginia State Bd. of Pharmacy v. Virginia Citizens Consumer Council, Inc.* that consumers could challenge a state restriction on prescription drug advertising.[71] The *Virginia State Board* case, the Second Circuit stated, exemplified the Supreme Court's commitment to the notion that the First

---

[67]*Id.*

[68]*Id.*

[69]842 F.2d 603 (2nd Cir.), *cert. denied*, 109 S.Ct. 377 (1988).

[70]*Id.* at 606 (citations omitted).

[71]425 U.S. 748 (1976).

Amendment protects not just speakers, but those who wish to receive information. "A challenge by news agencies must certainly be permitted when the restrained speech, as here, concerns allegations of corruption by public officials in obtaining federal contracts," the court wrote.[72]

Despite its favorable resolution of the standing question, the Second Circuit concluded that a media challenge to a restraint directed at some third party was not properly classified as a prior restraint. According to the court, a prior restraint halts the publication of specific information in the hands of the press so that it does not reach the public. In cases in which the gagged party is not challenging the restraint, the court reasoned, the free expression rights of the challenging media entity are not infringed in the same way as a direct restraint on the press. Moreover, the news agencies challenging the gag order in *Dow Jones* were not subject to sanctions for its violation, the court stated. "For this reason the order is considerably less intrusive of First Amendment rights than one directly aimed at the press," the Second Circuit reasoned.[73] Further, the gagged parties (i.e., the lawyers and defendants in the Wedtech case) were free to challenge the order and had not done so. As a result, the gag order could not be appropriately characterized as a prior restraint on the press.

Because the court said the prior restraint doctrine was not the appropriate legal category, the Second Circuit next discussed the constitutional standard necessary to balance First Amendment interests with Sixth Amendment fair trial concerns in the case of participant gag orders. The standard the court identified, taken from *Sheppard v. Maxwell,* was "whether there is a 'reasonable likelihood' that pretrial publicity will prejudice a fair trial."[74] As used in the *Sheppard* case, however, this standard had been intended for an evaluation of whether the judge should continue the case or change its venue. The Second Circuit concluded that the highly publicized Wedtech case, which had been plagued by leaks during the confidential grand jury proceedings prior to the trial, met the "reasonable likelihood" standard. The extensive and sensational publicity surrounding the case convinced the Second Circuit that the findings of the lower court were not "clearly erroneous"—a weak form of appellate review that asks only if no reasonable judge could have reached the conclusion in question.

The Second Circuit also found that the lower court had adequately considered other, less restrictive alternatives to the gag order. The entire range of *Sheppard* measures, including change of venue, jury sequestration, and searching voir dire, "must be explored and ultimately rejected as inadequate—individually and in combination."[75] In the case before it, the Second Circuit agreed with the lower court that such measures had been unable to stop grand jury leaks, and would also prove unavailing in the trial.

Although the U.S. Supreme Court refused to hear an appeal from the Second Circuit's decision in *Dow Jones,* three justices wrote a dissent to the denial of

---

[72]842 F.2d at 609.

[73]*Id.* at 608.

[74]*Id.* at 610, citing Sheppard v. Maxwell, 384 U.S. 333, 363 (1966).

[75]*Id.* at 611.

certiorari.[76] Justice White, joined by Justices Brennan and Marshall, argued that the Court should take the case to resolve the issue of whether media challenges to participant gag orders should be treated as prior restraints. The dissenters gave no clear indication of how they would decide the substantive issue, but indicated that it was of sufficient importance for the Court to consider, given conflicting lower court decisions.

In 1989, the Second Circuit struck down a participant gag order challenged by the press under the *Dow Jones* "reasonable likelihood" standard. In *In re New York Times Co.*,[77] a federal district judge had ordered attorneys in a criminal case not to speak to the media from the beginning of voir dire until the verdict was returned. The Second Circuit wrote that the threshold for imposing a participant gag order challenged by the media had not been met in *New York Times* because, unlike *Dow Jones*, there was no indication that counsel for either party would be willing to speak to the press. In *Dow Jones*, the court reasoned, the government had opposed the gag order, thereby suggesting prosecutors might wish to speak to the press. On the contrary, in *New York Times*, the district court made no finding even suggesting that a willing speaker existed. "Not only has there been no showing that prejudice may result from statements made to the press by counsel, but there has been no showing that statements are likely to be made at all," the Second Circuit wrote.[78] This lack of a putative willing speaker apparently caused the appellate court to find that the *Dow Jones* test had not been met, although *The New York Times* court did not explicitly perform any balancing under that test.

The U.S. Court of Appeals for the Ninth Circuit upheld a participant gag order challenged by the media in a 1986 case, *Radio & Television News Assn v. U.S. Dist. Court.*[79] In *RTNA*, the Ninth Circuit rejected a media challenge to a district court's gag order aimed at defense counsel. As the Second Circuit did in *Dow Jones*, the Ninth Circuit in *RTNA* determined that the press was sufficiently affected by the gag order to have standing to challenge its constitutionality.

The *RTNA* court, like the *Dow Jones* court, determined that the attorney gag order was not a prior restraint on the press. On the contrary, the court said, the press "remains free to direct questions at trial counsel. Trial counsel simply may not be free to answer."[80] The Ninth Circuit advanced three arguments for its position that the gag order was not a prior restraint as to the media. First, a participant gag order was, the Ninth Circuit reasoned, more like a restriction on press *access* than a direct restraint of speech. The court cited U.S. Supreme Court holdings in a series of cases that the press has only the same right to gather information as the public, and may be restricted from gaining access to certain sources, such a prisoners.[81] In the prison

---

[76]Dow Jones & Co. v. Simon, 109 S. Ct. 377 (1988).

[77]878 F.2d 67 (2nd Cir. 1989).

[78]*Id.* at 68.

[79]781 F.2d 1443 (9th Cir. 1986).

[80]*Id.* at 1446.

[81]The Ninth Circuit cited Pell v. Procunier, 417 U.S. 817 (1974) and Saxbe v. Washington Post Co., 417 U.S. 843 (1974).

cases, the Supreme Court declined to balance interests, and simply declared that the First Amendment required no affirmative duty on the part of government to make information available to the press that is not available to the general public. Second, the Ninth Circuit wrote that trial lawyers could, on their own initiative, refuse an interview in the absence of any gag order. In such a situation, no First Amendment violation could be established, the Ninth Circuit wrote. Third, the court reasoned that, although the government could not forbid the press to publish "leaks" by government officials, the press could not successfully challenge an order by a government agency directing its employees *not* to engage in "leaking" to the press. Like its first argument, this point emphasized that government has no duty to provide information to the press. These three arguments—fact situations the Ninth Circuit found analogous to participant gag orders in criminal cases—persuaded the court that "the media's collateral interest in interviewing trial participants is outside the scope of the protections offered by the first amendment."[82]

The Ninth Circuit explicitly rejected applying a strict scrutiny standard to the gag order, holding that the appropriate standard was "whether the restrictions imposed are reasonable and whether the interests [of the government] override the very limited incidental effects of the [order] on first amendment rights."[83] This test came from a dissenting opinion by Chief Justice Burger in a case involving access to criminal proceedings. In addition, the gag order was required to serve a legitimate purpose. Applying the reasonableness standard, the *RTNA* court found, with almost no discussion, that the lower court's determination that statements by trial counsel might affect a fair trial or threaten the integrity of the judicial process was not unreasonable. As a result, the order was held to be constitutional.

The U.S. Court of Appeals for the Sixth Circuit adopted a contrary position when it held, in 1975, that a gag order aimed at participants in a civil case was a prior restraint, although the order was challenged by the media. In *CBS, Inc. v. Young*,[84] the Sixth Circuit considered a gag order to be aimed at attorneys and court personnel, as well as "all parties concerned with this litigation, whether plaintiffs or defendants, their relatives, close friends, and associates. . . ."[85] The civil case in which the order was issued was a consolidated personal injury and wrongful death action arising from the Ohio National Guard firing on students at a demonstration at Kent State University in 1970.

The Sixth Circuit summarily concluded that the media had standing to challenge the order, citing *dicta* from *Branzburg v. Hayes* to the effect that freedom of the press would be "eviscerated" without some protection for news gathering.[86] The *Young* court then concluded that a prior restraint characterization was appropriate because, "[a]lthough the news media are not directly enjoined from discussing the

---

[82]781 F.2d at 1447.

[83]*Id.* at 1447, quoting Globe Newspaper Co. v. Superior Court, 457 U.S. 596, 616 (1982) (Burger, C.J., dissenting).

[84]522 F.2d 234 (6th Cir. 1975).

[85]*Id.* at 236.

[86]408 U.S. 665, 681 (1972).

case, it is apparent that significant and meaningful sources of information concerning the case are effectively removed from them and their representatives."[87] The court, citing the U.S. Supreme Court's line of editorial contempt cases (discussed in chapter 3), applied a version of the clear and present danger test, requiring that the gagged speech must create a clear and imminent threat to a fair trial to uphold the restraint. The *Young* court held that this threshold had not been met in the case before it, basing its decision, in part, on the "innocuous" nature of the newspaper articles submitted to support the gag order.[88]

The Sixth Circuit also rejected the application of the *Pell v. Procunier*[89] and *Saxbe v. Washington Post Co.*[90] line of cases. In those cases, the Supreme Court rejected First Amendment challenges to rules limiting media access to prisoners for interviews. The *Young* court emphasized that, in *Pell*, alternate means of communication were available, including letters, and other sources could provide information to the press about prison conditions.

Although *Young* was a civil action, a federal district court in another circuit followed similar reasoning in a criminal trial in 1987. In *Connecticut Magazine v. Moraghan*, a district court in the Second Circuit struck down a participant gag order issued in a Connecticut state court.[91] The case involved a defendant charged with dismembering his wife's body with a chain saw and putting parts of her body through a wood-chipping machine. Because of the sensational nature of the case, the state trial judge issued an order forbidding attorneys in the case from making any public statements until the trial ended. Connecticut Magazine challenged the order by a motion, which was subsequently returned to the magazine with a statement that the magazine lacked standing to challenge the gag order.

The federal district court, citing *Young*, easily disposed of the standing question. It found that the gag order's effect on the magazine's news-gathering ability was a sufficient harm to bestow standing.

On the merits of the gag order, the district court found that the order was "a prior restraint on the right to gather news and derivatively on publication."[92] As a result, the court applied the three-prong *Nebraska Press* test to determine the constitutionality of the gag order. On the first prong of *Nebraska Press*, the *Connecticut Magazine* court held that the state court had appropriately determined that the widespread publicity about the case was reasonably likely to impair the defendant's right to a fair trial. Here the *Connecticut Magazine* court seemed to adopt a "soft" reading of the *Nebraska Press* first prong, avoiding Chief Justice Burger's language that prior restraints were constitutional only if it was "clear that further publicity, unchecked, would so distort the views of potential jurors that 12 could not be found

---

[87]522 F.2d at 239.

[88]*Id.* at 240.

[89]417 U.S. 817 (1974).

[90]417 U.S. 843 (1974).

[91]676 F.Supp. 38 (D.Conn. 1987).

[92]*Id.* at 42.

who would . . . fulfill their sworn duty."[93] Instead, a mere likelihood that a fair trial might be impaired was deemed adequate under *Nebraska Press.*

The gag order foundered, however, on the second prong of *Nebraska Press*, which required that alternatives to a gag order must be examined to determine if such alternatives, alone or in combination, could adequately ensure a fair trial. Because the state judge had not made findings analyzing alternatives to the gag order, the *Connecticut Magazine* court concluded that the gag order could not stand. The federal court also found the gag order unconstitutionally overbroad because it forbade lawyers to make "any statements about the case to the media, rather than prohibiting only those statements that raise a 'reasonable likelihood of prejudicial impact.' "[94] Thus, the order was not narrowly tailored enough to pass muster.

The U.S. Court of Appeals for the Tenth Circuit has also applied prior restraint doctrine in a media challenge to a participant gag order, although in a civil context. In *Journal Pub. Co. v. Mecham*,[95] decided in 1986, the Tenth Circuit considered a case in which a federal district judge had directed a jury *not* to discuss its verdict after a civil trial. The judge's order, in part, admonished jurors that "[y]ou should not discuss your verdict after you leave here with anyone." Journal Publishing Company challenged the order as a violation of the First Amendment.

Discussing the First Amendment standard appropriate to decide the case, the Tenth Circuit cited both the "clear and imminent" danger standard from *CBS, Inc. v. Young*[96] and the compelling interest, or strict scrutiny, test. Although the court cited both constitutional tests, it did not distinguish between them, or explicitly suggest how they were to be applied. One commentator has suggested that clear and present danger is a specialized form of strict scrutiny,[97] but the Tenth Circuit never explained how it would apply the tests. Instead, the appeals court simply concluded that the order violated the "narrowly tailored" prong of strict scrutiny because it "contained no time or scope limitations and encompassed every possible juror interview situation."[98] The Tenth Circuit made it clear that it considered the order to be a prior restraint, but noted that some more limited order might pass constitutional scrutiny.

When gagged participants, rather than the media, have challenged gag orders, courts have generally applied some form of heightened scrutiny. Although restraints on participants—challenged by the participants, rather than the press—are beyond the scope of this chapter, it may be worth noting that courts have generally applied less scrutiny to such orders than to direct prior restraints on the press. For example, a 1991 Supreme Court case, *Gentile v. State Bar of Nevada*,[99] upheld a "substantial

---

[93] 427 U.S. at 596

[94] 676 F.Supp. at 43 (citations omitted).

[95] 801 F.2d 1233 (10th Cir. 1986).

[96] 522 F.2d 234, 240 (6th Cir. 1975).

[97] Anton, When Speech is not Speech: A Perspective on Categorization in First Amendment Adjudication, 19 Wake Forest L. Rev. 33, 47 (1983).

[98] 801 F.2d *at 1236.*

[99] 111 S.Ct. 2720 (1991).

likelihood" of prejudice standard in a case involving discipline of an attorney for out-of-court statements. *Gentile* involved statements made by a Nevada lawyer during a press conference on the day after his client was indicted. The Court stated that lawyers are not entitled to the same degree of protection as the media under such cases as *Nebraska Press*. The Court explained the distinction by noting that lawyers have traditionally been granted less First Amendment protection than the press, in part because of their status as officers of the court. In general, prior restraints against participants are less constitutionally suspect than restraints against the press,[100] and were, in fact, discussed with approval in both *Sheppard v. Maxwell*[101] and *Nebraska Press*.[102]

CONCLUSION

The federal courts have reached mixed results in cases involving media challenges to restraints on criminal justice information. It appears that all reported cases in the federal courts involving direct restraints on the press have struck down the restraints, with the exception of the *Noriega* case. However, even those cases striking down prior restraints may result in some doctrinal confusion, particularly depending on whether they actually engage in the balancing suggested in *Nebraska Press* or merely state a result with little analysis.

Cases involving gag orders directed at trial participants challenged by the media have yielded conflicting results. These cases reveal a tendency toward a reduced level of scrutiny for such gag orders. The courts that have chosen to regard participant gag orders as prior restraints naturally have been more likely to hold them unconstitutional. But even those courts have not settled on a consistent approach to balancing the interest in free expression against the governmental interests involved.

---

[100]*See e.g.*, In re Russell, 726 F.2d 1007 (4th Cir. 1984) (applying "reasonable likelihood" test to uphold gag order applied to witness). *But see* U.S. v. Ford, 830 F.2d 596 (6th Cir. 1987) (applying clear and present danger test to strike down gag order aimed at criminal defendant).

[101]384 U.S. 333, 360-63 (1966).

[102]427 U.S. 539, 564 (1976).

-5-

Postpublication Sanctions

The Supreme Court has consistently struck down attempts to enforce postpublication sanctions for truthful reports of information concerning the criminal justice system. The Court has rejected both criminal and civil liability for truthful reporting. In four cases decided between 1975–1989, the Court made it plain that it would strictly scrutinize such sanctions, although the Court did not categorically rule out sanctions.

POSTPUBLICATION SANCTIONS
IN THE SUPREME COURT

In a 1975 decision, *Cox Broadcasting Corp. v. Cohn*,[1] the Court reversed a civil damage award against a broadcaster who revealed the name of a deceased rape victim. In *Cox*, a television news reporter learned the name of the rape victim from police records made available to him, with no legal impropriety, in the trial of six youths charged with the murder and rape. After the reporter broadcast the victim's name, the victim's father filed a civil action for invasion of privacy. The privacy claim was based on a Georgia statute making it a misdemeanor for the media to "print and publish, broadcast, televise, or disseminate . . . the name of any female who may have been raped. . . ."[2]

A Georgia state court upheld the father's privacy action against the broadcaster's First Amendment challenge; the Georgia Supreme Court agreed. The state high court ruled that the criminal statute underlying the privacy claim was a valid limitation on free expression, and that no public interest was served by revealing the victim's identity.

---

[1] 420 U.S. 469 (1975).

[2] *Id.* at 471 n.1.

The U.S. Supreme Court, with one justice dissenting, reversed the Georgia court, noting the important role the press plays in reporting on government operations. "The commission of crime, prosecutions resulting from it, and judicial proceedings arising from prosecutions . . . are without question events of legitimate concern to the public," Justice White wrote for the Court.[3] Justice White explicitly recognized the importance of privacy concerns, but pointed out that revealing information contained in public documents was not grounds for an invasion of privacy action even under many common law formulations of the tort. The majority concluded that, "the First and Fourteenth Amendments command nothing less than that the States may not impose sanctions on the publication of truthful information contained in official court records open to the public."[4]

The Court's resolution of *Cox* did not involve a heightened scrutiny or balancing approach, but a "bright line" rule against postpublication sanctions for publication of truthful information obtained from public documents. Justice White's opinion expressed concern that any other rule would lead to "timidity and self-censorship" by the media.[5] The Court expressly invited states to protect privacy interests they deemed important by reconsidering which official court records should be released to the public.

In 1978, the Court unanimously struck down a state court decision against the media, this time one involving a criminal conviction for publication of truthful information. In *Landmark Communications, Inc. v. Virginia,*[6] the Court considered a case in which a Virginia newspaper, the *Virginian Pilot*, reported the status of a complaint against a state judge pending before the Virginia Judicial Inquiry and Review Commission. In the process, the newspaper identified the judge—a misdemeanor under a Virginia statute. The newspaper's parent company, Landmark Communications, was found guilty of violating the statute, and was fined $500. Unlike the rape victim's identity in *Cox,* the judge's identity was not part of an official record available to the public. On the contrary, all documents before the review commission were expressly declared to be confidential.

The Supreme Court of Virginia upheld Landmark's conviction, utilizing the clear and present danger test. The state high court found that revelation of the judge's identity constituted a clear and present danger to the work of the commission and the administration of justice. The functions served by confidentiality, the court asserted, were the protection of judges' reputations from frivolous complaints, upholding confidence in the judicial system by preventing publication of unfounded complaints, and "protection of complainants and witnesses from possible recrimination by prohibiting disclosure until the validity of the complaint has been ascertained."[7]

---

[3]*Id.* at 492.

[4]*Id.* at 495.

[5]*Id.* at 496.

[6]435 U.S. 829 (1978).

[7]*Id.* at 833.

The U.S. Supreme Court, in an opinion written by Chief Justice Burger, held that the statute that forbade revealing the judge's identity violated the First Amendment. The Court declined to announce a categorical rule that truthful reporting about public officials was always protected expression, but instead chose to weigh the interests protected by confidentiality against the free expression rights of the newspaper. The majority distinguished *Landmark* from *Cox* by noting that the former involved information mandated confidential by law, whereas the latter dealt with information gleaned from public records.

In balancing confidentiality against free expression, the Court assumed, for purposes of argument, that confidentiality served legitimate state interests. The Court's choice of a test to balance those interests against the First Amendment interests of the newspaper was curious, however. The Court "question[ed] the relevance" of the clear and present danger test adopted by the Virginia high court, but nevertheless proceeded to apply that test. The Court cited a series of earlier cases striking down punishment by contempt for out-of-court statements under the clear and present danger test, and concluded that the threat to the administration of justice in those cases constituted a more serious danger than the article in question in *Landmark*.[8] Thus, the article before the Court could not attain the status of a clear and present danger, and the conviction must fall, the Court concluded. With little explication of the balance involved, the Court held the statute unconstitutional as applied to *Landmark*. As in *Cox*, the Court invited more stringent security measures to prevent information from falling into the hands of the press, but held that, once the press obtained and printed truthful information, sanctions violated the First Amendment. Justice Stewart, concurring in the judgment, concluded that the state's interest in protecting its judiciary was of sufficient magnitude to constitutionally punish those who revealed confidential proceedings. However, Justice Stewart said punishment could not, consistent with the First Amendment, extend to newspapers.

The Court's next major examination of postpublication sanctions came in 1979 in *Smith v. Daily Mail Publishing Co.*[9] In *Smith*, the Court unanimously declared unconstitutional the criminal prosecution of a newspaper for revealing confidential information. In this case, the confidential information was the name of a juvenile who allegedly shot a 15-year-old classmate. A West Virginia statute prohibited publication of the name of any child involved in a juvenile court proceeding.[10] In *Smith*, the newspaper obtained the juvenile's name by asking witnesses and law enforcement officials at the scene of the crime.

Chief Justice Burger, writing for the Court, stated that whether the statute was characterized as a prior restraint or a sanction after publication was irrelevant; even a postpublication sanction required demonstration of "a need to further a state interest of the highest order."[11] The Court cited *Landmark* extensively, but moved

---

[8] The Court cited Bridges v. California, 314 U.S. 252 (1941); Pennekamp v. Florida, 328 U.S. 331 (1946); Craig v. Harney, 331 U.S. 367 (1947); and Wood v. Georgia, 370 U.S. 375 (1962).

[9] 443 U.S. 97 (1979).

[10] *Id.* at 98.

[11] *Id.* at 103.

away from *Landmark's* use of the clear and present danger test toward the classic strict scrutiny formulation—with the phrase "state interest of the highest order" apparently being used synonymously with "compelling state interest." The Court cited cases such as *Near v. Minnesota*[12] and *Nebraska Press Assn v. Stewart,*[13] as examples of First Amendment cases in which "the most exacting scrutiny" had been applied.[14] From this brief reference, it might be inferred that Chief Justice Burger regarded the clear and present danger test and strict scrutiny as functionally equivalent. That is, Burger cited *Nebraska Press*, which had explicitly applied clear and present danger language, as an example of exacting scrutiny. As in *Landmark*, the Court avoided an explicit account of the balancing process, but simply asserted that the state's interest in protecting juvenile offenders and encouraging their rehabilitation was constitutionally insufficient to uphold the statute. The state interest was fine as a matter of policy, the Court suggested, but was not of sufficient importance to override the constitutional rights embodied in the First Amendment when it came to punishing the media. "The magnitude of the State's interest in this statute is not sufficient to justify application of a criminal penalty to respondents," Chief Justice Burger wrote.[15]

The Court also pointed out that only newspapers were subject to the statute, excluding electronic media or other forms of printed communication. The underinclusiveness of the statute was an additional constitutional infirmity, the Court wrote, because the statute did not, as a result, "accomplish its stated purpose."[16] Other communication media could, with impunity, publish the names of juvenile offenders, and thus frustrate the state's interest in protection and rehabilitation of juveniles.

Justice Rehnquist, concurring in the judgment, agreed that the West Virginia statute was unconstitutional because of its underinclusiveness, but contended that a properly drafted statute punishing publication of juveniles' names could serve an interest of the highest order, and thus pass constitutional scrutiny. The notion of underinclusiveness would become important in the Court's next major postpublication sanctions case.

In 1989, the Court held unconstitutional damages awarded to a rape victim in an invasion of privacy suit against a newspaper that had published her name. In *The Florida Star v. B.J.F.*, a weekly newspaper had identified B.J.F. as the victim of a robbery and sexual assault.[17] The newspaper, which had an internal policy against identifying rape victims, published the report after a trainee reporter obtained the information from a sheriff's department report available in the department's press room. The victim's name was not a matter of public record under Florida law, and was erroneously made available in *B.J.F.* B.J.F. based her privacy action on a Florida statute making it a misdemeanor to print or broadcast a sexual offense victim's

---

[12]283 U.S. 697 (1931).

[13]427 U.S. 539 (1976).

[14]443 U.S. at 102.

[15]*Id.* at 104.

[16]*Id.* at 105.

[17]109 S.Ct. 2603 (1989).

identity, or identifying information, "in any instrument of mass communication."[18] A Florida jury awarded B.J.F. $75,000 in compensatory damages and $25,000 in punitive damages. A state appellate court upheld the award, and the Florida Supreme Court declined to review the case.[19]

The U.S. Supreme Court, in a 6–3 decision, reversed the state courts, applying the balancing formula from *Daily Mail*. That formula requires that liability serve a need to further a state interest of the highest order. The Court rejected *Cox* as determinative because, although both *Cox* and *B.J.F.* involved rape victim identification statutes, the information in *Cox* came from a court record and implicated the media's role as the watchdog of government activity in general, and of judicial proceedings in particular. In contrast, the information in *B.J.F.* came from a confidential police record and involved no judicial proceedings. This distinction, the Court stated, required an independent weighing of the conflicting interests of privacy and free expression in *B.J.F.*[20]

The Court identified the state's interest in forbidding identification of rape victims as consisting of three related interests: protecting victims' privacy, safeguarding victims from retaliation, and encouraging victims to come forward. The Court found these interests to be "highly significant."[21] Nevertheless, the Court rejected the plaintiff's invasion of privacy suit for three reasons. First, the sheriff's department had disseminated the victim's name, thus placing the information in the public domain. Second, the plaintiff recovered on a negligence *per se* basis (i.e., tort liability was established without proof of the elements of invasion of privacy). In other words, liability inevitably followed the determination that the newspaper violated the state criminal statute. The Court stated that negligence *per se* was too sweeping an approach to the delicate First Amendment issue at hand. Courts must, the majority asserted, make case-by-case determinations of liability when speech and press interests are at stake. Finally, the statute was underinclusive, in that it penalized only media of mass communication and not "the backyard gossip who tells 50 people that don't have to know."[22] The selective prohibition of only mass communicators rendered Florida's attempt to punish truthful information constitutionally inadequate, the Court wrote.

The majority opinion concluded with a caveat about the scope of *B.J.F.* The Court emphasized the limited nature of its holding by noting that it was not creating categorical First Amendment protection for truthful publication, nor holding that identification of rape victims could never be punished under state law. The Court said its holding was merely that, "where a newspaper publishes truthful information which it has lawfully obtained, punishment may lawfully be imposed, if at all, only when narrowly tailored to a state interest of the highest order. . . ."[23]

---

[18]*Id.* at 2605 n.1.

[19]*Id.* at 2607.

[20]*Id.* at 2608

[21]*Id.* at 2611.

[22]*Id.* at 2612-13.

[23]*Id.* at 2613.

The Court's opinion in *B.J.F.* nowhere holds that the privacy interests of rape victims are not "of the highest order." Rather, the Court found the state's method of protecting those interests inadequate. Presumably, a state scheme that dealt with the three concerns by limiting government dissemination of information, increasing the standard of fault, and eliminating underinclusiveness might pass constitutional muster. The *B.J.F.* opinion called victims' privacy interests "highly significant" without explicitly labeling them "of the highest order," but the implication seems to be that it was not the state's interest in protecting victims that was constitutionally infirm. *B.J.F.* suggests that an invasion of privacy suit, or a state criminal statute, that rectified the three difficulties in question could well survive strict scrutiny review.

Justice White, joined by Chief Justice Rehnquist and Justice O'Connor, dissented from the Court's *B.J.F.* decision. Justice White asserted that, unlike *Cox*, the police report naming B.J.F. should not, under Florida law, have been available to the press. Moreover, it was held in a room with a sign stating that "the names of rape victims were not matters of public record and were not to be published."[24] Also, B.J.F., unlike the juvenile offender in *Daily Mail*, was the victim of a crime, not its perpetrator. For these reasons, Justice White contended that the strict scrutiny test applied in *B.J.F.* placed too much emphasis on the public's right to know and too little on crime victims' rights of privacy.

LOWER COURT DECISIONS

Cox and its progeny appear to have largely settled, for the moment, the constitutional validity of postpublication sanctions, including civil liability for invasion of privacy. Although the precise constitutional standards are somewhat unclear in that quartet of cases, the results are unequivocal. The lower federal courts have considered few postpublication cases, but those few have resulted in victories for the media with some form of balancing applied.

For example, in a 1984 case, the U.S. Court of Appeals for the Seventh Circuit struck down an Indiana statute punishing anyone who identified an individual named in a sealed criminal information before the person was arrested. In *Worrell Newspapers of Indiana, Inc. v. Westhafer*,[25] a reporter had been threatened with contempt under the statute if she revealed the name of an as-yet unapprehended arson suspect. The name was contained in a sealed information.

The reporter did not publish the name of the suspect, but later brought a declaratory judgment action seeking to have the statute declared unconstitutional under the First Amendment. An Indiana federal district court applied strict scrutiny, and "held that the State's interest in apprehending criminals was sufficiently compelling to overcome the constitutional infirmity. . . ."[26] The district court also found the statute to be narrowly tailored to serve the state's interest.

---

[24]*Id.* at 2616 (White, J., dissenting).

[25]739 F.2d 1219 (7th Cir. 1984).

[26]*Id.* at 1221.

On appeal, the Seventh Circuit declared the statute unconstitutional, citing *Landmark, Cox,* and *Daily Mail,* among other cases. The Seventh Circuit expressed no quarrel with the state's goal of sealing records to aid in the apprehension of criminals. Nor did the appeals court deny that Indiana could punish those who held positions in the criminal justice system for revealing that information. However, applying strict scrutiny, the court found the interest in arresting criminals not "sufficiently compelling to justify the prohibition of publication by *any* person, including members of the press, of the contents of a sealed document. . . ."[27] The court cited a series of both postpublication and prior restraint cases in which a variety of governmental interests were held to be insufficiently compelling to override First Amendment protection,[28] but did not explicitly document how it arrived at its measurement of the magnitude of the state's interest in *Westhafer.*

The Seventh Circuit also found the Indiana statute to be overly broad by virtue of imposing sanctions on those not employed within the criminal justice system. As the Supreme Court did in the *Cox* line of cases, the Seventh Circuit seemed to invite the state to strengthen its internal procedures to prevent dissemination of the information sought to be kept secret. Once that information was in the hands of the press, however, postpublication sanctions could not survive constitutional scrutiny.

Finally, the Seventh Circuit rejected the statute under a separate balancing test—the clear and present danger standard. The state had argued that the flight of an individual mentioned in a sealed information was a clear and present danger to its ability to apprehend suspects. Citing *Landmark,* the appellate court rejected this argument with little discussion, characterizing the state's concerns as "remote and speculative."[29] The court noted that the statute applied to *all* cases of a sealed information, regardless of whether there was a danger of flight by the accused. Thus, the statute could not pass muster under the clear and present danger test.

A post-*B.J.F.* district court decision also demonstrates the deference that federal courts have granted the media in cases involving postpublication sanctions. In *Scheetz v. Morning Call, Inc.,*[30] a police officer and his wife sued a newspaper for publishing stories about an alleged assault by the officer on his wife. The newspaper obtained the information from confidential police records. The stories detailed the alleged assault and its aftermath, including that the police department did not follow up on the case. Moreover, the article quoted the local police chief as stating that some domestic violence claims are exaggerated or faked. The plaintiffs filed counts for civil rights violations and invasion of privacy, among other causes of action.

The district court, citing the *Cox* line of cases, concluded that there was no absolute privilege for the press to publish truthful information, at least when that information was obtained unlawfully. In *Scheetz,* the plaintiffs claimed the newspaper had conspired with an unknown officer to obtain the confidential reports. The

---

[27]*Id.* at 1223.

[28]*Id.* at 1223 n.4.

[29]*Id.* at 1225.

[30]747 F.Supp. 1515 (E.D. Pa. 1990).

court read both *Landmark* and *B.J.F.* as reserving the question of postpublication liability when information was gained unlawfully. However, the court in *Scheetz* found that, regardless of how the information was obtained, the First Amendment rights of the newspaper outweighed the privacy interests of the plaintiffs in the case at hand. The court noted that the focus of the articles was not the alleged assault, but the actions of the police department and the attitudes of police officials toward domestic violence. Applying strict scrutiny, the court held that the privacy interests of the plaintiffs were not of sufficient magnitude to pass the compelling interest test.

The *Scheetz* court's discussion of its balancing methodology is both extensive and confusing. The court noted that First Amendment rights are normally accorded strict scrutiny, whereas privacy rights have been evaluated under either a rational basis or "an intermediate scrutiny/sliding scale test."[31] As a result of the disparate levels of scrutiny, the court concluded it must weigh the constitutional claim more heavily than the privacy claim. This unusual approach of comparing levels of scrutiny, rather than directly balancing interests, appears to be a significant departure from standard judicial practice. It appears that the *Scheetz* court moved away from balancing specific interests against each other to a higher level of abstraction—balancing the balancing tests themselves.

The court also seemed to find the nature of the story—illuminating matters of public import, rather than merely reporting the facts of an isolated criminal complaint—an important component in its balancing process. Yet nowhere in the *Cox* line of cases is this distinction deemed important. Reporting truthful information received constitutional protection in those cases, even if the press reported only the identity of the victim of an isolated criminal act. Using those facts to "illuminate" a broader public concern, such as police indifference toward domestic violence, was not explicitly required to invoke strict scrutiny. On the contrary, the *Scheetz* court regarded the broader social import of the story in that case to bring it nearer the "core of the First Amendment. Only the most compelling countervailing interests could possibly yield liability."[32]

The *Scheetz* decision, although explicating the balancing process more thoroughly than the U.S. Supreme Court has generally done, seemed to add two unique features. First, the comparison of levels of scrutiny between the competing interests—free expression and privacy—yielded at least a tentative hypothesis that free expression should prevail. Second, the court reserved the most exacting scrutiny only for cases in which the news story is not simply the report of a factual event, but uses the event to illustrate a broader theme of government misconduct or neglect. Referring in *dicta* to stories whose significance is more fact-bound, the court stated as follows: "This sort of story lies far from the core of the First Amendment, and the privacy claims may well prevail."[33] The requirement that the story's "theme" be broader than the facts it reports to gain full First Amendment

---

[31]*Id.* at 1534.

[32]*Id.* at 1533.

[33]*Id.* at 1533.

protection seems to diminish the protection provided by the *Cox–B.J.F.* line of cases, and might encourage the sort of editorial timidity and second-guessing those cases sought to prevent.

CONCLUSION

Cox and its progeny appear to have so settled the issue of postpublication sanctions in favor of uninhibited publication that few cases appear in the reports of the federal courts. Yet the mechanisms by which those cases were decided leave unanswered questions that seem to leave this area of the law less settled than a superficial examination might suggest. Some statements by the Court, particularly those in *B.J.F.* regarding government dissemination, the standard of fault, and underinclusiveness, may herald new avenues of attack for prosecutors and private plaintiffs. Moreover, as in much of the Court's use of heightened scrutiny, the actual process of balancing interests is so vague that little guidance is provided to lower courts seeking to apply the approach to novel fact situations. For example, the *Scheetz* case, although merely one district court opinion, seems to exemplify the doctrinal confusion that can result from a scrutiny structure that is vague and ill-defined at best.

-6-

Access to Proceedings

The First Amendment right of access to trial proceedings is of far more recent vintage than constitutional limitations on prior restraints and subsequent punishments. Although courts have long recognized some form of common law right to attend criminal trials, the U.S. Supreme Court did not declare a constitutional right to be present at trials until 1980. The Court subsequently extended that right to other proceedings, including voir dire and pretrial hearings. The right to attend is not absolute, however. The press and public may still be excluded, provided the trial court applies a heightened scrutiny analysis to protect the First Amendment interests at stake.

Lower courts have extended the First Amendment right of access to encompass other proceedings, including pretrial suppression hearings, bail hearings, and other proceedings. These lower court decisions have used varying levels of scrutiny to test the constitutionality of closures. There seems to be little consistency among courts either in the choice of test or the apparent commitment to the value of openness in court proceedings.

THE SUPREME COURT AND ACCESS

The U.S. Supreme Court began its creation of a First Amendment right of access to criminal proceedings in 1980.[1] In *Richmond Newspapers, Inc. v. Virginia,*[2] the Court held that the right to attend criminal trials was implicit in the First Amendment guarantees. The case arose when a criminal defendant faced a fourth trial on charges of murder. The first trial had resulted in a conviction that was reversed on

---

[1]In Gannett Co. v. DePasquale, 443 U.S. 368 (1979), the Court concluded that the Sixth Amendment right to a public trial only applied to criminal defendants, and not to the public or press.

[2]448 U.S. 555 (1980).

appeal, whereas the next two trials had ended in mistrials. At the beginning of the fourth trial, the defendant's counsel asked the judge to close the trial to the public. The request was not opposed by the prosecutor. The trial judge agreed, without a hearing, to close the trial. Later, after a media challenge, the trial judge upheld the closure order. In arguing for the closure, the defendant's counsel cited the possibility of "leaks" to the media, which might publish inaccurate information, and "the fact that 'this is a small community.' "[3] The defendant was subsequently found not guilty.

Chief Justice Burger, writing for a plurality of the Court, held that the First Amendment required that the trial be open to the public. Chief Justice Burger first noted the historical openness of trials in Anglo-American law. From before the Norman Conquest to colonial America, Chief Justice Burger wrote, openness was "one of the essential qualities of a court of justice."[4]

Aside from the traditional openness of criminal trials, the plurality noted that access to trials encouraged the perception that trials were fair and discouraged perjury and biased decision making. Moreover, open trials have a cathartic effect on the community, the plurality asserted. Outrage and the urge to vigilante action may follow crimes, but "the open processes of justice serve an important prophylactic purpose, providing an outlet for community concern, hostility, and emotion."[5]

In declaring a First Amendment right of access to criminal trials, the plurality acknowledged that the Court had never before directly stated a right of access under the First Amendment. However, the *Richmond Newspapers* plurality found that the First Amendment right to receive information, based in the speech and press clauses, and the First Amendment right of assembly combined to ensure access to places that had historically been open to the public, and where access served an important functional role in ensuring fairness.

Finally, the plurality rejected the argument that no right of access to trials existed because no constitutional provision explicitly guaranteed it. The plurality cited other unenumerated rights, such as privacy, as examples of important rights not found in the Constitution or its amendments. Chief Justice Burger stated that "the right to attend criminal trials is implicit in the guarantees of the First Amendment; without the freedom to attend such trials, which people have exercised for centuries, important aspects of freedom of speech and 'of the press could be eviscerated.' "[6] The plurality distinguished cases denying a First Amendment right of access, such as *Saxbe v. Washington Post Co.*[7] and *Pell v. Procunier.*[8] Both *Saxbe* and *Pell* involved access to penal institutions, Chief Justice Burger stated, which "do not share the long tradition of openness" associated with criminal trials.[9]

---

[3]*Id.* at 561.

[4]*Id.* at 567, quoting Daubney v. Cooper, 10 B. & C 237, 240, 109 Eng. Rep. 438, 440 (K.B. 1829).

[5]*Id.* at 571.

[6]*Id.* at 580, quoting Branzburg v. Hayes, 408 U.S. 665, 681 (1972).

[7]417 U.S. 843 (1974).

[8]417 U.S. 817 (1974).

[9]448 U.S. at 576 n. 11.

After determining that a First Amendment right of access to trials existed, the plurality articulated a heightened scrutiny analysis for the closure order in *Richmond Newspapers*. Chief Justice Burger found that the trial judge had made no specific findings to justify the closure order, and had not adequately considered alternatives such as sequestration of witnesses or jurors. In language that suggested some form of heightened scrutiny, the plurality stated that "[a]bsent an overriding interest articulated in findings, the trial of a criminal case must be open to the public."[10] The opinion did not clarify what magnitude of state interest would qualify as "overriding," nor how the overriding standard compares to a compelling interest.

In a concurrence, Justice Brennan evoked strict scrutiny when he wrote that the Court need not, in the case at hand, decide what interests would be sufficiently compelling to justify closure of a trial. Justice Brennan also noted additional functional justifications for open trials not mentioned in Chief Justice Burger's opinion, including the notion that open trials could assist in locating key witnesses unknown to the parties by bringing the proceedings to the attention of those witnesses.

In 1981, the Court struck down a Massachusetts statute mandating closure in cases involving sexual assault against minors. In *Globe Newspaper Co. v. Superior Court*,[11] a Massachusetts state court had applied the statute by closing the rape trial of a defendant charged with the rape of three minor females. The *Boston Globe* appealed the closure order to the Supreme Judicial Court of Massachusetts, which chose to defer consideration of the constitutional claim until the U.S. Supreme Court's decision in *Richmond Newspapers*—then pending—was handed down. After *Richmond Newspapers* was decided, the Supreme Judicial Court held that the traditional openness of criminal trials did not apply to sexual assault cases. The state high court also held that the statute mandating closure "furthered 'genuine state interests,'"[12] which did not require evaluation on a case-by-case basis.

After an appeal to the U.S. Supreme Court, Justice Brennan, writing for the majority, held the mandatory closure rule unconstitutional. The majority stated the traditional strict scrutiny formulation as its standard of review: "It must be shown that the denial is necessitated by a compelling government interest, and is narrowly tailored to serve that interest."[13] Massachusetts' interests in the closure were twofold, according to Justice Brennan. First, the state sought to protect sexually assaulted minors from the trauma and humiliation that might result from public and press attendance at a trial, and thus protect their psychological well-being. Second, the state wanted to encourage victims of sexual assault to come forward. Presumably, a closed proceeding provided such encouragement. As to the first state interest, the Court found it to be "compelling," but not sufficiently narrowly tailored. Psychological harm and trauma to the victim from public proceedings could be

---

[10]*Id.* at 581.

[11]457 U.S. 596 (1981).

[12]*Id.* at 602.

[13]*Id.* at 607 (citations omitted).

addressed on a case-by-case basis, rather than by a categorical rule. A trial court could determine in each case the gravity of potential harm based on "the minor victim's age, psychological maturity and understanding, the nature of the crime, the desires of the victim, and the interests of parents and relatives."[14]

The state's second interest—encouraging sexual assault victims to come forward—was simply too speculative, the Court asserted. The majority apparently determined, without saying so explicitly, that this interest was not "compelling." The Court stated that no empirical data supported the notion that closing proceedings increased minor victims' willingness to report sexual assaults. Further, "logic and common sense"[15] suggested that closure would not be a great inducement, particularly because the press in Massachusetts could easily and legally learn the victim's identity and obtain a transcript of the testimony given during the closed proceeding. Moreover, the majority stated, the notion of encouraging victims to come forward "proves too much" because it could easily apply to victims of a great variety of crimes.[16] This argument, which might apply to any criminal case, "runs contrary to the very foundation of the right of access recognized in *Richmond Newspapers*: namely, 'that a presumption of openness inheres in the very nature of a criminal trial under our system of justice.' "[17]

Chief Justice Burger, in a dissenting opinion joined by Justice Rehnquist, argued that the *Globe Newspaper* majority had misapplied the test of *Richmond Newspapers*. That case, according to Chief Justice Burger, required a historical tradition of openness. Such a tradition was lacking in sexual assault cases, particularly when minor victims were involved, the dissent asserted. The dissent decried the strict scrutiny approach of the majority, characterizing it as a "wooden application of [a] rigid standard."[18] Because Massachusetts made a transcript of the closed proceeding available, the dissent found *Globe Newspaper* distinguishable from cases seeking to prevent dissemination of information about government. The proper First Amendment test, Chief Justice Burger argued, would be "whether the restrictions imposed are reasonable and whether the interests of the Commonwealth override the very limited incidental effects of the law on First Amendment rights."[19] This low level of First Amendment scrutiny, akin to mere rationality review, was sufficient to protect First Amendment rights, the dissent contended. Chief Justice Burger also attacked the majority's claim that neither empirical data nor common sense supported a compelling state interest in encouraging minor victims to report sexual assault. The prospect of public testimony might well discourage children and their

---

[14] *Id.* at 608.

[15] *Id.* at 610.

[16] *Id.* at 610.

[17] *Id.* at 610, quoting *Richmond Newspapers*, 448 U.S. at 573.

[18] *Id.* at 615 (Burger, C. J., dissenting).

[19] *Id.* at 616, citing, *inter alia*, Pell v. Procunier, 417 U.S. 817 (1974) and Saxbe v. Washington Post Co., 417 U.S. 817 (1974).

parents from reporting rape, the dissent claimed. In a footnote, the dissent cited several studies demonstrating the difficulty rape victims experienced in giving public testimony.[20]

In 1984, the Court extended the First Amendment right of access, holding the right of access to include not just criminal trials, but voir dire—the examination of potential jurors before a trial begins. In *Press-Enterprise Co. v. Superior Court of California*[21] (*"Press Enterprise I"*), a California trial court had closed the voir dire proceedings in a rape and murder trial. Of 6 weeks of voir dire, only 3 days were open to the public. Press-Enterprise Co. sought transcripts of the voir dire proceedings after the jury was chosen and after the trial concluded. Both requests were denied. The trial judge stated in his denial of the posttrial motion that "some of the jurors had some special experiences in sensitive areas that do not appear to be appropriate for public discussion."[22]

As in *Richmond Newspapers*, Chief Justice Burger wrote the opinion for the Court's majority in *Press-Enterprise I*. Chief Justice Burger's opinion from the outset seemed to assume that the Court was deciding not merely the right of the press to obtain the transcripts, but the right of the press to be present at the voir dire proceedings. The opinion traced the ancient roots of open voir dire proceedings in much the same way that *Richmond Newspapers* explored the historical tradition of open trials. After concluding that voir dire was traditionally an open proceeding, the Court articulated the standard of review. The *Press-Enterprise I* Court stated that a presumption of openness "may be overcome only by an overriding interest based on findings that closure is essential to preserve higher values and is narrowly tailored to serve that interest."[23] Although the adjectives *overriding* and *higher* were left undefined by the Court, the statement of the standard came immediately following a quote from *Globe Newspaper,* stating that case's classic strict scrutiny formulation requiring a compelling interest. The proximity of these two standards in the *Press-Enterprise I* opinion, with no suggestion by the majority that they were in any way conflicting, suggests that the *Press-Enterprise I* standard is more or less equivalent to strict scrutiny. The Court also required that trial courts make specific findings as to the interest served by closure.

The Court further stated that if closure were ordered to ensure juror privacy, "the constitutional values sought to be protected by holding open proceedings may be satisfied later by making a transcript of the closed proceeding available within a reasonable time," so long as the released transcript adequately protected the jurors' privacy.[24] The Court was unclear whether providing a transcript—presumably redacted in some manner to protect juror privacy—made the strict scrutiny inquiry unnecessary, or whether the transcript in lieu of attendance in open court was only an option after strict scrutiny had been satisfied.

---

[20]*Id.* at 618 n. 7.

[21]464 U.S. 501 (1984).

[22]*Id.* at 504.

[23]*Id.* at 510.

[24]*Id.* at 512.

The *Press-Enterprise I* Court, examining the record before it, found that the trial court had not made the requisite findings to warrant closure, nor had the trial court explored alternatives to closure, the Court wrote. The Court stated that a compelling interest in juror privacy might be established "when interrogation touches on deeply personal matters that person has legitimate reasons for keeping out of the public domain."[25] The majority noted that a juror who had been a rape victim, for example, might establish a compelling privacy interest. In concurrence, Justice Marshall urged that a trial court be required to use the least restrictive means available to advance a compelling interest in closing voir dire proceedings. For example, Justice Marshall suggested transcripts of juror responses be released while concealing juror identity in cases in which privacy interests were "compelling." "Only in the most extraordinary circumstances can the substance of a juror's response to questioning at *voir dire* be permanently excluded from the salutary scrutiny of the public and the press," Justice Marshall wrote.[26]

In 1986, the Court further expanded the right of access to criminal proceedings to encompass preliminary hearings. In *Press Enterprise Co. v. Superior Court*[27] ("*Press-Enterprise II*"), a nurse was accused of murdering 12 patients by injecting them with large doses of a heart drug. On a motion by the defendant, a California trial court excluded the press and public from the preliminary hearing in the case, which had attracted national news coverage. The closure was premised on protecting the defendant's Sixth Amendment right to a fair trial. After the pretrial ended, and the defendant was bound over for trial, the court refused to release transcripts of the proceeding, again based on the possibility of prejudicing the defendant's fair trial rights.

The California Supreme Court upheld the lower court on two grounds. First, the state high court said, earlier U.S. Supreme Court cases, such as *Press-Enterprise I* and *Globe Newspaper Co.,* applied only to bona fide trials. Second, the state supreme court reasoned that the closings in *Press-Enterprise I* and *Globe* had been based on privacy rights of victims and potential jurors—presumably a weaker governmental interest than the Sixth Amendment interest present in *Press-Enterprise II*.

The U.S. Supreme Court, in a majority opinion written by Chief Justice Burger, reversed the California Supreme Court. The majority rejected the California court's characterization of the preliminary hearing as an event completely separate and distinct from the trial. "[T]he First Amendment question cannot be resolved solely on the label we give the event, i.e., 'trial' or otherwise, particularly where the preliminary hearing functions much like a full-scale trial,"[28] the Court wrote.

The Court considered two factors in determining if the First Amendment required access to the preliminary hearing. First, the Court asked whether the proceeding was one that had historically been open to the public. The *Press-Enter-*

---

[25]*Id.* at 511.

[26]*Id.* at 520-21 (Marshall, J., concurring in the judgment).

[27]478 U.S. 1 (1986).

[28]*Id.* at 7.

prise II Court found that preliminary hearings had indeed traditionally been open. Second, the Court considered "whether public access plays a significant positive role in the functioning of the particular process in question."[29] On the latter point, the Court determined that California preliminary hearings essentially functioned like a minitrial, in which criminal defendants could, among other things, cross-examine witnesses, present evidence, and be represented by counsel. Thus, the preliminary hearings were sufficiently like trials to be brought under the general principle that public scrutiny promoted all the positive values of openness established by *Richmond Newspapers*. These included protecting against biased proceedings, providing a public perception of fairness, and creating a cathartic community release in the face of violent crime. Moreover, the Court noted that "the preliminary hearing in many cases provides 'the sole occasion for public observation of the criminal justice system.' "[30]

Once the preliminary hearing in *Press-Enterprise II* was found to have passed these two tests, the Court said a qualified First Amendment right of access attached, which required a heightened scrutiny inquiry to justify closure. The standard the Court set forth was the "higher values" formulation from *Press-Enterprise I*, supplemented with the following description of the required lower court findings: "first, there is a substantial probability that the defendant's right to a fair trial will be prejudiced by publicity that closure would prevent and, second, reasonable alternatives to closure cannot adequately protect the defendant's fair trial rights."[31] Because the California Supreme Court had adopted a lower standard of review—the "reasonable likelihood" of prejudice test—the *Press-Enterprise II* Court reversed the lower court. A mere risk of prejudice was not sufficient to support closing a hearing to which the First Amendment right of access attached, the Court wrote. Moreover, the California Supreme Court had failed to consider whether alternatives, such as careful voir dire, might mitigate the impact of any prejudicial publicity.

As in *Press-Enterprise I*, Chief Justice Burger's majority opinion in *Press-Enterprise II* purported to decide a case based on denial of a transcript to a hearing. However, the language of the opinion leaves no doubt that the question decided is one of access to the proceeding, not merely to a written transcript after the proceeding has taken place. Both *Press-Enterprise I* and *Press-Enterprise II* raised questions about the extent to which the opinions constitute *dicta*, but lower federal courts have consistently treated the opinions as authoritative not just as to transcripts, but on the question of access to proceedings as well.

Richmond Newspapers and its progeny leave little doubt that the First Amendment protects access to some criminal proceedings. As to trials, the issue appears to be settled at the federal court level. No reported cases have upheld the complete closure of a trial since *Richmond Newspapers*. As a result, the following section

---

[29]*Id.* at 8.

[30]*Id.* at 12 (citation omitted).

[31]478 U.S. at 14.

does not consider that question. The extent of the First Amendment right of access to other proceedings the Supreme Court has actually addressed is considerably less clear. Moreover, the extent to which *Richmond Newspapers* and its progeny translate to broader access rights to criminal proceedings to which the Court has not spoken is a source of continuing disagreement among lower federal courts.

LOWER COURT ACCESS DECISIONS

Voir Dire Hearings

Despite the *Press-Enterprise I* Court's holding that there is a First Amendment right to attend voir dire, or jury selection, the lower federal courts have permitted closed voir dire proceedings. The small number of federal cases[32] considering closure are about evenly divided between those requiring open proceedings and those upholding closure. In one of the latter cases, the U.S. Court of Appeals for the Fourth Circuit approved a closed voir dire proceeding in 1991 in *In re South Carolina Press Association*.[33] In that case, the Fourth Circuit considered a federal district court's closure of voir dire in a case involving extortion by South Carolina state legislators. The legislators were charged with accepting money in exchange for certain votes in the South Carolina General Assembly. The case also involved claims by the defendants that the prosecutions were racially motivated. The Fourth Circuit stated that the process of picking a jury involved sensitive issues, including potential jurors' racial views and attitudes toward public officials. The investigation spawned a number of separate criminal prosecutions. In the prosecution considered by the Fourth Circuit, the trial judge decided that "frank and full responses from potential jurors, which are essential to voir dire, would be chilled if they felt that their remarks would be published in the press. . . ."[34]

The Fourth Circuit held that the lower court had correctly closed the voir dire proceeding. The appellate court noted the strict scrutiny language from *Press-Enterprise I*, but stated its own three-part test for closing proceedings. That test, which the court had used previously in other cases, required findings that "(1) there is a substantial probability of that the defendant's right to a fair trial will be prejudiced by publicity; (2) there is a substantial probability that closure would prevent that prejudice; and (3) reasonable alternatives to closure cannot adequately protect the defendant's fair trial rights."[35] This test is quite similar to the standard stated by the Supreme Court in *Press-Enterprise II*, although the Supreme Court's standard in

---

[32]In addition to the cases discussed in the text, see U.S. v. Edwards, 823 F.2d 111 (5th Cir. 1987) (no First Amendment right of access to supplemental voir dire hearing); U.S. v. Peters, 754 F.2d 753 (7th Cir. 1984) (overturning closure of voir dire hearing); U.S. v. Brooklier, 685 F.2d 1162 (9th Cir. 1982) (overturning closed voir dire on procedural grounds); In re Greensboro News Co., 727 F.2d 1320 (4th Cir. 1984) (upholding closure of voir dire hearing).

[33]946 F.2d 1037 (4th Cir. 1991).

[34]*Id.* at 1039.

[35]*Id.* at 1041.

the latter case lacked the "substantial probability" language with regard to the efficacy of closure in preventing prejudice.[36] The *Press-Enterprise II* standard thus appeared to require something closer to certainty that closure would be effective in preventing prejudice to the defendant.

In determining the danger of prejudice, the Fourth Circuit noted that the case involved highly charged issues, including bribery, drug abuse, sting operations, and allegations of racial persecution. These emotional issues had persuaded the trial court to authorize a pre-voir dire questionnaire to potential jurors inquiring about their attitudes and prejudices. This questionnaire had ensured respondents that their answers would be viewed only by the parties and court personnel. The questionnaire, with its promise of confidentiality, was used extensively in the voir dire examination of potential jurors. The Fourth Circuit considered the existence of the questionnaire an important factor in the determination of the likelihood of prejudice.

The *South Carolina Press Association* court accepted, and quoted liberally from, the trial court's evaluation of the three prongs of the test. First, a substantial likelihood of prejudice existed because the court said jurors would not respond honestly to questioning if they believed the press would report their answers. The trial court noted that, in an earlier prosecution of a legislator arising from the sting operation, "[e]ven without the press at the hearing, the potential jurors were sometimes reluctant to speak frankly before the court and it was only after the repeated assertions of the court that the proceedings were private that these jurors began to respond."[37] The trial court found, and the Fourth Circuit agreed, that a substantial probability of prejudice to the defendant existed if the voir dire proceeding were conducted in public because the jurors would not truthfully disclose their views in public. This finding of likely prejudice was based *solely* on chilling juror responses because the jury was sequestered, and thus presumably isolated from any coverage of the voir dire proceeding. In other words, the hearing was closed not to prevent publicity, but to create a nonthreatening environment in which jurors could freely express their views and, presumably, personal prejudices.

As to the second prong of the Fourth Circuit's test—a substantial probability that closure would prevent the prejudice—the Fourth Circuit agreed with the trial court's conclusory statement that the closed hearing would elicit frank responses, and thus would prove effective. The third prong—reasonable alternatives are inadequate to protect the defendant's Sixth Amendment rights—similarly was met with little difficulty by the trial court, whose analysis the Fourth Circuit accepted almost without question. Counsel for the press suggested alternatives such as side bar conferences on particularly sensitive matters or juror identification by number only. The court rejected these alternatives as less than satisfactory. In the case of the side bar alternative, "the juror would have to request the side bar after the question has already been posed, which arguably chills the witness' response."[38]

[36]478 U.S. at 14
[37]946 F.2d at 1042.
[38]*Id.* at 1042.

The court also rejected juror anonymity by numbering the jurors. "[E]ven if the juror is assigned a number, they are still aware of the presence of the press in the courtroom."[39] Thus, the court found no alternative adequate to ensure truthful juror responses, which were required to safeguard the fair trial rights of the defendant. The *South Carolina Press Association* court further found the right to a fair trial a sufficiently "high value" under the *Press-Enterprise II* formulation, requiring "an overriding interest based on findings that closure is essential to preserve higher values and is narrowly tailored to serve that interest."[40] In concluding its opinion, the Fourth Circuit stated that "under the very unusual circumstances of these cases, no reasonable alternatives to closure" would protect the defendant's Sixth Amendment rights.[41]

In a decision contrary to *South Carolina Press Association,* the U.S. Court of Appeals for the D.C. Circuit in 1987 summarily reversed a closed voir dire in *Cable News Network, Inc. v. U.S.*[42] *Cable News Network* included, like *South Carolina Press Association,* a pre-voir dire questionnaire, the results of which suggested to the trial judge that jury privacy would be implicated in voir dire proceedings. The questionnaire did not expressly promise confidentiality. The Court's concern in *Cable News Network* focused on juror privacy *qua* privacy; the D.C. Circuit did not expressly consider the Sixth Amendment rights of the defendant as affected by chilled juror speech during questioning. That is, only the privacy rights of the jurors, not how that privacy would affect their impartiality (and thus the defendant), were at issue.

The D.C. Circuit read *Press-Enterprise I* differently than had the *South Carolina Press Association* court. Citing language from *Press-Enterprise I,* the court said that the trial court was required to make "individualized findings that specific jurors had compelling reasons for wishing to keep private responses to particular questions which, in each case, outweighed the value to the public of an open *voir dire.*"[43] The trial court had not done so in *Cable News Network.* Rather, the court had allowed all jurors who wished to do so to be questioned *in camera.* The jurors were not required to demonstrate any specific privacy claim. The trial court stated that no objective standard was available to evaluate such a privacy interest. This entire approach was inconsistent with *Press-Enterprise I,* the D.C. Circuit found.

In addition, the D.C. Circuit held that the trial court had erred by failing to require jurors to make an *affirmative* request for *in camera* voir dire. Quoting language from *Press Enterprise I,* the D.C. Circuit ruled that jurors could not "elect closed voir dire simply by remaining mute."[44] The appellate court said this procedure encouraged limits on access to voir dire, even when individual juror privacy interests might be insignificant.

---

[39]*Id.* at 1042.

[40]478 U.S. at 9-10.

[41]946 F.2d at 1044.

[42]824 F.2d 1046 (D.C. Cir. 1987).

[43]*Id.* at 1049.

[44]*Id.* at 1049.

In a 1989 case, the U.S. Court of Appeals for the Sixth Circuit overturned a voir dire closing using audio technology because the trial court had not met the "overriding interest" standard of *Press-Enterprise I*. In *In re Memphis Pub. Co.*,[45] a former head basketball coach at Memphis State University had been charged with income tax evasion and other criminal offenses. As a result of tremendous pretrial publicity, the trial judge "decided to use a device which emitted white noise during voir dire proceedings . . . ."[46] The white noise device prevented spectators in the courtroom, including the press, from hearing the questioning of potential jurors. When the use of the device was challenged by the press, the trial court said the defendant's Sixth Amendment right to a fair trial was in danger if the questioning was made public. The judge ordered that a transcript of the voir dire proceedings be made available after the jury was selected.

The Sixth Circuit reversed the closing via technology, holding that the strict scrutiny test of *Press-Enterprise I* had not been met. The *In re Memphis Pub. Co.* court said that a "naked assertion by the district court . . . that the defendant's Sixth Amendment right to a fair trial 'might well be undermined,' without any specific finding of fact to support that conclusion,"[47] did not meet the standard required by both *Press-Enterprise I* and *Press-Enterprise II*.

Both *Cable News Network* and *In re Memphis Pub. Co.* used an oft-repeated strategy in cases reversing closed proceedings. The appellate court states the standard—generally a form of heightened scrutiny—and then reverses the lower court primarily because of a lack of specificity in its findings. The actual *content* of the scrutiny test is not discussed; there is no explication of what might qualify as a "compelling" or "overriding" interest. Rather, the appellate court simply declares that the case before it is inadequate to meet the standard. That inadequacy stems not from substantive insufficiency, but a procedural flaw in the form of insufficiently specific findings of prejudice or of some other, higher interest. The net effect of this style of opinion is to easily dispose of the pending case. However, the guidance such opinions offer for future cases is limited, and the heightened scrutiny formulation is left as a shadowy outline with little substantive force.

Pretrial Suppression Hearings

The few federal courts considering the question of First Amendment access to pretrial suppression hearings, with no direct guidance from the U.S. Supreme Court, have adopted varying standards of review in determining when Sixth Amendment fair trial interests override the First Amendment interest in access to proceedings. The Supreme Court did consider public access to a pretrial suppression hearing in *Gannett v. DePasquale*,[48] but the *Gannett* Court focused on the Sixth Amendment

---

[45]887 F.2d 646 (6th Cir. 1989).

[46]*Id.* at 647.

[47]*Id.* at 648.

[48]443 U.S. 368 (1979). Because *Gannett* is a Sixth Amendment case, it receives only brief mention in this study, which concentrates on cases interpreting the First Amendment.

guarantee of a public trial in upholding the order excluding the press and public. The Court's holding was based on the notion that the Sixth Amendment public trial clause gave the press and public no affirmative access right, but belonged solely to the defendant. The *Gannett* Court discussed, without deciding, a possible First Amendment right of access to proceedings, but that right was not fully articulated until the *Richmond Newspapers* decision.[49] Since *Gannett*, only a handful of federal courts have addressed the issue, and not all of those cases were decided on the merits. [50]

Pretrial suppression hearings are proceedings in which courts consider whether to allow into evidence in a criminal trial items of evidence that may have been obtained by government misconduct. For example, if government agents such as police obtained the item of evidence through an illegal search, in violation of the Fourth Amendment, the so-called "exclusionary rule" may require that the evidence be "suppressed." Unlike the hearing in *Press-Enterprise II*—a preliminary hearing that functioned much like a mini-trial—a pretrial suppression hearing only seeks to determine whether certain evidence should be presented to the jury. The concern in many closures of pretrial suppression hearings is that evidence that may be suppressed will be reported on by the media, thus coming to the attention of potential jurors despite subsequent exclusion of the evidence. Under these circumstances, courts may fear that defendants in highly publicized cases will not receive fair trials because evidence excluded from the trial will nonetheless be widely discussed in the press. As a result, jurors may decide the case based on outside information not presented during the trial.

Some courts considering access to pretrial suppression hearings have suggested only modest scrutiny of closure orders. For example, in *U.S. v. Criden*,[51] the U.S. Court of Appeals for the Third Circuit held in 1982 that a district court need only determine that closure was necessary to protect the defendants' fair trial rights. In *Criden*, Philadelphia Newspapers challenged denial of access to a transcript of a closed pretrial suppression hearing, which the appellate court treated as identical to a challenge to the closure. The case involved prosecutions of defendants in the "Abscam case," a highly publicized government sting operation.

The *Criden* court, writing before either of the *Press-Enterprise* cases, first concluded that a First Amendment right of access attached to pretrial proceedings. The court noted that the Supreme Court in *Richmond Newspapers* had attached

---

[49]Justice Blackmun, in a concurrence and dissent to *Gannett*, created a test for Sixth Amendment access rights by the public that would later come to be applied in First Amendment access cases. Justice Blackmun argued that the Sixth Amendment should require open proceedings for the public and press unless the criminal defendant could demonstrate that closure was "strictly and inescapably necessary" to protect a fair trial. *Id.* at 440. This standard required an accused to show a substantial probability of irreparable damage to his or her Sixth Amendment rights, a substantial probability that alternatives such as those described in *Sheppard* would not protect those rights, and a substantial probability that closure would effectively protect against the harm.

[50]In addition to the cases discussed in the text, see Johnson Newspaper Corp. v. Morton, 862 F.2d 25 (2d Cir. 1988) (closure of suppression hearing held to be moot after transcript made available).

[51]675 F.2d 550 (3rd Cir. 1982).

importance to the historical tradition of openness. Although "there was no counter-part at common law to the modern suppression hearing,"[52] the *Criden* court found that pretrial proceedings had become increasingly important in modern criminal procedure. Often, the court said, these hearings may be the *only* proceeding because criminal cases may result in a plea bargain prior to a full-scale trial. Without a First Amendment right of access to such proceedings, "beneficial public scrutiny may never take place if not at the hearing itself," the court said.[53]

After concluding that a First Amendment right of access applied to pretrial suppression hearings, the *Criden* court suggested a relatively low level of scrutiny to determine the constitutionality of the closure. After the trial court has examined and rejected alternatives, specifically and on the record, as inadequate, the trial court need only determine "that closure is necessary to protect effectively against the perceived harm."[54] This "necessary" test appears significantly less stringent than a strict scrutiny "compelling interest" approach. The *Criden* court did not apply the test, however, because of the paucity of findings from the court below. Instead, it vacated the lower court's order.

Another 1982 opinion, this one by the U.S. Court of Appeals for the Ninth Circuit, seemed to set forth a higher standard of review for denial of access to a pretrial suppression hearing. In *U.S. v. Brooklier*,[55] the Times Mirror Company challenged closure of a suppression hearing in a RICO prosecution against alleged Mafia members. The Ninth Circuit agreed with the Third Circuit's *Criden* decision that a First Amendment right of access applied to pretrial suppression hearings, but stated no specific test. The *Brooklier* court, in a separate section of its opinion, adopted Justice Blackmun's formulation that a closure must be "strictly and inescapably necessary in order to protect the fair-trial guarantee."[56] Although the "strictly and inescapably necessary" standard appeared in a section of the court's opinion dealing with closure of a bail hearing, other courts have interpreted the Ninth Circuit's *Brooklier* opinion as applying that standard to closure of pretrial suppression hearings as well.[57]

One year later, in 1983, the U.S. Court of Appeals for the Second Circuit adopted a more lenient constitutional standard of review for closures of pretrial suppression hearings. In *Application of the Herald Co.*,[58] the Second Circuit considered the closure of a suppression hearing in a prosecution against Michael Klepfer. Klepfer was charged with making false statements to government agents concerning a criminal investigation of Raymond J. Donovan, President Reagan's nominee for

---

[52]*Id.* at 555.

[53]*Id.* at 557.

[54]*Id.* at 561-62.

[55]685 F.2d 1162 (9th Cir. 1982).

[56]*Id.* at 1167, quoting Gannett Co. v. DePasquale, 443 U.S. 368, 440 (1979) (Blackmun, J., concurring in part and dissenting in part).

[57]*See* Application of the Herald Co., 734 F.2d 93, 99 (2nd Cir. 1984).

[58]734 F.2d 93 (2nd Cir. 1984).

secretary of labor. Klepfer sought a pretrial hearing to suppress statements he had made to investigators because, he argued, they were obtained in violation of his constitutional rights. Despite argument by counsel for the Herald Company, the trial judge closed the hearing and later denied access to a transcript of the hearing.

The Second Circuit noted that the U.S. Supreme Court cases seemed to establish that First Amendment protection existed for access to pretrial suppression hearings. The appellate court acknowledged that pretrial suppression hearings were not historically open, as were trials. Nevertheless, a "functional argument" operating in such cases as *Richmond Newspapers* suggested that a First Amendment right of access arose in cases in which "public interest serves important public purposes," such as scrutiny of the criminal justice system.[59] The court found that a majority of Supreme Court justices had accepted the "functional argument," rather than a view of First Amendment access based solely on the historical openness of proceedings. Thus, functional considerations alone could, independently, justify a finding of First Amendment access to a proceeding.

However, the Second Circuit noted that the Supreme Court was unclear on the standard of review courts should apply in determining the scope of that protection. After an extensive discussion of tests, ranging from mere reasonableness to strict scrutiny, the Second Circuit stated it would adopt a standard requiring a "significant risk of prejudice to the defendant's right to a fair trial or of danger to persons, property, or the integrity of significant activities entitled to confidentiality, such as ongoing undercover investigations or detection devices."[60] The *Herald* court said it was "reluctant" to adopt any more rigorous form of scrutiny that would suggest First Amendment access rights were constitutionally equal to rights of free expression.[61] This reluctance appeared to stem from the Second Circuit's general First Amendment philosophy—consistent with that of the U.S. Supreme Court—that news gathering should not be elevated to a status equal to freedom to disseminate information. In addition to its "significant risk of prejudice" standard, the court said the trial court must consider alternatives, although the trial court need not find that closure is necessarily the least restrictive alternative. The trial court must merely "reach a reasoned conclusion that closure is a preferable course to follow to safeguard the interests at issue."[62] The Second Circuit also authorized trial judges to set forth findings on confidential matters in sealed records.

The Second Circuit, applying its newly created standard to the *Herald* case, struck down the closed proceeding. The court said the trial court had not sufficiently detailed adequate grounds for closure, although the appellate court admitted grounds might be available. The *Herald* court said the trial judge had set forth, "in a conclusory fashion," grounds for closure: "'the potential harm to this defendant' and 'tainting of any future proceedings by pre-trial disclosures.' "[63] The Second

---

[59]*Id.* at 97.

[60]*Id.* at 100 (citations omitted).

[61]*Id.* at 100.

[62]*Id.* at 100.

[63]*Id.* at 101.

Circuit remanded the case for further consideration by the trial court. Although the standard created in *Herald* is stricter than mere "reasonableness," it is difficult to predict its true rigor because the standard was not applied by the Second Circuit.

Bail Hearings

The U.S. Supreme Court has not ruled on whether bail hearings should be open to the press and public. However, at least three lower federal court decisions have upheld closure of bail hearings under varying levels of scrutiny.

The first federal case to recognize a First Amendment right of access to bail hearings was *United States v. Chagra*,[64] decided in 1983. In *Chagra*, an El Paso attorney and others were charged with conspiracy to assassinate a federal judge who was killed in San Antonio. Joseph Chagra was charged both in the conspiracy case and a separate tax evasion case. The charges were highly publicized. When Chagra moved for a reduction in his bail—set at $1,500,000—he also asked that the hearing be closed, over the objection of several newspapers. Chagra specifically sought closure of portions of the hearing dealing with a statement he made to F.B.I. agents. Chagra claimed the statement, if made public, would jeopardize his right to a fair trial. A federal magistrate closed the hearing, and this decision was upheld by the district court.

On appeal, the Fifth Circuit recognized a qualified First Amendment right of access to bail hearings, but upheld the closure on a "likelihood of prejudice" standard. The *Chagra* court, writing prior to the *Press-Enterprise* decisions of the Supreme Court, held that a defendant seeking closure must demonstrate three things. First, the defendant's "right to a fair trial will likely be prejudiced by conducting the hearing publicly."[65] Second, alternative measures are inadequate. Finally, closure would effectively protect the defendant's Sixth Amendment rights. The Fifth Circuit contrasted this lesser standard with Justice Blackmun's "strictly and inescapably necessary" test from his partial dissent in *Gannett Co. v. De-Pasquale*.[66] The Fifth Circuit found that the less rigorous standard was adequate, and that the district judge had applied the lesser test "in substance."[67]

The *Chagra* court found that the district court had failed to consider one alternative remedy—that of a change of venue to another state. The district judge had explicitly considered only a change of venue within Texas, where publicity about the case was great. However, the Fifth Circuit called this error harmless.

In 1984, the U.S. Court of Appeals for the First Circuit upheld a bail hearing closure, but declined to settle on a constitutional standard of review. As in *Chagra*, the court in *In re Globe Newspaper Co.* recognized a First Amendment right to attend bail hearings.[68] The *Globe* case involved a racketeering prosecution that

---

[64]701 F.2d 354 (5th Cir. 1983).

[65]*Id.* at 365.

[66]443 U.S. 368, 440 (1979) (Blackmun, J., dissenting).

[67]701 F.2d at 365.

[68]729 F.2d 47 (1st Cir. 1984).

included allegations of conspiracy to murder a grand jury witness. Some of the evidence against the defendants consisted of conversations intercepted by electronic surveillance. The prosecution used some of these recorded conversations in the bail hearing.

A federal magistrate closed the bail hearing based on both the prejudicial effect of the recorded conversations on the defendants' Sixth Amendment fair trial rights and the defendants' privacy rights under a federal statute known as Title III.[69] Electronic surveillance authorized under Title III places severe restrictions on the uses to which surveillance materials may be put, and provides criminal and civil penalties for the disclosure of unlawful wiretaps, which also cannot be presented in any court. The First Circuit stated no specific reason to suspect that the Title III material in *Globe* was illegally obtained; the court merely pointed out that the complexity of the statute could easily lead to unintentional violations of the statute in gathering surveillance.

The First Circuit held that the balance between the fair trial and privacy concerns of the defendants and the First Amendment right of access must be decided in favor of the closure. In *Globe*, the First Circuit declined to specify a standard of review, but stated that the closure order in this case satisfied either Justice Blackmun's more exacting "strictly and inescapably necessary" standard or the lesser "likelihood of prejudice" standard adopted by the *Chagra* court. The court noted that if the Title III material were eventually found to be lawful and admissible, public access would then follow either at the trial or through availability of transcripts of the bail hearing. In that case, the court said, delayed access was not as great a harm as denied access. However, if the Title III surveillance material were found to be illegally obtained and inadmissible at trial, "the widespread publicity attending a premature release of that material will injure beyond repair the privacy right protected by Title III."[70] That disclosure would also endanger the Sixth Amendment fair trial rights of the defendants, the *Globe* court wrote. With no citation to authority or evidence, the court stated that if damaging statements by the defendants were "blazoned in the media before trial,"[71] exposed jurors would have a difficult time ignoring them despite instructions. The First Circuit did not discuss alternatives, such as a careful voir dire.

The *Globe* court found that the closure satisfied Justice Blackmun's "strictly and inescapably necessary" test.[72] First, the surveillance material represented a "substantial probability" of "irreparable damage" to the defendants' fair trial rights.[73] Second, the Title III material established a substantial probability that alternatives would not protect the defendants, although the First Circuit did not explicitly discuss alternatives. The court reasoned that the Title III material altered the balance

---

[69]18 U.S.C. 2510 et seq.

[70]729 F.2d at 57-58 (citations omitted).

[71]*Id.* at 58.

[72]443 U.S. at 440 (Blackmun, J., dissenting).

[73]*Id.* at 441-42.

because "disclosure itself is the injury to be avoided."[74] Finally, there was a substantial probability that closure would effectively protect the defendant's rights, according to the *Globe* court.

The court noted that sensitive Title III material could be referred to without disclosing its contents. Indeed, the court pointed out that this had been done by referring to numbered paragraphs in the process of appealing the *Globe* case. However, the First Circuit found this approach of using numbered paragraphs during the bail hearing inadequate as an alternative to closing the bail hearing. The First Circuit wrote that, "we find ample support for the magistrate's determination that the parties should be able freely to discuss that material in their initial presentations to the court."[75] The court also reasoned that First Amendment access rights should be given less weight in the initial stages of criminal proceedings, such as bail hearings.

In a 1990 bail hearing case, a federal district court applied a test much like the Blackmun formulation and approved closure. In *U.S. v. Gotti*,[76] a judge for the Eastern District of New York held closure constitutional in a case against reputed Mafia boss John Gotti and other defendants. Gotti and his co-defendants were charged with a variety of racketeering and conspiracy offenses.

The district court applied the *Press-Enterprise II* test, similar to Justice Blackmun's test used by the First Circuit in the *Globe* bail hearing case. That test required, first, that there be a substantial probability of injury to the defendants' fair trial rights, and, second, that reasonable alternatives would not protect those rights. The *Gotti* court found this standard met by government evidence in the form of Title III surveillance materials. The government proposed to introduce these materials at the bail hearing. The *Gotti* court said it could not discuss the specifics of its finding of "a substantial probability" under *Press-Enterprise II* without disclosing the Title III material. "A recital of specific findings to demonstrate that conclusion would necessarily require divulging the contents of those excerpts and would thus defeat the very purpose for which the defendants' request for closure is made," the court wrote. Thus, the *Gotti* court declared the first prong of the *Press-Enterprise* test established without any specific discussion of how the test was met.

The court dealt with the second prong—examination of reasonable alternatives—in summary fashion. The court stated with no discussion that redaction was not a reasonable alternative. The court also wrote that a change of venue created problems because of the constitutional right of the defendants to be tried in the state where the crime was committed and a federal statutory right to be tried in the judicial district where the crime was committed. Moreover, the court rejected voir dire with the statement that the undisclosed Title III material was so prejudicial that it would "create a pattern of deep and bitter prejudice throughout the community from which a jury will be selected so as to pose voir dire problems that are real and not just

---

[74]729 F.2d at 58.

[75]*Id.* at 58.

[76]753 F.Supp. 443 (E.D.N.Y. 1990).

imagined."[77] Thus, the court held that the bail hearing could constitutionally be closed, although it noted that the interest in public and press access might be evaluated differently in later proceedings in the case.

Change of Venue Hearings

A hearing for a change of venue is generally a pretrial proceeding in which a criminal defendant seeks to have the trial moved to a locale in which, supposedly, a more fair trial may take place. In what may be the only federal court decision on First Amendment access to a change of venue proceeding, the U.S. Court of Appeals for the Fourth Circuit reversed a lower court's determination that a closed proceeding was constitutional. At issue in *In re Charlotte Observer*[78] was a change of venue for the Rev. Jim Bakker and a co-defendant, both charged with fraud in connection with Bakker's ministry. Bakker and his co-defendant sought a change of venue based on prejudicial publicity. A federal magistrate assigned to hear the motion, on his own initiative, closed the hearing to avoid the media re-publishing all the prejudicial information that would be discussed in the support of the motion. The magistrate initially entered the closure order without notice or a hearing, but later held a hearing and determined that closure was proper.

The Fourth Circuit struck down the closure order, applying the strict scrutiny language of *Press-Enterprise II*—that closure must preserve higher values and be narrowly tailored. The appellate court noted that the magistrate was not concerned so much with new prejudicial information as with media repeating earlier prejudicial statements in the course of explaining whatever decision the magistrate reached on the change of venue motion. Further, the magistrate, although stating that "he had 'carefully considered possible alternatives to closure,'" nonetheless concluded that "he '[could] conceive of none' and simply discounted without any elaboration the efficacy of the only alternative he identified—jury *voir dire*."[79]

The Fourth Circuit disagreed with the magistrate's conclusion that, under *Press-Enterprise II*, the prejudicial publicity from the voir dire hearing had a substantial probability of prejudicing the defendants' fair trial rights. The appellate court noted that any prejudicial publicity involved had already been circulated, and that its re-publication alone was the crucial issue. "Assessing whether any finite amount of pretrial publicity is damaging enough to warrant concern for fair trial rights is hard enough, assessing whether a discrete bit more would tip the scale probably defies rational prediction," the court wrote.

Next, the Fourth Circuit concluded that closing the hearing was not a practical remedy to prevent re-publication of prior prejudicial information. Even assuming an open hearing would result in a great deal of publicity, the court wrote, a closed hearing would incite even greater speculation and re-publication. The court noted

---

[77] *Id.* at 448.

[78] 882 F.2d 850 (4th Cir. 1989).

[79] *Id.* at 853.

that, under the *Press-Enterprise II* test, if closure would not prevent the harm, "that alone suffices to make it constitutionally impermissible."[80]

Finally, the Fourth Circuit concluded that the magistrate had not adequately considered the possibility of a thorough jury voir dire as an alternative to closure. The court cited highly publicized cases, such as those involving the Watergate defendants and John DeLorean, in which juries "were satisfactorily disclosed to have been unaffected (indeed, in some instances blissfully unaware of or untouched) by that publicity."[81] The Fourth Circuit stated that voir dire could be assumed to protect against jury bias in nearly all cases. The court also noted that the magistrate's assessment of closure betrayed an inadequate grasp of the First Amendment value of openness as a guarantor of both fairness and the appearance of fairness in criminal proceedings.

Plea and Sentencing Hearings

In what is apparently the only reported federal court decision on the issue, the U.S. Court of Appeals for the Fourth Circuit decided in 1986 that a First Amendment right of access extended to both plea and sentencing hearings. The case, *In re Washington Post Co.*,[82] arose when a federal district court, at the request of the government, closed the plea and sentencing hearings of a Ghanaian national charged with espionage against the United States. The United States and the government of Ghana had reached an agreement under which the defendant would plead *nolo contendere* to two counts in the indictment. Under the agreement, the parties would then jointly move for a suspended sentence. The defendant would then be exchanged for individuals held in Ghana on charges of spying on behalf of the United States.

The government's closure motion maintained that an open proceeding would "jeopardize the success of the exchange and pose a threat to the lives of persons subject to the jurisdiction of the Government of Ghana."[83] A *Washington Post* reporter was excluded from the plea hearing, and told that no reason for the closure would be forthcoming. A *Post* reporter was also ejected from the subsequent sentencing hearing.

On appeal, the Fourth Circuit held that *Richmond Newspapers* and its progeny required that the proceedings be open. The court reasoned that plea and sentencing hearings could both be considered parts of the trial, thus directly controlled by the holding in *Richmond Newspapers*. However, even if plea and sentencing hearings were considered separate proceedings from the trial, they were nonetheless integral parts of the criminal prosecution to which a First Amendment right of access should attach, the Fourth Circuit wrote.

---

[80]*Id.* at 855 (citations omitted).

[81]*Id.* at 855 (citations omitted).

[82]807 F.2d 383 (4th Cir. 1986).

[83]*Id.* at 386.

The Fourth Circuit concluded that the district court could not simply accept a claim of national security as grounds for closing the proceedings. The appellate court determined that the district court was required to follow the three-part test of *Press-Enterprise II* and make specific factual findings of the need for closure. The Court vacated the orders closing the hearings, but noted that the hearings had already taken place, thus precluding remand of the case.

Particular Witness Testimony

Two recent federal district court decisions have considered, with mixed results, closed proceedings for the testimony of witnesses in situations deemed to be particularly sensitive. In 1990, the U.S. District Court for the District of Columbia closed a videotaped deposition by former President Ronald Reagan in *U.S. v. Poindexter*.[84] The court, in a criminal prosecution of former National Security Advisor John M. Poindexter, evinced "a deep concern about the risk of public disclosure in the course of President Reagan's testimony of sensitive national security and foreign policy information."[85] After a number of news organizations asked to attend the deposition, the court held that it would conduct an *in camera* deposition, after which it would release an edited videotape of the proceedings. Classified information would be removed from the edited tape, the court said.

The district court defined the deposition as a pretrial proceeding, and thus subject only to a qualified right of access, as stated in the *Press-Enterprise II* two-part inquiry requiring a historical tradition of openness and a functional role for access in ensuring fairness. Examining the historical tradition of access to such proceedings, the court said, without citation, that there was no such tradition because "the provision of evidence by former or sitting Presidents of the United States has been extremely rare, and in each such instance the court having jurisdiction has had to fashion procedures tailored to the particular situation."[86] Moreover, the court wrote that a federal statute, the Classified Information Procedures Act (CIPA), required that pretrial proceedings involving classified information be held *in camera*. The court did not explain how a statute enacted by Congress could control its decision on the First Amendment access issue, although the implication seems to be that the requirement of closed proceedings under CIPA was one component of the "historical tradition" inquiry under *Press-Enterprise II*.

As to the functional interest served by access, the district court declared, with little discussion, that the possibility that Reagan's testimony would include information damaging to national security meant that "the public interest could well be injured by the attendance of press representatives at the deposition."[87] The district court implied in a footnote that, because the initial two-part inquiry suggested that

---

[84]732 F.Supp. 165 (D.D.C. 1990).

[85]*Id.* at 166.

[86]*Id.* at 167.

[87]*Id.*

no qualified right of access existed, it would not be necessary to apply the heightened scrutiny test of *Press-Enterprise II*.[88]

The *Poindexter* court concluded that it could meet the Supreme Court's *Press-Enterprise II* concerns for both fairness and the appearance of fairness in criminal proceedings by ordering the release of the videotape as soon as it had been edited. "Immediate post-editing disclosure of the videotape will give assurances of fairness to both the public and the accused . . . ," the court wrote.[89] The court pointed out that access was not being denied—merely delayed. Somewhat ironically, a second order by the district court 1 week later denied media access to the videotape until after it had been introduced into evidence.[90]

Although *Poindexter* resulted in closed proceedings, a 1992 district court decision applied strict scrutiny to deny a request for closed proceedings during testimony in the criminal trial of a male physician charged with inseminating female infertility patients with his own sperm. Prosecutors in the case sought to close the courtroom when the patients, whose children were allegedly fathered by the defendant, testified against him. In *U.S. v. Jacobson*,[91] the U.S. District Court for the Eastern District of Virginia held that the government had a compelling interest in protecting the patients' children from learning about their true paternity. The court found that "keeping secret the true identity of the parents and their children is necessitated by the compelling and overriding governmental interest in the psychological health and welfare of the children involved in the matter."[92] According-ing to the court, public disclosure of the circumstances of their conception could cause the children "significant psychological harm."[93]

Despite finding a compelling governmental interest in closing the trial during the patients' testimony, the court held that closure was not sufficiently narrowly tailored to pass constitutional muster. Reasonable and less drastic alternatives to closure, the court wrote, were the use of pseudonyms during the testimony of the patients, exclusion of sketch artists during the patients' testimony, and redaction of the patients' names from documents filed in the case. Although these measures would result in less public information about the case, the court found they were sufficiently narrow and would obviate the need to close the proceedings altogether.

CONCLUSION

Although the Supreme Court has addressed the issue of access to court proceedings in a series of cases, the question of access to any particular proceeding remains in

---

[88]*Id.* at n. 7.

[89]*Id.* at 170.

[90]U.S. v. Poindexter, 732 F. Supp. 170 (D.D.C. 1990).

[91]785 F.Supp. 563 (E.D.Va. 1992).

[92]*Id.* at 568.

[93]*Id.*

doubt, particularly for those proceedings about which the Court has not directly spoken. Even where strict scrutiny has been applied to closure orders, federal courts have in some instances upheld closure. Lower courts appear generally to have applied lower levels of scrutiny, sometimes approaching mere reasonableness, to proceedings not considered by the Supreme Court.

-7-

Defects in the System

The techniques of constitutional interpretation established by the Supreme Court to balance the right of the press to report on the criminal justice system against other rights have led to varied results in the lower federal courts. On the one hand, the scrutiny structure has led to the eradication of most direct prior restraints on the press. Moreover, post-publication sanctions for press reporting on criminal justice have been virtually eliminated. On the other hand, prior restraints on participants in criminal trials, when challenged by the media, are upheld with little scrutiny in some federal courts. Also, press access to criminal proceedings, even if given some relatively high level of constitutional scrutiny, has been frustrated in a number of situations that arguably should have resulted in open proceedings.

This chapter summarizes the uses of constitutional scrutiny in the cases considered in this study. Next, the chapter offers a practical critique of the scrutiny structure as it is applied to cases involving the First Amendment and the criminal justice system. This critique seeks to suggest some defects in the scrutiny structure that may extend beyond the cases at hand. Although the lower court cases considered in this study may, in some instances, be of little precedential value at the national level, the kinds of judicial reasoning they exemplify suggest ways in which higher courts might better guide lower courts in their attempts to accommodate First Amendment interests and the other concerns at stake in the criminal justice system.

SUMMARY OF FINDINGS

In the prior restraint cases examined in this study, the federal courts have treated almost all direct restraints on the press as anathema. The strength of the judicial reluctance to directly gag the press has resulted in a line of U.S. Supreme Court cases striking down prior restraints. However, it was not until *Nebraska Press* that a clear standard was established. That standard—a three-part inquiry based on the clear and present danger test—requires courts to examine the nature and extent of pretrial coverage, possible alternatives, and the extent to which a prior restraint would prove effective in protecting the defendant from prejudice. The three-prong *Nebraska Press* test has been applied by lower federal courts to routinely strike down prior restraints. Moreover, some lower courts holding prior restraints unconstitutional have done so without explicit balancing of any kind; a mere citation to *Nebraska Press* often has been deemed sufficient. The only published exception to the lack of direct prior restraints in the criminal justice context at the federal level is the *Noriega* case, in which the district court said it could not apply *Nebraska Press;* the Eleventh Circuit mentioned the *Press-Enterprise II* test, but did not perform any explicit balancing under that test.

Federal courts have been divided on the issue of media challenges to restraints on trial participants. Some federal courts considering the issue have upheld such restraints, reasoning that the heavy burden against prior restraints is inapplicable when the restrained party is not challenging the order. Those courts have applied weak standards of review, such as whether a "reasonable likelihood" of prejudice existed or whether the restraint was reasonable. The federal courts equating media challenges to participant restraints with direct prior restraints have held them unconstitutional, applying either *Nebraska Press* or some variation of the "clear and imminent" threat to a fair trial standard.

Postpublication sanctions against the press in the criminal justice context appear to have been universally declared unconstitutional, at least in reported federal cases. The Supreme Court has applied differing levels of scrutiny, ranging from a categorical bar against postpublication sanctions, in *Cox Broadcasting Corp. v. Cohn,*[1] to both clear and present danger and strict scrutiny formulations in cases following *Cox*. Although, the reported lower court decisions have applied strict scrutiny, as discussed later in this chapter, they have not always done so in ways seemingly envisioned by the Supreme Court.

The federal decisions involving access to criminal proceedings are much less clear. The Court's *Richmond Newspapers* line of cases provides a variety of standards of review, ranging from an "overriding interest" standard to a "compelling interest" standard to a "substantial probability" of prejudice test. Although all these tests resulted in the Court concluding that the proceeding at hand should have been open, lower courts have frequently been reluctant to open proceedings on which the Court has not directly ruled. In such situations, lower federal courts have generally adopted some lower level of scrutiny to weigh the First Amendment interest in access against the countervailing government interest in closure.

Lower federal courts considering closure of preliminary hearings have upheld closure using a "necessary" test or a "likelihood of prejudice" standard. Other courts have struck down closure of preliminary hearings, applying standards such as a "significant risk of prejudice" or the "substantial probability" test from *Press-En-*

---

[1]420 U.S. 469 (1975).

terprise II. Reported lower federal court decisions considering voir dire, pretrial suppression hearings, and trial testimony of particular sensitivity have resulted in some open and some closed hearings, whereas bail hearing cases have apparently always resulted in closure being upheld. The only reported cases considering change of venue and plea and sentencing hearings have struck down closure as unconstitutional.

PROBLEMS WITH THE EXISTING STRUCTURE

The cases examined in this study suggest a number of problems with the scrutiny structure as it has been developed in the federal courts. This section critiques the existing scrutiny structure and, in the conclusion, offers suggestions for dealing with some of those criticisms.

The Conflict Problem

Perhaps the greatest difficulty with the use of heightened scrutiny in cases in which the press seeks to cover criminal proceedings is the notion of two fundamental rights in conflict: the received view of a conflict between the cherished rights of free speech and press, and the inviolable right of a criminal defendant to receive a fair trial. Under the received view, these two rights are regarded as in some way incompatible. When judges perceive two rights in conflict, the most natural response is to balance the conflicting rights (i.e., employ some judicial test, like strict scrutiny, that sorts out conflicting interests). As a number of scholars have pointed out, however, this notion of constitutional rights in conflict may be in error.

Do the First Amendment's expression clauses conflict with the Sixth Amendment's fair trial provision? More precisely, does the Sixth Amendment empower government to suppress speech by private actors that may interfere with the conduct of an impartial trial? A majority of at least one federal appellate panel, discussed in chapter 4, has held that it does not; a number of scholars have reached the same conclusion. There is no question that the Sixth Amendment requires government to provide a fair trial. The point raised by those disagreeing with the received view is that private actors, such as the news media, are not under a similar obligation by the terms of the Sixth Amendment. Nor, according to advocates of this view, can government require the press to assist it in meeting its obligations under the Sixth Amendment.

The crucial issue is whether the Sixth Amendment—as part of the Bill of Rights, a series of restraints on government—allows government to control the conduct of citizens to assist it in doing its duty. As Judge Goodwin pointed out in *CBS v. U.S. Dist. Ct. for C.D. of California,*[2] the Sixth Amendment only suggests that "the

---

[2]729 F.2d 1174 (9th Cir. 1983).

government may not perform governmental acts that deprive a person of a fair trial."[3] The Sixth Amendment does not—either by its terms or, logically, by its inclusion in the Bill of Rights—authorize government to limit other constitutional rights of citizens. The fact that the Sixth Amendment operates as a restraint on government conduct does not necessarily suggest that government is thereby empowered to restrain others. Oregon Supreme Court Justice Hans A. Linde has argued that a constitutional right "is a claim that runs against the government—usually not a claim that the government do something *for* you or me, but that it refrain from doing something *to* us."[4] As a result, constitutional rights do not create rights or remedies against private parties acting solely for themselves and not on behalf of government. In the criminal justice setting, constitutional rights do not allow one party—a defendant—to assert a right to limit the conduct of another party—the media. According to Linde, the notion of a conflict between fair trial and free press rights "lets the state turn two constitutional limitations on its powers into a classic example of 'let's you and him fight.' It asks defendants and reporters to trade off their rights between themselves or let a court do it for them. But this is not constitutional law."[5]

Constitutional scholar Laurence Tribe stated the point as follows: "If our system of justice is functioning properly, government is prohibited from trying an accused in a prejudicial atmosphere; if pre-trial publicity prevents the impaneling of an impartial jury, the defendant is entitled by the sixth amendment to a dismissal of the charges against him."[6]

If the Sixth Amendment does not create governmental power to interfere with the gathering and dissemination of news about the criminal justice system, the use of heightened scrutiny formulations to balance First and Sixth Amendment concerns is clearly in error. In fact, the concept of a conflict or battle between fair trial and free press rights is an illusory one. Such a conclusion would not foreclose the balancing of other interests, however. For example, the privacy rights of witnesses or jurors could still be balanced against the First Amendment, at least if those privacy rights rose to constitutional dimensions.

The Abstractness Problem

One of the difficulties that seems to recur as courts try to apply various levels of scrutiny to fair trial–free press issues is the level of abstraction at which First Amendment interests are considered. That is, often judicial analyses focus on a concrete, pressing problem, such as the fair trial rights of an accused or the privacy interests of witnesses or jurors. These real concerns, which involve important rights

---

[3]*Id.* at 1184 (Goodwin, J., concurring).

[4] Linde, Fair Trials and Press Freedom—Two Rights Against the State, 13 Willamette L.J. 211, 217 (1977).

[5]*Id.* at 218.

[6]L. Tribe, American Constitutional Law 625-26 n. 15 (1978).

of parties before the court to be tried impartially or to protect their privacy, render the First Amendment interests at stake shadowy at best. As First Amendment scholar Rodney Smolla noted, "the use of the balancing approach tends to result in relatively low protection for speech, because when balancing is employed, speech tends to be devalued as just another social interest to be considered in the mix."[7]

Lower federal courts rarely discuss—or even acknowledge, other than a boiler-plate citation or two—the salutary effect on both actual and perceived fairness that may result from uninhibited press coverage of the criminal justice system. Likewise, lower court opinions rarely express the view that press coverage might encourage judges and other officials to act more responsibly, expose perjury from complainants and other witnesses, lead to the discovery of additional evidence, or reveal jurors who for one reason or another should not be allowed to sit on a given case. Lower federal courts rarely examine the range of benefits that Chief Justice Burger expressed as flowing from open trials in *Richmond Newspapers*—benefits that could equally be argued to flow from an absence of prior restraints on participants or from other measures that allow for uninhibited press coverage of, and thus public awareness about, criminal proceedings.

The result of this lack of attention to concrete societal benefits arising from unencumbered First Amendment rights often seems to be an inflation of the importance of the governmental interest in limiting coverage. The governmental interest, whether privacy or the Sixth Amendment, becomes the exclusive focus of the analysis and may tend to win the day by its very immediacy. First Amendment interests may be given brief mention by citation to, for example, *Nebraska Press* or *Richmond Newspapers*, but the First Amendment concerns that infused those cases are not a focus of analysis. Often in the lower courts, the defendant's Sixth Amendment rights are concrete, while the First Amendment interests at stake have a certain abstract unreality. "Free speech is a wonderful notion," the courts frequently imply, "but we have more serious concerns at the moment."

An example of this mode of analysis is found in *In re South Carolina Press Association*,[8] discussed in chapter 6. In that case, the U.S. Court of Appeals for the Fourth Circuit permitted a closed voir dire proceeding with no examination of the First Amendment values advanced by open jury selection. The Fourth Circuit chose to focus on the threat to a fair trial posed by open questioning of jurors, who might conceal their true attitudes if those attitudes were to be open to public scrutiny. The court completely avoided the issue of how public scrutiny of the process of selecting jurors might advance the fairness of the process. It could be argued that open jury selection could prevent perjury by a potential juror with an ax to grind by allowing the public to be aware the juror is being considered. Further, the Fourth Circuit did not discuss the value of open proceedings in increasing public confidence in the judicial system and discouraging unfairness by parties and officers of the court alike.

[7]R. Smolla, Free Speech in an Open Society 40 (1992).
[8]946 F.2d 1037 (4th Cir. 1991).

In short, the *South Carolina Press Association* court infused its analysis with none of the sensitivity to the value of open proceedings that characterized *Richmond Newspapers* and its progeny. The concerns of the Sixth Amendment were regarded as real and concrete, whereas the First Amendment concerns seem strictly *pro forma*. The Fourth Circuit's reference to "the press" as the interested party suggests the court's failure to appreciate that the First Amendment values of openness are public values that are aimed at enhanced fairness in all criminal proceedings. In other words, by characterizing the interest in openness as one solely belonging to the press, and not to the public at large, the Fourth Circuit implicitly devalued the First Amendment interest at stake. The underlying message seems to be that enhanced fairness for criminal defendants is served by closed courtrooms, and that such fairness would be safeguarded if only it were not for an intrusive media presence. The *South Carolina Press Association* court conducted its First Amendment analysis by discounting the First Amendment and assuming that the Sixth Amendment right to a fair trial is advanced best in secrecy. The First Amendment interests at stake had no real substance.

The same abstract view of First Amendment values can be seen in numerous other cases in this study. As long as the value of uninhibited press and public scrutiny of criminal justice continues to be considered at a high level of generality, it is a simple matter for courts to conclude that other interests should be paramount, whether the standard is a "compelling interest," a "reasonable likelihood," or a "clear and present danger." Unless judges perceive some important interest worth protecting, the height of the formulaic hedge placed around that interest may be of little help. Interestingly, a different Fourth Circuit panel noted this very phenomenon of abstractness when it struck down a magistrate's order closing a change of venue hearing in the *Charlotte Observer* case discussed in chapter 6.[9] The court stated that the closure order reflected no appreciation for the value of open proceedings to guard both actual and perceived fairness in criminal proceedings. The lower court's failure to grasp the value of openness, the Fourth Circuit suggested, contributed to its erroneous view of alternatives to a closed hearing. Although higher courts cannot force lower courts to share presumptions about the instrumental value of allowing vigorous public scrutiny of criminal justice, they can require lower courts to conduct the analysis in a way that accounts for value of openness.

The Fact-Bound Problem

Few would dispute that the notion of *stare decisis* to some extent guarantees that a prior case determines the result in a later case to the extent that the later case conforms factually to the earlier one.[10] However, federal courts' use of heightened

---

[9]822 F.2d 850 (4th Cir. 1989).

[10]Blacks' Law Dictionary defines *stare decisis* as the notion that "when court has once laid down a principle of law as applicable to a certain state of facts, it will adhere to that principle, and apply it to all future cases, where facts are substantially the same. . . ." Black's Law Dictionary, p. 1261 (1979).

scrutiny sometimes discloses a fact-bound judicial approach that unduly limits First Amendment rights. This fact-bound approach is characterized by a subservience to precedent so long as the exact factual configuration of the earlier case is present. However, in cases somewhat less on all fours with the precedential case, judges tend to lose sight of the underlying First Amendment principles in the face of what are often characterized as "unique" or "unusual" cases. This cramped view of *stare decisis* causes some judges to abandon heightened scrutiny, rather than recalibrate the test to the facts before the court while retaining sensitivity to the First Amendment values involved. The argument suggested here is not that changed facts never require different standards of review. Rather, when First Amendment interests are at stake, judges cannot escape the responsibility of engaging in a serious analysis of *why* those facts require less or no scrutiny. Simply declaring a case "unique" is not, by itself, an adequate basis on which to treat First Amendment rights less deferentially when the same free expression interests are present in both the precedential case and the case at hand.

In the *Noriega* case, discussed in chapter 4, both the district court and the Eleventh Circuit declined to consider seriously the tremendous burden on the government to justify a prior restraint on CNN, regardless of duration. For example, the district court refused to apply the *Nebraska Press* three-prong test because of CNN's refusal to turn over the Noriega tapes for review. The court claimed this refusal made it impossible to apply the *Nebraska Press* standard, the first prong of which required an evaluation of the extent of prejudice. Without the tapes, the court said, it could not perform the analysis required by the first prong.

Although that may have been the case, the court abandoned its responsibility to the First Amendment too soon. The court, lacking the tapes, could have *assumed* that the material was prejudicial and moved on to the other prongs of *Nebraska Press*, all of which must be satisfied to support a prior restraint. Had it done so, the court might have determined that some alternative short of a restraint on the media would adequately protect Noriega's right to a fair trial (the second prong), or that a prior restraint was not an effective means to ensure a fair trial (the third prong). As to alternatives, the trial judge could have sequestered the prosecution team, as indeed he later ordered, because it was prosecutors, not the public, whom the judge feared gaining knowledge of Noriega's defense strategy from the tapes. Alternatively, the judge might have assumed the prosecutors were already aware of the contents of the tapes, which after all were recorded by the government. In that case, the restraint might have failed the effectiveness prong of *Nebraska Press* because if Noriega's strategy were already known to the government, no restraint could have prevented the harm to his defense.[11]

Although the alternative analysis discussed above may be subject to debate, what is not arguable is that the trial judge in the *Noriega* case never even attempted to carry out the mandate of *Nebraska Press*. Because of "the unique nature of the problem,"[12] the court simply abandoned heightened scrutiny and ordered a restraint

---

[11]I am indebted to my friend Sig Splichal for some of these insights on the *Noriega* case.

[12]752 F.Supp. at 1036.

on material in the hands of the media. Because of its fact-bound view of precedent, the trial court, faced with a somewhat different factual configuration than that in *Nebraska Press*, did not try to recalibrate the *Nebraska Press* test to preserve that case's underlying concern of limiting prior restraints in criminal cases. Had the *Noriega* court engaged in a serious analysis, retaining as much of the *Nebraska Press* Court's animating concerns as possible, it might have reached the same result. Instead, the trial court simply threw up its hands in the face of a novel fact situation and made no attempt to accommodate the First Amendment interests at stake. The "fact-bound problem" emerges when, as in *Noriega*, courts significantly reduce or abandon the level of constitutional scrutiny in prior cases when called on to decide cases with unusual facts.

The fact-bound problem is evident in a number of access cases discussed in chapter 6, in which courts forbade public access to proceedings on which the Supreme Court has not ruled. Despite the First Amendment interests outlined in *Richmond Newspapers* and its progeny, lower courts have frequently applied diminished standards of scrutiny to other proceedings, often with no explicit justification. For example, in *U.S. v. Criden*,[13] the U.S. Court of Appeals for the Third Circuit settled on a lower level "necessary" test to justify closure of a pretrial suppression hearing. The court said this less-than-strict scrutiny of such closures was the appropriate constitutional standard, despite its acknowledgment that the public may have no other opportunity to oversee such cases because plea bargaining may well take place at the conclusion of the suppression hearing. The court did not mention the broader public policy concern of how the judicially created exclusionary rule should operate, and whether the public should have an opportunity to see such a rule in action. The *Criden* court did discuss the societal interests in open proceedings raised in *Richmond Newspapers,* and the "uniquely irretrievable loss that would be incurred by the public through the denial of the right to attend the hearing."[14] Nevertheless, faced with a variation on the *Richmond Newspapers* facts, the *Criden* court adopted a lower level of scrutiny. Again, the essential First Amendment concerns had not changed between the two cases, but a change in the factual pattern caused the court to take those concerns less seriously by promulgating a less protective standard.

The Vagueness Problem

One of the most serious shortcomings of the scrutiny structure, as pointed out by many commentators, is its vagueness.[15] The levels of scrutiny devised by the courts often seem to be mere rhetorical devices to disguise the prejudices of judges, rather than precise formulations designed to reach constitutionally valid results. There is no doubt all legal formulations are subject to some judicial interpretation, and there

---

[13] 675 F.2d 550 (3rd Cir. 1982).

[14] 675 F.2d at 558.

[15] Galloway, Means-End Scrutiny in American Constitutional Law, 21 Loyola of L.A. L. Rev. 449, 487 (1988); T. Emerson, Toward a General Theory of the First Amendment 54 (1963).

is no doubt that legal decision making can never be reduced to geometric precision. Nonetheless, the scrutiny structure as presently articulated leaves wide latitude for lower courts to reach almost any result with little substantive guidance from above. There seems to be little question that a more rigorously defined structure could possibly limit the discretion of lower court judges. As Professor John Ely has written: "One doesn't have to be much of a lawyer to recognize that even the clearest verbal formula can be manipulated. But it's a very bad lawyer who supposes that manipulability and infinite manipulability are the same thing."[16] Clearer guidance from higher courts on the application of heightened scrutiny could no doubt constrain the discretion of lower court judges and lead to some increased level of legal certainty.

One of the first areas of uncertainty encountered in heightened scrutiny is the meaning of adjectives such as *compelling, overriding, clear and present,* and *imminent.* The Supreme Court has been less than clear on the meaning of these terms. In 1968, in *U.S. v. O'Brien,*[17] Chief Justice Warren suggested that there was little distinction between the terms: "To characterize the qualities of the governmental interest which must appear, the Court has employed a variety of descriptive terms: compelling; substantial; subordinating; paramount; cogent; strong."[18] Although Warren's remark did not specifically state that there was no difference between these terms, it implied that all the terms were part of a single standard, and it noted the "imprecision" inherent in the terms. Later commentators have nevertheless suggested that most justices regard at least some of the terms as denoting different degrees of magnitude.[19] One commentator pointed out that "the analytical structures are so flexible and the tests so vague that judges are left at large to decide cases on the basis of personal bias."[20] Another commentator stated that balancing tests "give a view of judicial review that is intuitional, if not incomprehensible."[21]

In the cases examined in this study, the U.S. Supreme Court has been less than clear in its expositions of how lower courts should weigh conflicting interests. In the prior restraint area, the Court in the seminal *Near* case never stated a standard, but merely noted that only in exceptional cases could prior restraint be applied constitutionally. Likewise, the *per curiam* opinion in the Pentagon Papers case did not establish a guiding standard for lower courts other than noting a heavy presumption against prior restraints. The individual justices' opinions in that case did suggest various tests, but none was accepted by a majority of the Court. *Nebraska Press* brought firmer doctrinal ground, but the *Nebraska Press* test is still subject to considerable interpretation by lower courts, particularly with regard to

---

[16]J. Ely, Democracy and Distrust 112 (1980).

[17]391 U.S. 367 (1968).

[18]*Id.* at 367-77 (citations omitted).

[19]*E.g.,* Stone, Content-Neutral Restrictions, 54 U. of Chicago L. Rev. 46, 49-50 (1987).

[20]Galloway, Means-End Scrutiny in American Constitutional Law, 21 Loyola of L.A. L. Rev. 449, 487 (1988).

[21]Henkin, Infallibility Under Law: Constitutional Balancing, 78 Colum. L. Rev. 1022, 1048 (1978).

the first prong of the test, which asks the court to consider "the nature and extent of pretrial coverage."[22] Some courts, such as the U.S. Court of Appeals for the Ninth Circuit in the DeLorean case,[23] have seized on language from Chief Justice Burger's opinion stating that prior restraints could only pass constitutional muster if it is "clear that further publicity, unchecked, would so distort the views of potential jurors that 12 could not be found who would . . . fulfill their sworn duty."[24] When courts infuse the first prong of *Nebraska Press* with this rigorous language, the test becomes quite strict. However, some courts have adopted a "soft" reading of this prong. For instance, a federal district court in *Connecticut Magazine v. Moraghan*[25] found that a reasonable likelihood that publicity would prejudice a defendant's fair trial rights was constitutionally sufficient under *Nebraska Press*. The weakness of a "reasonable likelihood" approach is that trial courts can summarily decide that this vague standard is met in almost any high-profile criminal case.

The postpublication sanction cases are also plagued with vague standards that provide little assistance to lower courts. Although it could be argued that the absence of federal cases upholding postpublication sanctions suggests a solidly grounded First Amendment jurisprudence, a case can be made that the future of this area of the law is less clear than might be desired. Although the first case in the quartet of Supreme Court decisions on postpublication sanctions, *Cox Broadcasting v. Cohn*,[26] set forth a categorical bar to sanctions in cases involving publicly available documents in criminal trials, the next three cases in the series exhibit vagueness about how lines should be drawn.

In *Landmark Communications, Inc. v. Virginia*,[27] the Court said it applied the clear and present danger standard, but nowhere in the opinion gave any sense of when the danger of speech might rise to that level. The Court simply declared the danger less than "clear and present" in the case at hand. In *Smith v. Daily Mail*,[28] the Court shifted from the clear and present danger standard to what seemed to be strict scrutiny, holding that a postpublication sanction could only pass constitutional muster by furthering "a state interest of the highest order."[29] As in most strict scrutiny cases, this "highest order" was never classified in a manner that would allow other courts to make the determination in any but the most impressionistic manner. Nor was the Court explicit about whether the "highest order" interest is less than, more than, or the same as a "compelling" interest. After setting this ill-defined standard, the Court did not explicitly perform any balancing using the test, but declared, *ipse dixit*, that the interest in *Daily Mail* was insufficient to support the postpublication sanction.

---

[22]427 U.S. at 562.

[23]CBS v. U.S. Dist Ct. for C.D. of California, 729 F.2d 1174 (9th Cir. 1983).

[24]427 U.S. at 569.

[25]676 F.Supp. 38 (D. Conn. 1987).

[26]420 U.S. 469 (1975).

[27]435 U.S. 829 (1978).

[28]443 U.S. 97 (1979).

[29]*Id.* at 103

In the most recent case in the *Cox* series, *The Florida Star v. B.J.F.*,[30] the Court seemed even less concerned with defining a "highest order" interest. Rather, the Court declared the state's interest in punishing the press "highly significant," and seemed to assume for the remainder of the opinion that the "highest order" standard had been met. It may be that Justice Marshall's opinion did not actually reach the question of the magnitude of the state interest; the issue is nowhere explicitly decided in *B.J.F.* Nonetheless, the tone of the opinion seems to suggest that the state's interest in protecting rape victims is constitutionally sufficient to overcome the free speech interests at stake.

The difficulty with *Landmark, Daily Mail,* and *B.J.F.* is that nowhere in those cases is the potential litigant, lawyer, or lower court judge given even a rough sketch of what such an animal as a "clear and present danger" or a "highest order" interest might look like. Nor does the Court explain whether such state interests, once identified, are of such magnitude in all circumstances, *a priori*, or only rise to these levels *in relation to* a specific set of facts or a specific opposing First Amendment interest.

The lack of guidance offered by the trio of cases following *Cox* is paralleled in the few federal lower court decisions considering postpublication sanctions. In *Worrell Newspapers of Indiana, Inc. v. Westhafer*,[31] the U.S. Court of Appeals for the Seventh Circuit declared unconstitutional an Indiana statute punishing publication of the identity of an unapprehended suspect in a sealed criminal information. The *Westhafer* court, citing *Cox* and its progeny, found the state's interest in apprehending criminals insufficiently compelling to impose sanctions under the First Amendment. Like the Supreme Court in the *Cox* line of cases, the Seventh Circuit made no attempt to define when an interest becomes compelling, or to actually examine the state's interest in the case before it using some objective criteria of "compellingness." Thus, the Seventh Circuit's *Westhafer* opinion provides almost no guidance for future cases unless they involve facts virtually identical to *Westhafer*. All that is learned from the Seventh Circuit is that this particular interest is not compelling—not how, why, or in what manner. This almost uniform vagueness in heightened scrutiny cases may contribute to the fact-bound problem discussed elsewhere in this chapter. If standards of decision do not give some independent basis for evaluating future cases, but only provide impressionistic conclusions concerning the instant case, courts considering novel fact situations in the future are perhaps more likely to take a more limited view of precedent—effectively confining prior cases to their facts. The unclear standards in heightened scrutiny cases provide no path for the growth and evolution of First Amendment law based on more or less objective criteria.

The vague standards of the Supreme Court may also be responsible for lower court adventures like that in *Scheetz v. Morning Call, Inc.*[32] In *Scheetz*, a federal

---

[30]109 S.Ct. 2603 (1989).

[31]739 F.2d 1219 (7th Cir. 1984).

[32]747 F.Supp. 1515 (E.D. Pa. 1990).

district court in a postpublication sanctions case advanced the unique proposition that the highest degree of First Amendment scrutiny should be reserved only for news stories that illuminate broad themes of public importance. In *Scheetz*, that theme was police indifference to domestic violence, illustrated by the case of a police officer's wife whose claim of violence toward her by her husband was ignored by officials. The corollary of the *Scheetz* court's ruling is that stories about isolated events not illustrative of some broader theme, although involving public scrutiny of the criminal justice system, are entitled to less than exacting scrutiny. In short, the *Scheetz* court embarked on a constitutional analysis completely foreign to the U.S. Supreme Court's approach in *Cox* and its progeny. Although *Scheetz* may be viewed as a judicial anomaly, the idiosyncratic interpretation of the *Scheetz* court may be encouraged in a legal environment lacking solid guidelines for First Amendment analysis.

Vagueness is also endemic in the standards for courtroom access promulgated by *Richmond Newspapers* and its progeny. *Richmond Newspapers* articulated an "overriding interest" standard that may or may not be equal to strict scrutiny.[33] In *Globe Newspapers,* decided shortly after *Richmond Newspapers,* the majority stated a classic strict scrutiny formulation, allowing closure only if government could show a compelling interest and a narrowly tailored means of achieving that interest. *Press-Enterprise I* repeated *Richmond Newspapers'* "overriding interest" standard, adding a "narrowly tailored" prong. *Press-Enterprise II* stated that the closure required findings that "closure is essential to preserve higher values and is narrowly tailored to serve that interest."[34] The *Press-Enterprise II* Court further stated that "higher values-narrowly tailored" standard was embodied in the requirement of specific findings of a substantial probability of prejudice to the defendant's Sixth Amendment rights and the inadequacy of reasonable alternatives. This "substantial probability" standard, although not defined with any clarity, was declared to be more demanding than a mere "reasonable likelihood" of prejudice.

Thus, *Richmond Newspapers* and its progeny do not even share the same language in their doctrinal formulations, much less offer clear guidance as to what those standards might mean in practice. Lower courts have developed a patchwork of standards for proceedings about which the Supreme Court has not spoken. These standards have ranged from a requirement that closure be "necessary" to protect Sixth Amendment rights[35] to a standard requiring a "likelihood of prejudice."[36] As in *Richmond Newspapers* and its progeny, nowhere do these lower court opinions set forth objective criteria for determining when the standard is met, other than the impressionistic speculation of the particular judge.

---

[33]448 U.S. at 581.

[34]478 U.S. at 13-14 (citing *Press-Enterprise I*).

[35]U.S. v. Criden, 675 F.2d 550, 561-62 (3d Cir. 1982) (suppression hearing).

[36]U.S. v. Chagra, 701 F.2d 354, 364 (5th Cir. 1983) (bail hearing).

The Empirical Problem

One of the most striking problems with the scrutiny structure as applied to criminal justice and the media is the lack of empirical support for judicial decisions. Judges regularly advance sweeping generalizations about the effect of news coverage on potential jurors. In almost none of the cases examined in this study did judges give citations to (or even indicate awareness of) social scientific studies concerning the effect of prejudicial publicity. Decisions about the effect of news coverage are often at the heart of the judicial determination of whether the risk of prejudicial publicity rises to the level of a "compelling" or "overriding" interest or a "clear and present danger." Yet judges nearly always evaluate such risks in what appears to be a purely intuitive manner.

Of the Supreme Court cases examined in this study, only one cited empirical research to bolster a legal determination, and that citation came in a dissenting opinion. In *Globe Newspaper Co. v. Superior Court*,[37] the Court struck down a statute requiring judges to close the courtroom when minor victims of sexual crimes gave testimony. The majority opinion, written by Justice Brennan, claimed that there was no social scientific evidence to support the dissenters' view that closed courtrooms would result in more victims pressing charges. In support of the majority's contention that the mandatory closure rule would not support the state's interest in encouraging sex crime victims to come forward, Justice Brennan pointed to the lack of "empirical support for the claim that the rule of automatic closure . . . will lead to an increase in the number of minor sex victims coming forward and cooperating with state authorities."[38] The majority cited no empirical evidence of its own for the contrary view.

Chief Justice Burger, joined in dissent by then-Justice Rehnquist, cited two studies that, he asserted, demonstrated the psychological damage that public testimony could cause minor victims. Burger also pointed out that the empirical data the majority claimed were lacking—that closed proceedings would encourage victims to come forward—could never be obtained if the statute was declared unconstitutional. "It makes no sense to criticize the Commonwealth for its failure to offer empirical data in support of its rule; only by allowing state experimentation may such empirical evidence be produced," Burger wrote.[39]

This brief battle over empirical data is the first and last time the notion of social science rears its head in the cases described in this study. In the vast majority of cases, judges appear to believe they can make determinations about the social and psychological effects of news coverage using only legal materials and common sense. For example, in *U.S. v. Gotti*,[40] a 1990 case in which a federal district court closed a bail hearing, the district judge simply declared that the Title III surveillance materials to be discussed at the bail hearing, if released, would "create a pattern of

---

[37] 457 U.S. 596 (1981).

[38] 457 U.S. at 609.

[39] *Id.* at 617.

[40] 753 F.Supp. 443 (E.D.N.Y. 1990).

deep and bitter prejudice" in the community.[41] The judge made no attempt to substantiate this claim. The U.S. Court of Appeals for the Fourth Circuit reached an opposite, but equally unsupported, conclusion in *In re Charlotte Observer.*[42] In that case, involving a change of venue hearing for the Rev. Jim Bakker and a co-defendant, the Fourth Circuit declared that voir dire was an adequate remedy to protect against biased juries in nearly all circumstances. The Fourth Circuit did cite other highly publicized trials, such as the Watergate and DeLorean cases, as examples of cases in which potential jurors were virtually untouched by even massive pretrial publicity. This selective use of a few instances to formulate a general rule is a more serious attempt to substantiate the effects of publicity than most courts make, but it unquestionably falls short of even the most elementary standards of social scientific rigor.

Although social scientific investigation of prejudicial publicity cannot be said to have arrived at definitive answers, there is a body of literature that could offer some guidance to judges. For example, one 1981 review of empirical research stated that experimental and field studies have shown that pretrial publicity can affect public knowledge of a crime and juror willingness to speculate about a defendant's guilt, "but these studies do not provide evidence that the publicity has as much power to affect the actual jury verdict as has been commonly assumed, or that the effects cannot be overcome by careful use of the legal remedies of change of venue and *voir dire* examination."[43] Other studies seem to show that greater knowledge of case facts can tend to bias jurors in favor of conviction.[44] One scholar, Norbert L. Kerr, said in 1991 that "the clear thrust of [social science] evidence is that jurors' attitudes are affected by extreme exposure to pretrial publicity, that their verdicts are affected as well, and that the existing remedies, with some exceptions, do not deal with the problem entirely."[45]

Many studies are of somewhat limited value because of unreal conditions, such as mock trials, or because of potentially questionable self-reporting by jurors in actual trials. Although empirical evidence is inconclusive, attention to social

---

[41]*Id.* at 448.

[42]882 F.2d 850 (4th Cir. 1989).

[43]Buddenbaum, Weaver, Holsinger, and Brown, Pretrial Publicity and Juries: A Review of Research, Research Report No. 11, School of Journalism, Indiana University (1981). *See also* Simon, Does the Court's Decision in *Nebraska Press Association* Fit the Research Evidence on the Impact on Jurors of News Coverage?, 29 Stan. L. Rev. 515 (1977) ("results show that when ordinary citizens become jurors, they assume a special role in which they apply different standards of proof, more vigorous reasoning and greater detachment" *Id.* at 528).

[44]*E.g.,* Wright, Local Newspaper and Television Reliance and Perceptions of a Criminal Defendant (paper presented at national convention of the Speech Communication Association, 1991, Atlanta, Georgia).

[45]Panel One: What Empirical Research Tells Us and What We Need to Know About Juries and the Quest for Impartiality, 40 Am. U. L. Rev. 547, 551 (1991). For a thorough review of the literature, see Wright, Local Newspaper and Television Reliance and Perceptions of a Criminal Defendant (paper presented at the national convention of the Speech Communication Association, 1991, Atlanta, Georgia).

science research may give courts some basis—other than sheer speculation—on which to build assumptions about the effects of publicity. Moreover, some commentators contend that even if the effects of publicity are hard to measure with accuracy, research can help "critique existing remedies for minimizing the impact of bias. As a result, it helps us formulate better methods and employ them more effectively to reduce particularly overwhelming or distorting biases."[46]

CONCLUSION

This chapter suggested that the scrutiny structure could benefit from some retooling if it is to be maintained in cases involving First Amendment rights and the criminal justice system. First, federal courts must seriously consider whether the Sixth Amendment, textually or by implication, authorizes them to restrain First Amendment freedoms of the press and public to advance criminal defendants' fair trial interests. If judicial and scholarly criticism of this approach is valid, fair trial rights would be one interest no longer subject to balancing within the First Amendment scrutiny structure.

Next, lower courts need to infuse their analyses with concrete First Amendment values. The Supreme Court has generally given significant consideration to the instrumental value of uninhibited coverage of criminal justice, but lower courts have often treated First Amendment concerns as abstract and without substance. In heightened scrutiny analysis, this abstract approach to protection of speech may be unspoken because heightened scrutiny formulations purport to measure the strength of the opposing interest (e.g., "compelling" or "overriding"), rather than the magnitude of the speech interest. The trivialization of speech interests can only be identified by reading between the lines of the opinions, when relatively marginal interests are allowed to trump First Amendment concerns—even if the level of scrutiny applied is ostensibly an exacting one. The government interest—whether Sixth Amendment concerns, privacy concerns, or some other interest—is seemingly inflated because of the court's lack of concern for the speech interest at stake. As one commentator, addressing a different line of First Amendment cases, stated: "Even if speech-protective first amendment standards are ostensibly invoked, their application may be so relaxed and the judicial attitude may be so grudging as to alter the standard of review in fact."[47]

This problem, which is not unique to First Amendment jurisprudence, essentially involves a *de facto* lowering of the standard of review at the same time lip service, often in the form of a string citation, is given to the concerns that animated the creation of that standard of review. There is no easy solution to maintaining legal certainty through standards applied by judges who do not share the concerns of

---

[46]Minow & Cate, Who is an Impartial Juror in an Age of Mass Media?, 40 Am. U. L. Rev. 631, 661 (1991).

[47]Dienes, When the First Amendment is not Preferred: The Military and Other "Special Contexts," 56 U. Cin. L. Rev. 779, 828 (1988).

those who created the standards. Strict scrutiny in the hands of a judge with little regard for First Amendment values is likely to be less than strict.

One suggestion might be greater clarity in the scrutiny structure: What objective criteria might be used to identify a compelling interest? How dangerous must a clear and present danger be? The issue of vagueness in the standards of review appears inextricably linked with the problem of devalued First Amendment interests. Moreover, a system of analysis that required lower court judges to identify the First Amendment interests at stake might help focus judicial attention on the issue. For example, analytical attention to the kinds of First Amendment benefits discussed by the *Richmond Newspapers* Court (i.e., increased fairness, a public perception of fairness, reduced perjury, etc.) might be required as part of a revised balancing process. The current structure simply ignores the speech interests, and thus might contribute to their devaluation. It could be argued that concern for First Amendment interests is "built into" strict scrutiny and similar tests, but their application by some courts suggests that a mode of analysis that required explicit attention to the speech part of the legal equation might help focus judicial attention on important First Amendment values currently ignored. Clearly, requiring judges to recite a jurisprudential laundry list of competing values is not a magical solution to unarticulated balancing, but the requirement might make it more difficult for some judges to routinely devalue First Amendment interests.

Finally, some attention to social scientific literature and empirical data may be worth considering. For example, although research into effects of prejudicial publicity on jurors is still in its infancy, some awareness of empirical data might help judges in their determinations. For instance, the notion that mass communication is an all-powerful means of influencing potential jurors' minds is one that seems to haunt the judicial imagination. An awareness of the limits of that influence might help judges overcome what sometimes seems to be their fear of journalists and their apparent concern that publicity must invariably compromise the fair administration of justice. Moreover, empirical research may help judges make more informed choices among alternative remedies, such as change of venue and voir dire, designed to ameliorate the effects of prejudicial publicity.

-8-

A Proposal for a Categorical Solution

THE SCRUTINY STRUCTURE
AND THE FIRST AMENDMENT

As the critique developed in the previous chapter suggests, the scrutiny structure as it is presently applied has significant weaknesses. These weaknesses include the vagueness of current standards, the level of abstraction at which First Amendment interests are considered, and the unwillingness of lower courts to extend protection beyond the factual scenarios in which Supreme Court precedents were created. But an even more basic issue raised by the cases examined in this study is whether the First Amendment should be subject to balancing of any kind in the criminal justice context.

From a theoretical standpoint, the idea of heightened scrutiny in free press–fair trial cases seems suspect because of the important speech and press interests associated with ensuring a fair and effective justice system through open proceedings and uninhibited coverage. Few scholars or judges have taken the view that the First Amendment protects all speech, without qualification. With the possible exception of Justice Hugo Black, most students of the First Amendment have found that absolutism is, in the words of one treatise, "fundamentally too simplistic to be a viable method of analysis. . . ."[1] Many forms of speech—from treason to obscenity to perjury—are subject to significant government regulation. Many more, including commercial speech and broadcasting, have some degree of protection that nevertheless is subject to restriction in light of significant countervailing social policy goals. However, it also seems clear that there may be certain important categories

---

[1] R. Smolla, Smolla and Nimmer on Freedom of Speech: A Treatise on the First Amendment, 2-54 (1994).

of speech that are deserving of absolute or near-absolute protection. The criminal justice system, through which government exercises perhaps its most awesome power—that of depriving citizens of life and liberty—seems to be one domain in which unfettered public scrutiny and comment should be the rule. If one accepts the principle frequently reiterated by the Supreme Court—that open proceedings, are inherently fairer than closed proceedings—the value of free access to, and discussion about, criminal proceedings seems clear. Moreover, coverage of the criminal justice system, and examination of the government's activities in that system, seems without question to be a part of the Meiklejohnian notion of political speech, which the Court has held to be the core of the First Amendment. As Professor Meiklejohn noted: "Public discussions of public issues, together with the spreading of information and opinion bearing on those issues, must have a freedom unabridged by our agents. Though they govern us, we, in a deeper sense, govern them."[2]

Yet the use of heightened scrutiny mechanisms seems to belie the importance of uninhibited coverage of the criminal justice system. One solution to this difficulty might lie in jettisoning the scrutiny structure as applied to coverage of criminal proceedings altogether in favor of a regime of categorical protection. That is, courts could dispense with weighing governmental interests against speech interests, and instead protect speech about the criminal justice system categorically.

Commentators have frequently advocated two distinct strategies for resolving the tension between protecting speech and providing for other conflicting interests deemed worthy of protection. One strategy, the interest-balancing approach, includes the type of heightened scrutiny formulations described in this study. Interest balancing presents courts with a grid of tests to determine whether the speech or government interest in regulating speech should prevail based on various degrees of weighting in favor of speech, as in strict scrutiny, in favor of the regulation, as in the rational basis test, or somewhere in between, as in midlevel scrutiny. Such formulations, regardless of their wording, are always subject to some degree of vagueness and unpredictability.

The second strategy, often referred to as the *categorical approach,* avoids case-by-case determinations of the strengths of competing interests, and instead focuses on whether the speech in question is the type of speech that, *a priori,* requires complete protection. If so, the speech is entitled to absolute protection, regardless of the strength of the competing interest. Advocates of categorical rules suggest that this approach provides more protection for speech and greater certainty in First Amendment doctrine. For example, Professor Laurence Tribe has supported the categorical approach with an appeal to its relative certainty:

Categorical rules thus tend to protect the system of free expression better because they are more likely to work in spite of the defects in the human machinery on which we must rely to preserve fundamental liberties. The balancing approach is contrast-

---

[2]Meiklejohn, The First Amendment is an Absolute, 1961 Supreme Court Review 245, 257.

ingly a slippery slope; once an issue is seen as a matter of degree, first amendment protections become especially reliant on the sympathetic administration of the law.[3]

To better appreciate and analyze the nature of the problem, it may be helpful to explore the debate in more comprehensive terms.

RULES VERSUS STANDARDS

The relative advantages of categorical determinations versus interest-balancing approaches is but one example of a broader debate that for many years has surfaced and resurfaced in numerous areas of law. Although different vocabularies are sometimes used, this debate is perhaps most frequently described as the issue of "rules" versus "standards." Categorical approaches to First Amendment law are the equivalent of rules, whereas interest-balancing approaches are the equivalent of standards. The debate has plagued so many areas of law for so long that legal scholar Pierre Schlag has asserted that no resolution of the debate is possible: "It is an arrested dialectic: There is no moment of synthesis."[4] Armed with somewhat more optimism than Professor Schlag—and perhaps a great deal more naiveté—this section attempts to explore this dialectic in hopes of discovering some helpful principles for the resolution of the problem of categorical versus interest-balancing approaches to First Amendment law in the criminal justice context.

Judge Richard Posner explained the rules versus standards debate with reference to the rules of the road.[5] An example of a *rule*, which is a seemingly clear and determinate legal directive, would be a law that required all school bus drivers to stop at all railroad tracks, even if no warning lights were flashing and the warning gate was not down. A *standard* is a legal directive that creates seemingly greater discretion, such as the familiar negligence standard that requires drivers to exercise "due care." The broader and more nebulous "due care" standard might be helpful for deciding a large number of cases in which the facts and circumstances remain to be seen. Flexibility is the key here. No one could possibly "codify" all possible traffic mishaps to provide clear rules of liability for each and every accident that has ever happened or may happen in the future. However, the narrow and determinate command to stop at railroad crossings, no matter what the circumstances, which allows neither bus drivers nor judges much discretion in deciding if the requirement has been met, may be more appropriate for areas of human activity about which more is known in advance, where clear directions are possible, and where the interest being protected is sufficiently important to tolerate the inefficiencies that go along with reduced discretion.

[3]L. Tribe, American Constitutional Law 794 (1988).

[4]Schlag, Rules and Standards, 33 UCLA L. Rev. 379, 383 (1985). *See also,* M. Kelman, A Guide to Critical Legal Studies 15-63 (1987).

[5]R. Posner, The Problems of Jurisprudence 42-50 (1990).

As the rules versus standards debate has unfolded, a number of scholars have maintained that rules and standards are less binary oppositions than they are poles along a continuum. Some legal directives more rule-like, whereas others are more standard-like. Both kinds of directives are an attempt to "operationalize" certain background principles that are considered of social importance. For example, a background principle relevant to free speech law is the notion that government should not interfere with people's expressive autonomy unless their actions cause some clear harm to someone else. It can be operationalized through a rule-like directive ("no prior restraints") or a standard-like directive ("prior restraints are constitutional only when the speech creates an actual and imminent danger"). Legal scholar Kathleen M. Sullivan has stated that a "legal directive is 'rule'-like when it binds a decisionmaker to respond in a determinate way to the presence of delimited triggering facts. Rules aim to confine the decisionmaker to facts, leaving irreducibly arbitrary and subjective value choices to be worked out elsewhere."[6] In contrast, standard-like directives are worded in such a way as to increase the discretion of the judge by "collapsing decisionmaking back into the direct application of the background principle or policy to a fact situation."[7] The application to First Amendment law is clear: Categorical approaches (rules) are formulated after judges have already calculated the social value of the speech, and provide clear protection if that type of speech is present; interest-balancing approaches (standards) require judges in each case to weigh the value of the particular speech against other social goods.

Professor Sullivan argued that strict scrutiny is more rule-like than standard-like because of its tendency to be "strict in theory, but fatal in fact." However, a number of cases discussed in this study suggest that strict scrutiny-like standards used in media cases involving the criminal justice system vest considerable discretion in the judge to independently weigh the value of the speech and find it outweighed by other, more pressing needs. Variations on strict scrutiny, such as the "overriding interest" test used in access to court cases, seem to allow considerable discretion in lower courts to prevent access, whereas the version of strict scrutiny that the Supreme Court articulated in *B.J.F.* seems poised for a case in which privacy interests overcome speech interests. Thus, one might argue that the scrutiny structure—strict scrutiny and its innumerable variations—is less like a rule and more like a standard.

Assuming that the scrutiny structure is more standard-like than rule-like, what advantages might accrue in a First Amendment regime that propounded clear, categorical rules in media cases involving the criminal justice system? Justice Antonin Scalia, although almost certainly not predisposed to favor the constitutional modifications advocated here, recently discussed the general advantages of rule-like directives in a 1989 Harvard Law School lecture reprinted in the *University*

---

[6]Sullivan, The Supreme Court 1991 Term: Foreword: The Justices of Rules and Standards, 106 Harv. L. Rev. 22, 58 (1992).

[7]*Id.* at 58.

of Chicago Law Review.[8] The lecture, "The Rule of Law as the Law of Rules," provides a helpful summary of what have traditionally been regarded as some of the benefits of rules.

Justice Scalia argued that rules were to be preferred over more discretionary standards for a number of reasons. First, rules guarantee equal treatment of similar cases better than standards, which are often cast in the form of vague multifactor tests. Justice Scalia acknowledged that the sorts of generalizations that rules embody are often less than perfect because they limit judicial flexibility and necessarily conform imperfectly to complex phenomena. Nonetheless, the value of clear rules and the equal treatment they provide should not be underestimated. "When one is dealing, as my Court often is, with issues so heartfelt that they are believed by one side or the other to be resolved by the Constitution itself, it does not greatly appeal to one's sense of justice to say: 'Well, that earlier case had nine factors, this one has nine plus one.' "[9] Although rules, with their hard edges and clear boundaries, may result in some difficulties at the margins, Justice Scalia argued, the ability of rules to produce decisions that satisfy the basic human desire for equal treatment makes them generally preferable. As discussed in the previous chapter, the failure of the scrutiny structure to treat similar cases similarly, particularly in the field of access to courts, is one of its significant defects.

Second, Justice Scalia wrote, rules are infinitely preferable in a system of law in which the Supreme Court reviews only a tiny minority of lower court decisions. It may be years between Supreme Court decisions on a given question of law, during which time lower courts must struggle to apply standards with only the vaguest hints of how the balance should be struck. The desire for consistency and uniformity among diverse lower courts is a strong incentive for the Supreme Court to provide clear rules—again with the understanding that all rule-like generalizations are, to some extent, imperfect. In the context of media coverage of the criminal justice system, the cases discussed in this book have provided ample evidence of lower courts applying the scrutiny structure in ways that the Supreme Court would almost certainly not countenance. Yet the demands of the Court's caseload ensure that the Court will be unable to correct all the misapplications of its scrutiny structure.

Justice Scalia's third argument in favor of rules over standards emphasized the notion of *predictability*. To regulate their conduct, citizens need some advance warning of how legal disputes will be decided, should they arise. In a complex and litigious society, Justice Scalia argued, it is important that courts offer clear and relatively predictable directives to provide some sense of what the result will be in as-yet unlitigated circumstances. Rules provide at least a semblance of such predictability, whereas standards often do not. One might go further than Justice Scalia and argue that, at least in the First Amendment context, unpredictability has the added disadvantage of chilling or deterring speech in situations in which the law is unclear. For example, if editors and reporters are unsure about the extent to

---

[8]Scalia, The Rule of Law as a Law of Rules, 56 U. Chi. L. Rev. 1175 (1989).

[9]*Id.* at 1178.

which postpublication sanctions might apply, they may choose to forego publication of speech that is an important part of public discourse, rather than risk the uncertainties of standard-based jurisprudence.

The fourth advantage of rules over standards, according to Justice Scalia, is the way in which rules limit judicial discretion. By adopting a general rule, Justice Scalia argued,

> I not only constrain lower courts, I constrain myself as well. If the next case should have such different facts that my political or policy preferences regarding the outcome are quite the opposite, I will be unable to indulge those preferences; I have committed myself to the governing principle. In the real world of appellate judging, it displays more judicial restraint to adopt such a course than to announce that, "on balance," we think the law was violated here—leaving ourselves free to say in the next case that "on balance," it was not.[10]

Although one might quibble with the claim that general rules completely and successfully hem in judicial discretion, and a number of legal scholars have done more than just quibble, it seems beyond debate that rules are generally more effective at doing so than are multifactor balancing tests.

Justice Scalia's fifth argument in favor of rules is that, although rules limit judicial discretion, they also strengthen judicial resolve in difficult cases. Judges who face troublesome, unpopular decisions are given firm ground on which to reach the correct decision by clear rules, despite social pressure to reach some alternate result. In contrast, balancing tests may give some judges an easy way out of taking a principled stand because of the tests' vague contours and the relative ease with which different results can be justified. Justice Scalia provided the example of a convicted criminal defendant who must be released because of an improper police lineup. A general rule provides a solid foundation for such an unpopular decision, whereas a "totality of the circumstances" test leaves considerably more wiggle room for the faint-hearted jurist. The search for unpopular cases, however, need proceed no further than many First Amendment claims by the media. Media coverage of criminal trials is frequently subject to significant public condemnation, particularly when countervailing privacy claims are involved, despite the public good served by such scrutiny. Clear rules mandating both access and freedom to publish would protect First Amendment interests more consistently than the current system.

Justice Scalia's five claimed benefits of rules—encouraging equal treatment, promoting uniformity among diverse courts, advancing predictability for citizens, restraining judicial discretion, and strengthening judicial resolve—are not uniquely his contribution. They reflect views expressed for some time in the rules versus standards debate. Nonetheless, Justice Scalia's articulation captures the essence of the case for clear, general rules.

---

[10] *Id.* at 1179-80.

Other commentators have stated the case for rules as being supported by additional values.[11] Legal scholar Richard A. Epstein argued in favor of simple rules because of their economic efficiency.[12] Professor Sullivan pointed out that a number of political theorists, including Friedrich Hayek and John Rawls, have argued that, without clear and distinct rules announced in advance, governments can subvert individual rights. For example, Rawls wrote that the legal system "is a coercive order of public rules addressed to rational persons for the purpose of regulating their conduct and providing the framework for social cooperation. . . . If the bases of these claims are unsure, so are the boundaries of men's liberties."[13]

Undoubtedly, there are drawbacks as well as advantages to rules. Perhaps the most notable disadvantage, as mentioned earlier, is the relative inflexibility of rules. At the margins, rules may create unfairness by excluding from their ambit some cases that should be treated the same as those that fall under the rule—cases that a sliding scale might treat as analogous. For example, consider a rule that protects newspaper and broadcast journalists from being required to reveal their confidential sources in judicial proceedings. Such a rule (often called a *shield law*) may have the admirable goal of furthering the free flow of information by ensuring that potential whistleblowers will feel comfortable telling their stories to the press without fear that they will be identified later. The public benefits by learning about government corruption, unsafe business practices, and other unpleasantness that might otherwise never come to light. As frequently happens, however, because of bad drafting or for other reasons, the rule by its terms is limited only to newspaper or broadcast reporters, leaving magazine journalists, book authors, scholars, cable television reporters, and others unprotected. These excluded persons might well produce information just as significant, if not more so, to the public as the newspaper and broadcast journalists. If interpreted strictly by a court, the rule is, in legal terms, underinclusive.

Rules may also include within their scope cases that should not properly be treated the same as the paradigm rule cases. For example, a rule that legislators should be absolutely protected from defamation claims arising from their statements on the floor of the legislature may have considerable utility because it permits the public's business to be conducted without the perpetual threat of civil lawsuits hanging over officials' heads. However, perhaps the rule should not protect the unscrupulous officeholder who uses his or her position to ruin the reputation of an adversary when the speech has no discernible connection to the public's business. Such a rule, although reasonably certain in its application, is overinclusive.

Moreover, as culture and technology change, rules may lock in anachronisms that could be avoided by the use of adaptable standards. For example, consider a rule that requires seekers after public records—such as real estate records—to pay $2 to the records custodian for each record retrieved. Such a rule might reflect the

---

[11]*See generally*, J. Raz, The Authority of Law (1979).

[12]R. Epstein, Simple Rules for a Complex World (1995).

[13]J. Rawls, A Theory of Justice 235 (1972).

fair cost of retrieval services in an era of paper records, file cabinets, and photo-copiers. However, when technology changes and thousands of such records can simultaneously be transferred to and stored on a computer disk, the per-record charge becomes reprehensible. Thus, rules can be underinclusive, overinclusive, and resistant to change as knowledge or technology advances. In fact, as generalizations about a world that is constantly changing and in which hard-edged boundaries are scarce, rules are almost guaranteed to produce such dysfunctional results on at least some occasions.[14]

Rules are also subject to the objection that the domain created by a rule cannot be specified in advance clearly enough to compel later decision makers to decide particular cases under the rule. For a variety of reasons, either willfully or through some form of misperception, later decision makers may not see a case before them as falling under the rule, although the rule maker would have wanted the rule applied in that situation.[15] The variety of alternate rules available in most areas of legal doctrine sometimes makes the choice of rule problematic.[16] Even if the choice of the appropriate rule is reasonably clear, situations also inevitably arise that the rule maker simply never contemplated. At this point, everything seems up for grabs, despite the rule maker's best attempt to constrain discretion.[17] The fundamental difficulty is that the world does not neatly conform to linguistic categories. A rule specifying "no prior restraints" seems unambiguous, but the problem, made clear in earlier chapters, nonetheless remains: What exactly is a "prior restraint?" Is a short-term temporary restraining order a "prior restraint" in the same way that a permanent injunction is? Is an injunction against speech by lawyers and parties in

---

[14]For more on these problems with rules, see the excellent discussion in F. Schauer, Playing By the Rules: A Philosophical Examination of Rule-Based Decision-Making in Law and in Life (1991).

[15]This claim is closely related to the familiar objection, derived from Wittgenstein, that rules cannot dictate their own application. As explicated by philosopher Saul A. Kripke, this objection raises skeptical questions about human beings' ability to formulate rules that can govern situations not previously encountered by the rule-follower. Why, as Kripke asks, must $68 + 57$ equal "125" and not "5" for someone who has previously used the symbol "+" only for working with numbers smaller than 57? Perhaps the previous computations (employing the symbol "+") did not actually use the "plus" function, but the "quus" function, which compels the user to add two numbers if the second is less than 57, but otherwise to reach the answer "5." See S. Kripke, Wittgenstein on Rules and Private Language (1982). This objection is frequently answered by the claim that the problem simply doesn't arise for situated actors within a particular form of life—for example, judges.

[16]See, e.g., Cohen v. Cowles Media Co., 111 S.Ct. 2513 (1991) (majority and dissenters differed over choice of rule to apply in case involving broken media promise to confidential source).

[17]There is an enormous legal literature on the question of whether law is indeterminate, and thus incapable of limiting judges' discretion. Most commentators date the modern beginnings of this dispute from the Legal Realist movement of the 1920s and 1930s, although it is prefigured in the writings of Oliver Wendall Holmes. In recent years, the work of Critical Legal Studies scholars has often emphasized indeterminacy. A full discussion of all of the permutations of this argument is beyond the scope of this chapter, the philosophical assumptions of which include a significant degree of determinacy in legal doctrine. A few entry points into the indeterminacy literature include: A. Altman, Critical Legal Studies: A Liberal Critique (1990); Hasnas, Back to the Future: From Critical Legal Studies Forward to Legal Realism, or How not to Miss the Point of the Indeterminacy Argument, 45 Duke L.J. 84 (1995); Kress, Legal Indeterminacy, 77 Cal. L. Rev. 283 (1989).

a criminal case a "prior restraint" when challenged by the media? Has a "prior restraint" taken place if a judge does not issue a formal injunction, but simply makes veiled threats of later reprisal to reporters? As Judge Posner noted: "In the absence of a legislative definition judges have to decide what the word shall mean for legal purposes, not what it does mean."[18]

Despite these drawbacks—or inevitabilities—of rules, their virtues may outweigh their vices in certain circumstances. Judge Posner's school bus example is instructive: "School bus drivers must stop at all railroad crossings" is far less flexible than a rule requiring drivers to exercise "due care." Because the bus' cargo is so precious (i.e., the justification for the rule is so important), we may be willing to tolerate any inefficiencies and dysfunctions that the rule creates. Further, the problem of linguistic or conceptual confusion exists throughout human communication. It is not uniquely disabling to an argument in favor of rules. Even if some later cases to which the rule ideally should apply are not treated as falling under the rule, the institutional context and the general conventions of language will ensure that many "clear" cases will be decided using the rule. The next section argues that uninhibited scrutiny of the criminal justice system is vitally important, and that a categorical rule in the criminal justice domain would best serve that goal.

A CATEGORICAL RULE?

Because of the importance of public scrutiny of criminal proceedings, one solution to the doctrinal disarray brought about by the scrutiny structure might be to place speech about criminal justice in a category that cannot be abridged. That is, the Court could declare categorically that speech about the criminal justice system, such as coverage of court proceedings, could not be restrained or punished regardless of any competing interest. No balancing of interests would be required as long as the speech fit within the category. The Court could also declare that access to judicial proceedings could not be abridged, regardless of countervailing considerations.

As extreme as this suggestion may sound to some, a categorical approach is not without precedent. For example, the Court in *Cox Broadcasting Corp v. Cohn*,[19] discussed earlier, declared a categorical rule against postpublication sanctions imposed on the press based on the accurate publication of a rape victim's name obtained from judicial records. In *Cox*, the Court reversed a state court decision allowing a civil privacy action brought by the father of a murdered rape victim who had been identified by a television station. "The freedom of the press to publish [public record] information appears to us to be of critical importance to our type of government in which the citizenry is the final judge of the proper conduct of public business," the majority wrote. "In preserving that form of the government the First and Fourteenth Amendments command nothing less than that the States may not

---

[18]R. Posner, The Problems of Jurisprudence 46 (1990).

[19]420 U.S. 469 (1975).

impose sanctions on the publication of truthful information contained in official court records open to public inspection."[20] Any sort of sliding scale, the majority suggested—any concession to case-by-case determination of liability—would unavoidably lead to timidity by the press in providing the public with a full account of public proceedings. The Court's decision, with its appeal to predictability, suggests that freedom of expression is an often fragile right that simply will not be exercised when the boundaries of protection are unclear. The Court's logic also suggests Rawls' position that lack of clarity in individual liberties provides a dangerous opportunity for arbitrary governmental action. The categorical approach was abandoned in later cases in the *Cox* line in favor of heightened scrutiny, but such an approach applied generally to the kinds of cases discussed in this study might do a great deal toward removing the subjectivity and uncertainty of the current scrutiny structure.

The Supreme Court came close to articulating a categorical rule in *Nebraska Press Assn v. Stuart*,[21] dealing with prior restraints in the context of a criminal trial. As discussed more fully earlier, Justice Brennan's concurring opinion—advocating a categorical rule against the use of prior restraints to protect fair trial rights—came close to garnering five votes. Brennan argued that "there can be no prohibition on the publication by the press of any information pertaining to pending judicial proceedings or the operation of the criminal justice system, no matter how shabby the means by which the information is obtained."[22] Justice Brennan's opinion noted that trial judges have effective means of ensuring a fair trial for a criminal defendant that do not involve restraints on the press. Thus, a categorical rule would not involve sacrificing Sixth Amendment interests to free speech. Unlike the *Cox* majority, Justice Brennan and those who joined his opinion would have extended categorical protection even beyond the situation in which information was obtained through public records, at least when the case involved a prior restraint.

Justice Brennan's concurrence warned against the uncertainties of balancing tests. He pointed out that the prior restraint balancing tests suggested in earlier cases allowed "no judicial weighing of the countervailing public interest in receiving the suppressed information; the direct, immediate, and irreparable harm that would result from disclosure is simply deemed to outweigh the public's interest in knowing, for example, the specific details of troop movements during wartime."[23] National security is one thing, Justice Brennan suggested, but in the criminal justice context the prior restraint calculus provides no means of comparing the public interest in the information against possible harm to the defendant. "Arbitrary and excessive" use of prior restraints would be a distinct possibility, with an extra incentive to censor added into the mix when judges viewed media coverage as somehow reflecting on their own performance or competence. Justice Brennan was realistic about media abuse and sensationalism

[20]*Id.* at 495.
[21]427 U.S. 539 (1976).
[22]*Id.* at 588.
[23]*Id.* at 605.

when First Amendment rights were treated categorically, noting that such abuse would always accompany probing and informative media coverage. Nevertheless, he maintained that "the decision of what, when, and how to publish is for editors, not judges."[24] Had Justice Brennan's suggested rule been adopted, as it so nearly was, the later difficulties encountered in the *Noriega* case—in which a short-term prior restraint was allowed to stand—might have been avoided.

Perhaps the most interesting aspect of the *Cox* and *Nebraska Press* decisions is the precedential use to which they have been put in federal courts. As discussed in chapter 5, the *Cox* line of cases, although evolving from a categorical rule to a balancing approach, has nonetheless resulted in no reported federal case in which a subsequent punishment for publication was allowed to stand. Similarly, *Nebraska Press*—up until the *Noriega* decision in 1989—had generated no reported federal cases in which a direct gag order against the media had been upheld (although media challenges to gag orders directed toward participants have been rejected).

At least two possible lessons could be drawn from the aftermath of the *Cox* progeny and the *Nebraska Press* case. On the one hand, the argument could be made that a categorical rule is unnecessary because the balancing mechanisms used by later cases in both lines have been generally protective of First Amendment interests. Clearly, this argument has some merit. The argument becomes less compelling, however, when one considers what appears to be the weakening fabric of those balancing tests suggested by both *Noriega* in the prior restraint realm and the *B.J.F.* case in the postpublication sanction realm. Thus, although the results of the balancing tests employed were once clear, their continued vibrancy seems at least questionable as of this writing. On the other hand, a serious argument could be made that the subsequent histories of *Cox* and *Nebraska Press* make a strong case for the practical feasibility of categorical rules against infringement of speech in the criminal justice context. The fact that lower federal courts seem to have managed quite well for a number of years under balancing regimes that produced *de facto* categorical results takes the wind out of suggestions that a categorical rule is simply too extreme. It seems clear that federal courts have, at least ostensibly, been providing fair trials, despite their almost complete inability or unwillingness to abridge speech either prospectively or after the fact.

The near five-vote majority in *Nebraska Press* and the actual result in *Cox* are not the only exemplars of categorical First Amendment rules that would uphold speech regardless of the strength of countervailing interests. The Court's 1974 decision in *Miami Herald v. Tornillo*[25] struck down a Florida statute granting "right of reply" to political candidates who had been attacked by newspapers. The statute required the newspaper to print the candidate's reply to its criticism. In the process of striking down the statute, the Court created what appears to be a clear, categorical rule against forced access or "compelled speech" as applied to print media generally.[26]

---

[24]*Id.* at 613.

[25]418 U.S. 241 (1974).

[26]*But see* Red Lion Broadcasting Co. v. FCC, 395 U.S. 376 (1969) (upholding constitutionality of FCC-mandated right of reply as applied to broadcasters).

The *Tornillo* opinion, written by Chief Justice Burger, noted the many worthwhile social interests that might be advanced by some version of a public right of access to the media.[27] Nonetheless, *Tornillo* avoided balancing language of any kind, and simply held that government intervention into newspaper editors' discretion was unconstitutional, regardless of the important interests furthered by forced access. "The choice of material to go into a newspaper, and the decisions made as to limitations on the size and content of the paper, and the treatment of public issues and public officials—whether fair or unfair—constitute the exercise of editorial control and judgment," Chief Justice Burger wrote. "It has yet to be demonstrated how governmental regulation of this crucial process can be exercised consistent with First Amendment guarantees of a free press as they have evolved to this time."[28] Thus, *Tornillo* supports the view that some First Amendment interests (e.g., editorial discretion) require protection that puts speech beyond the reach of balancing formulations.

The categorical rule suggested in this chapter could be stated as follows: The First Amendment compels press and public access to all judicial proceedings involving a criminal defendant, regardless of countervailing considerations. Moreover, prior restraints of any duration and postpublication criminal sanctions against speech related to the criminal justice system violate the First Amendment, unless that speech is of a sort that would result in direct, immediate, and inevitable harm to national security. In addition, civil sanctions against reasonably accurate speech directly pertaining to criminal proceedings, as well as to pretrial events such as arrests, searches, interrogations, and the like, violate the First Amendment. These principles also apply to quasi-criminal proceedings that enforce ethics or disciplinary codes against public officials, including judges.

A few caveats might be in order. The rule against civil sanctions does not apply to libel suits. That might seem obvious given that the rule applies only to truthful speech, and that libel is by definition false. However, some speech may fall into the disputed zone between truth and falsity. In those circumstances, constitutional and common law libel jurisprudence is sufficiently protective of media statements about official proceedings and public officials. Moreover, reputational interests require recognition of some causes of action where damaging speech falls outside traditional libel protections. The "directly pertaining" language in the postpublication sanctions portion of the rule clearly builds in some judicial discretion. But the intention is that harmful speech that might be subject to a privacy action cannot be "bootstrapped" under the rule by some tangential connection to some event in the criminal justice system. The "reasonably accurate" language also creates room for discretion, but the intention is that, given the often slippery nature of "truth," protection should apply to all speech that represents at least a good faith attempt at accuracy.

---

[27]The *locus classicus* is Barron, Access to the Press—A New First Amendment Right, 80 Harv. L. Rev. 1641 (1967).

[28]418 U.S. at 258.

The approach suggested herein does not attempt to state an all-encompassing theory of First Amendment jurisprudence. For example, it does not suggest replacing all use of strict scrutiny or other balancing formulations with categorical "all-or-nothing" rules. Rather, the approach suggests that, within one limited domain of First Amendment law—speech about and access to the criminal justice system—balancing tests be set aside in favor of absolute rules that allow news gathering and dissemination to proceed unimpeded by courts and legislatures. The extent to which such a categorical approach might extend to reporting of other government proceedings, such as legislative and executive activities, would have to be determined after considerable attention to interests other than speech that might be affected.

Not all commentators have accepted the need for an absence of restraints on criminal justice reporting. For example, Professor Blasi advocated a rule allowing no restraints on publication about criminal defendants who hold public office. For other criminal defendants, however, Blasi found his "checking value" adequately provided for by a rule that allowed gag orders against either the press or trial participants if "the premature release of the information in question would almost certainly make it impossible for the defendant to be tried by a jury that is not strongly predisposed against him."[29] Yet the underlying theory of the checking value—that official misconduct and abuse of power will be minimized when government actions are closely observed—suggests that restrictions on coverage of criminal proceedings should not stand. One could plausibly argue that often public scrutiny should be the most intensive as to the very cases in which lawyers and judges wish to restrict access or dissemination of information.

The suggestion that a categorical rule should prevent restraints on news gathering and dissemination in the criminal justice context need not necessarily ignore other interests worthy of some degree of protection. First of all, it seems overwhelmingly clear that the *Sheppard* alternatives—intensive voir dire, sequestration, change of venue, and the like—are quite effective in ensuring an impartial jury. Although the empirical evidence is mixed, the actual results in high-profile trials in recent years suggest that most, if not all, direct restraints on the press are simply unnecessary. Moreover, judges might, when necessary, exercise considerably more imagination than is often demonstrated in lower federal court opinions in using alternatives to protect other important interests. For example, in *U.S. v. Jacobson*,[30] discussed in chapter 6, a district court protected the privacy interests of patients and children of an infertility physician by, among other measures, allowing the patients to use pseudonyms during their testimony. This technique protected an important privacy interest while maintaining an open proceeding without the need for any direct restraints on the press. Although one might quarrel with the court's decision to exclude sketch artists from the courtroom, the court's general approach to what it regarded as a compelling interest showed a flexibility and willingness to seek novel solutions that is lacking in many of the cases discussed in this study.

---

[29]Blasi, The Checking Value in First Amendment Theory, 1977 A.B.A. Res. J. 521, 636-37.

[30]785 F.Supp. 563 (E.D. Va. 1992).

CONCLUSION

There are no doubt many areas of free speech law in which balancing tests are appropriate. This chapter argues, however, that speech about and access to the criminal justice system are not among them. Rules are inevitably both inflexible and imperfect in a number of ways. But the argument here is that when the interest to be protected is sufficiently valuable, rules have their place in constitutional jurisprudence. As the distinguished legal scholar Frederick Schauer noted:

> The distinctive feature of rules, therefore, lies in their ability to be formal, to exclude from consideration in the particular case factors whose exclusion was determined without reference to the particular case at hand. This formalism of rules is not only conceptually sound and psychologically possible, but it also . . . is on occasion normatively desirable.[31]

Media coverage of the criminal justice system is one of those occasions.

The solution proposed here is clearly no panacea. Some legal scholars with a stake in the indeterminacy debate would no doubt suggest that clear rules are an impossibility, given the complexity of legal and social phenomena and the wide variety of jurisprudential tools in the hands of judges. Unquestionably, there is some merit to this argument. Considering the concrete alternatives available, however, the suggestion here is that imperfect rules might well perform better than the current standard-based doctrines.

---

[31]Schauer, Formalism, 97 Yale L.J. 509 (1988).

-Author Index-

A

Abraham, H., 17, 18, 20, 23
Altman, Andrew, 139
Anton, Martin Jack, 23, 83

B

Barron, Jerome, 143
Blackstone, Sir William, 65
Blasi, Vincent, 7–8, 144
Bodenhamer, David J., 41
Brown, Charlene J., 24, 25, 129
Buddenbaum, Judith M., 129
Bunker, Matthew D., 31

C

Campbell, Douglas S., 41–45
Cate, Fred H., 130
Chamberlin, Bill F., 24, 25
Corwin, E., 20
Cover, Robert, 17
Cox, Archibald, 21, 27

D

Day, David S., 11–12
Dienes, C. Thomas, 130
Dreschsel, Robert E., 63

E

Ely, John Hart, 12, 124, 124
Emerson, Thomas I., 2, 8–10, 11, 123
Epstein, Richard A., 138

G

Galloway, Russell W., 12, 123, 124
Gerald, J. Edward, 60
Goldfarb, Ronald, 41
Gottlieb, Stephen E., 3, 25, 28
Greenawalt, Kent, 6
Gunther, Gerald, 22, 29, 30

H

Hall, Kermit, 17, 18, 29
Harris, Robert, 16, 17
Hasnas, John, 139
Henkin, Louis, 124
Holsinger, Ralph L., 129
Horwitz, Morton J., 20

K

Kalven, H., Jr., 22
Kress, Ken, 139
Kripke, Saul A., 139

L

Levy, Leonard W., 25, 65
Linde, Hans A., 73, 119
Lusky, Louis, 20, 25

M

Mason, A. T., 17, 18, 19, 20, 23, 25
Mavrinac, Albert, 16
Meiklejohn, Alexander, 7, 133
Middleton, Kent, 63
Mill, John Stuart, 6–7

146

Minow, Newton N., 130
Murphy, P., 20
Murphy, Walter F., 25

O

Osborn, Chrysta, 12

P

Parsons, Patrick, 12
Pember, Don, 63
Posner, Richard A., 134, 140
Powell, Lewis F., Jr., 25
Pritchett, C., 27

R

Rawlings, Tom C., 25
Rawls, John, 138
Raz, Joseph, 138
Redish, Martin, 9
Rimmer, Tony, 63

S

Scalia, Antonin, 135–136
Schaur, Frederick, 139, 145
Schlag, Pierre, 134
Simon, Rita J., 129
Smolla, Rodney A., 7, 120, 132
Stone, Geoffrey, 10–11, 124
Stonecipher, Harry W., 24, 25
Sullivan, Kathleen M., 135
Swindler, W., 18

T

Tankard, James W., Jr., 63
Tribe, Laurence, 10, 119, 133–134

W

Weaver, David H., 129
Werhan, Keith, 11
Wolfe, C., 21, 22
Wright, John W., 129

-Subject Index-

A

Abrams v. United States, 7, 22, 29
Abscam case, *see U.S. v. Criden*
Access to trial proceedings, 80, 94–115
    Supreme Court cases, 94–101
    lower court cases, 101–114
        pretrial suppression hearings, 104–108
        bail hearings, 108–111
        change of venue hearings, 111–112
        plea and sentencing hearings, 112–113
        particular witness testimony, 113–114
Ad hoc balancing, 8–10
American Bar Association, 58, 60–61, 63
American Newspaper Publishers Association, 61
Application of Dow Jones & Co., Inc., 78–80
Application of the Herald Co., 106–108

B

Bakker, Rev. Jim, 111
Bad tendency test, 22, 28–29
Balancing, 2, 9–10, 25, 28–29, 60–61, 67, 68–69,
    70, 71, 81, 84, 87, 89–93, 118–119,
    120, 124, 125, 132–134, 137, 141–143
Bantam Books, Inc. v. Sullivan, 67n
Belo Broadcasting Corp. v. Clark, 72
Bench-bar-press guidelines, 63
Black, Hugo, 1, 35–36, 132
Blackmun, Harry A., 67, 106, 108–110
Blackstone, Sir William, 65
Board of Education v. Barnette, 27
Brandeis, Louis D., 17, 22, 29
Brandenburg v. Ohio, 29
Branzburg v. Hayes, 81, 95

Brennan, William J., 67, 68–69, 70, 72–73, 80, 96,
    128, 141–142
Bridges v. California, 34–36, 37, 39, 40
Bright line rule, 86
    see also postpublication sanctions
Burger, Warren, 11, 65, 68–69, 72, 81, 82, 87–88,
    95–97, 98, 99, 120, 125, 128, 143
Burr, Aaron, 34, 42

C

Cable News Network (CNN), 75–78, 122
Cable News Network, Inc. v. U.S., 103–104
Cardozo, Benjamin, 23
Carolene Products footnote, 33
Categorical approach, 133–145
CBS, Inc. v. Young, 81–82, 83
CBS v. U.S. Dist. Ct. for C.D. of California, 72–73,
    74, 118
Chandler v. Florida, 57n
Checking value, 7–8, 144
Clark, Thomas C., 57, 58, 59
Classified Information Procedures Act, 113
Clear and present danger test, 11, 21–23, 28–29,
    67, 68, 70, 78, 82, 83, 86–88, 91, 117,
    125, 126, 131
Cohen v. Cowles Media Co., 139
Committee on the Operation of the Jury System
    of the United States Judicial Confer-
    ence, 62
Compelling state interest, *see* strict scrutiny
Connecticut Magazine v. Moraghan, 82, 125
Consolidated Edison Co. v. Public Service Com-
    mission, 15n, 25n

Contempt power, 34–40, 60–61
Content distinction, 10–11, 32
Corbitt v. NBC, 70n
Court-packing, 18
Cox Broadcasting Corp. v. Cohn, 69, 70–71, 85, 87, 89, 91, 92, 117, 125, 126, 140–142
Craig v. Harney, 38–39, 40
Criminal justice system, *see* mass media, Fourteenth Amendment, and Sixth Amendment

D

Daubney v. Cooper, 95n
Deferential test, *see* rational basis test
DeLorean, John, 72, 112, 125, 129
Dennis v. United States, 29
Depression, 16, 17
Diversity rationale, 6
Douglas, William O., 39
Due process clause, 1, 16–18, 41, 42, 56–58

E

Estes v. Texas, 57–58
Exacting scrutiny, *see* strict scrutiny

F

Fair trial guarantees, *see* Fourteenth Amendment and Sixth Amendment
Fifth Amendment, 17
First Amendment
    see also content distinction, Fourth Amendment, prior restraint, scrutiny structure and Sixth Amendment
    and contempt power, 34–40, 60–61
    doctrine and free speech, 2–5, 28–33
    and media access to proceedings, 80, 94–115, 117
    protection for information recipients, 79, 95
    treated as abstract only, 119–121
First National Bank of Boston v. Belloti, 15n, 25n
The Florida Star v. B.J.F., 88–90, 92–93, 126, 135, 142
Fourteenth Amendment, 1, 16–17, 19, 23, 26, 27, 37, 45–46, 66, 86, 140–141
    see also due process clause and substantive due process
Fourth Amendment, 105
Frankfurter, Felix, 21, 24–25, 27, 37–39, 51, 53, 56
Free expression
    see balancing, content distinction, and First Amendment
Free press–fair trial issue, 34–63
    see also mass media and prejudicial publicity
    problems with received view, 118–119

studies on, 60–63
U.S. Supreme Court cases on, 41–64

G

Gag orders, *see* prior restraint
Gannett Co. v. DePasquale, 104–105, 108
Gentile v. State Bar of Nevada, 83–84
Globe Newspaper Co. v. Superior Court, 71, 96, 99, 127, 128
Goldblum v. National Broadcasting Corp., 74–75

H

Hand, Learned, 21, 29
Harlan, John M. II, 57, 58
Heightened scrutiny approach, *see* scrutiny structure
High-value speech, 11, 30
Holmes, Oliver Wendell, 6, 7, 17, 21–22, 28–29, 38, 50, 67, 139n
Holt v. United States, 49–50
Hopt v. Utah, 44–48, 50
Hughes, Charles Evens, 19–20, 23, 66
Hunt v. National Broadcasting Co., Inc., 74
Huron Publishing Co. v. Martin, 70n

I

Indeterminacy, *vii*, 139n
Individual autonomy rationale, 5–6
In re Charlotte Observer, 71–72, 111, 121
In re Globe Newspaper Co., 108–110
In re Greensboro News Co., 101n
In re Memphis Pub. Co., 104
In re New York Times Co., 80
In re South Carolina Press Association, 101–103, 120–121
In re Washington Post Co., 112–113
Intermediate scrutiny, 9–10, 12, 31–32, 92
    see also O'Brien test
Irvin v. Dowd, 41, 54–56

J

Jackson, Robert H., 27, 51–52
Jacobson v. Massachusetts, 21
Jehovah's Witness, 24, 27
Johnson Newspaper Corp. v. Morton, 105n
Jones v. Opelika, 24
Journal Pub. Co. v. Mecham, 83
Judicial review, 10, 11, 15–17, 20, 21, 22
    see also scrutiny structure, strict scrutiny
    judicial activism, 16–20, 22, 23
    judicial restraint, 18, 27
Juries in criminal trial proceedings, see mass media

K

Kent State University, 81
Kovacs v. Cooper, 24

L

Lambert v. Polk County, 70n
Landmark Communications, Inc. v. Virginia, 86–88, 91, 92, 125, 126
Legal predictability, 136–137
Legal Realism, 20, 139n
Levels of scrutiny, 18–21, 28, 78, 91–93, 97, 100, 108, 115, 121–123
Lochner era, 16–18
Lochner v. New York, 16–17
Los Angeles Times, 35
Lusky, Louis, 19–20

M

Marketplace of ideas, 6, 7
Marshall, John, 42
Marshall, Thurgood, 68, 78, 80, 99, 126
Marshall v. United States, 54
Mass media
     see also free press–fair trial issue, prior restraint, postpublishing sanctions, and prejudicial publicity
Mattox v. United States, 49
McIntyre v. Ohio Elections Commission, 30
Mechanical jurisprudence, 20
Medina Report, 61–62
Menendez v. Fox Broadcasting Co., 70n
Miami Herald v. Tornillo, 142–143
Minersville District v. Gobitis, 27
Munn v. Illinois, 21n
Murdoch v. Pennsylvania, 24

N

Near v. Minnesota, 23, 66–67, 69, 70, 88, 124
Nebraska Press Association v. Stuart, 4, 65n, 66, 68, 69, 70, 71, 75, 78, 83, 88, 116, 123, 124, 141, 142
Nebraska Press test, 71–74, 76–77, 82–83, 117, 120, 122–123, 124,125
New Deal, 17, 18
The New York Times, 67
New York Times Co. v. U.S., 67, 69, 70n, 73, 124

O

O'Brien test, 3, 9, 11
O'Connor, Sandra Day, 78, 90
obscenity, 33
Oklahoma Publishing Co. v. District Court, 69

P

Palko v. Connecticut, 23
Pell v. Procunier, 80n, 82, 95
Pennekamp v. Florida, 37–38, 40
Pentagon Papers, *see New York Times Co. v. U.S.*
Poindexter, John M., 113
Posadas de Puerto Rico Associates v. Tourism Co., 32
Postpublication sanctions, 23, 85–93, 117, 143
     Supreme Court cases, 85–90, 125
     lower court cases, 90–93, 126
Predictability, *see* legal predictability
Preferred position doctrine, 24–25
Prejudicial publicity
     impartial juries, 41–60
     studies about, 60–63, 128–130
Press-Enterprise v. Superior Court (Press-Enterprise II), 77, 98–100, 101–103, 104, 105, 110–114, 117, 127
Press-Enterprise v. Superior Court of California (Press Enterprise I), 98–100, 101, 103–104, 127
Prior restraint, 23, 65–84, 122, 139–140, 143
     see also postpublication sanctions and privacy
     applied to trial participants, 78–84, 117
     beneficial absence of, 120
     cases struck down, 70–75
     cases upheld, 75–78
     Supreme Court doctrine, 66–69
Privacy, 70, 71, 85–86, 88–93, 96–97, 99, 103, 109, 119
Progressivism, 20

R

Radio & Television News Assn. v. U.S. Dist. Court 80, 81
Rational basis test, 11, 27, 32–33, 133
Rationality review, 97
Reagan, Ronald, 113
Reardon Report, 60
Reasonableness, 107–108
Red Lion Broadcasting Co. v. FCC, 142n
Reed, Stanley F., 37
Rehnquist, William H., 88, 90, 97, 128
Reynolds v. United States, 42–44, 48, 50
Richmond Newspapers, Inc. v. Virginia, 4, 94–96, 97, 98, 100–101, 105–106, 107, 112, 117, 120, 121, 123, 127, 131
Rideau v. Louisiana, 56–57, 58
Roberts, Owen J., 26
Roosevelt, Franklin D., 17, 18
Rules, 135–140
     a categorical rule, 140–144
     see also standards

S

Saxbe v. Washington Post Co., 80n, 82, 95
Scalia, Antonin, 135–136
Scheetz v. Morning Call, Inc., 91–93, 126–127
Schenck v. United States, 21–22, 28–29
Schneider v. State, 26
Scrutiny structure, 2–5, 8–9, 12, 26
    see also intermediate scrutiny, *O'Brien* test,
        postpublication restraint, prior re-
        straint, strict scrutiny, and scrutiny
        structure critique
    and a categorical rule, 140–144
    and the First Amendment, 132–134
    origins of, 15–33
    rules versus standards, 134–140
    studies on, 10–13
    Supreme Court formulations of, 34–60
Scrutiny structure critique
    abstractness problem, 119–121
    conflict problem, 118–119
    empirical problem, 128–130
    fact-bound problem, 121–123
    vagueness problem, 123–127
Shelton v. Tucker, 28n
Shepherd v. Florida, 51–52
Sheppard v. Maxwell, 58–60, 61, 62, 79, 83, 105n, 144
Simmons v. United States, 48–49
Simon & Schuster v. New York State Crime Victims Board, 31
Simpson, O.J., vii, 1
Sixth Amendment, 1, 9, 10, 41, 45–46, 52, 62, 68–69, 70, 73, 74, 75, 77, 99, 102–103, 104–105, 105n, 108, 109, 118–119, 120, 127, 130, 141
Skinner v. Oklahoma, 26
Smith v. Daily Mail Publishing Co., 70–71, 87, 89, 90, 91, 125, 126
Spies v. Illinois, 45, 50
Standards, 135–136
Standards of review, *see* levels of scrutiny
Standing, 78–79
Stare decisis, 121–123
Stevens, John P., 69
Stewart, Potter, 58, 67, 68, 87
Stone, Harlan Fiske, 2–3, 15–16, 17, 18–21, 22, 23
Strict scrutiny, 3, 11, 15, 22–23, 24–27, 30–32, 33, 81, 83, 85, 88, 90, 92, 96, 97, 98, 101, 104, 107, 111, 114, 125, 131, 133, 135

Stroble v. California, 52–53
Stroud v. United States, 50–51
Substantive due process, 16–18

T

Time, place, and manner doctrine, 12
Turner Broadcasting System v. F.C.C., 31

U

U.S. Supreme Court
    see First Amendment, judicial review, and
        scrutiny structure
U.S. v. Brooklier, 101n 106
U.S. v. Burr, 42
U.S. v. Carolene Products, 2–3, 15–16, 19–21, 22, 23, 24, 25, 27, 28, 33
    see also *Carolene Products* footnote
U.S. v. Chagra, 108–109
U.S. v. Criden, 105–106, 123
U.S. v. Dennis, 68n
U.S. v. Edwards, 101n
U.S. ex rel. Darcy v. Handy, 53
U.S. v. Gotti, 110–111
U.S. v. Jacobson, 114, 144
U.S. v. McKenzie, 71–72
U.S. v. Noriega, 75–78, 84, 117, 122–123, 141
U.S. v. O'Brien, 3, 32, 124
    see also *O'Brien* test
U.S. v. Peters, 101n
U.S. v. Poindexter, 113–114

V

Vietnam, 67
Virginia State Bd. of Pharmacy v. Virginia Citizens Council, Inc., 78–79

W

Waite, Morrison R., 43–44
Warren, Earl, 3, 32, 124
The Washington Post, 67
Watergate, 72, 112, 129
West Virginia Board of Education v. Barnette, 6
White, Byron R., 67, 69, 80, 86, 90
Whitney v. California, 22, 29
Wood v. Georgia, 39–40
Worrell Newspapers of Indiana, Inc. v. Westhafer, 90–91, 126
WXYZ, Inc. v. Hurd, 70